# Contemplation and Action

# in World Religions

# Contemplation and Action
# in World Religions

Selected Papers from the Rothko Chapel Colloquium
"Traditional Modes of Contemplation and Action"

Edited by

Yusuf Ibish and Ileana Marculescu

A Rothko Chapel Book
Distributed by
University of Washington Press, Seattle and London

© Rothko Chapel, Houston, 1978, 1977
Distributed by University of Washington Press
Printed in the United States of America

Library of Congress Catalogue Card Number: 78-61504
ISBN: 0-295-95634-8 (paper)

To John de Menil
(1904–1973)

# Acknowledgments

We are deeply indebted to Professor Yusuf Ibish, Chairman of the Department of Islamic Studies of the American University of Beirut, for having organized the colloquium "Traditional Modes of Contemplation and Action" and seeing it through to its conclusion. The steering committee he invited took an active part in the planning, and we wish here to thank individually Msgr. Georges Khodr, Metropolitan of Mount Lebanon, Seyyed Hossein Nasr, director of the Imperial Iranian Academy of Philosophy, and Awadh Kishore Saran, professor of sociology at the University of Jodhpur.

Professor Ibish had chief editorial responsibility for all colloquium publications. Also serving on the editorial committee for this abridged edition of the papers were Leo Alting von Geussen, Frederick Franck, Ileana Marculescu, and Francesco Pellizzi. Dr. Marculescu, moreover, undertook the basic task of abridging the selected papers and also contributed introductory notes. We further acknowledge the help of Harris Rosenstein, of the Institute for the Arts, Rice University, with the final editing. Professor Thomas Michel, S.J., Department of Middle Eastern Languages and Culture, Columbia University, and earlier Dr. Kamel Refaey, of Houston, helped us in our efforts to attain consistency in the transliteration of Arabic; Barbara Stoler Miller, Professor of Oriental Studies, Columbia University, provided similar help with the Sanskrit. Other important editorial assistance was given by Pamela Bloom. Sister Frances King provided valuable notes on the colloquium discussions. Special thanks are due to all of them.

The Board of the Rothko Chapel

# Foreword

What man indeed can know the intentions of God?
Who can divine the will of the Lord?

Wisd. of Sol. 9:13

O Mankind! Be careful of your duty to your Lord
who created you from a single soul.

Qur'an IV, 2

"The human race is facing the greatest crisis in its history because religion itself is being weighed in the balance"[1] wrote Thomas Merton in his essay "Mysticism in the Nuclear Age," and he added: "You cannot save the world merely with a system. You cannot have peace without charity. You cannot have social order without saints, mystics, and prophets."[2]

Such a crisis, such a need calls for humility: no one religion, no one ideology can expect to convert the world to goodness. But, from whatever quarter the saints appear, the perfume of their saintliness will reach over the borders of their religion, of their culture, engaging everyone in the same pursuit.

The Rothko Chapel, where the colloquium "Traditional Modes of Contemplation and Action" took place, was meant as a sanctuary for all, a "No-man's-land for God." It emerged from unpredictable events, after many accidents. It was born from the work and passion of a great artist and from the sponsor's commitment to brotherhood, to "otherness."

The place was consecrated on February 27, 1971. The ceremony was conducted by Eastern Orthodox, Catholic and Protestant dignitaries, by Rabbis and Moslems. Two and a half years later, the colloquium on contemplation and action helped to shape the vocation of the Rothko Chapel.

It had been prepared by a journey that John de Menil made to Rome, Geneva, Paris, Taizé and Beirut, to Lagos, Ife, Abidjan and Bouaké, to Cairo, Tehran and Delhi, to Dharmsala, Madras and Kancheepuram. The warm welcome, the openmindedness he found everywhere confirmed him in his wish to have a truly ecumenical encounter at the Rothko Chapel. An encounter where the initiative would be taken by the East, rather than held tightly by the West.

In the fall of 1971, in Lebanon, John de Menil met Yusuf Ibish, professor at the American University of Beirut. In May 1972 he invited him to Houston to draw plans. The visit resulted in a timeless bond of friendship, and in a colloquium organized by Dr. Ibish. The Rothko Chapel provided the hospitality.

It was an active hospitality guided by the thought that "no one has the right to say that his view of God is the only view," as one of the authors wrote in this book. It was a warm welcome, stimulated by the Qur'an's affirmation that "every nation has a prophet" and strengthened by the conviction that tradition is a fire to which each generation brings its own wood. And, after all, "the depths of God can only be known by the spirit of God" (I Cor. 2:11).

*Dominique de Menil*

[1] *A Thomas Merton Reader*, Revised Edition ed. Thomas P. McDonnell (Garden City, N.Y.: Image Books, 1974), p. 371.
[2] Ibid., p. 375.

8

# Contents

9

# Introduction

To introduce a book, i.e., to present its characteristic features, to elucidate its inner articulation and evaluate its place within a larger cultural context is, after all, not such an obstructive endeavor. A book must speak for itself anyhow, and an introduction merely suggests a possible way to begin listening. Things are nevertheless different and more complex when the same book, besides its expressed message, stands also as a *sign:* it represents a definite form achieved by a multiform experience. It thus becomes the access into a space which, of course, we enter through the established concepts of our language, a space which we are supposed to explore with the words of our common human tribe, but which we most probably will never entirely exhaust either by words or concepts. At this point, then, a sign, *the* sign, arises: something which is given and yet to come; a mark along the path of the research so that the peregrination may never stop and yet not go astray. A sign "neither speaks nor keeps silent" (Heraclitus): it is an everlasting introduction to adventure.

And, undoubtedly, this Colloquium pertains to adventure: an adventure in encounter; an adventure in language. As we all know (or perhaps have we forgotten it?) a meeting is not necessarily an *encounter* (often just the reverse). May it be so only because the encounter somehow precedes itself, (be)comes from the invisible realm of beings in such a way that, when realized, brings forth a creative (re)discovery of what, unsuspected, was already there? And that this — let us call it inward dimension (in contrast to the more horizontal level of "meeting") — implies a free and living transcending of one's self; not my transcending *of* another but *toward* another. By all means, the participants at the Colloquium, being

11

both qualified scholars and persons spiritually alive to their own respective traditions, might have been tempted to confront notions, ideas, and information (as in any respectable scholarly meeting), or to satisfy themselves merely with the delighted recognition of a preexisting, diffuse "unity of all" (religions, traditions, beliefs). But, in a somehow unexpected move, they found themselves impelled to "go beyond" (precisely because there is no true *tradition* except a living one) and to explicitly acknowledge that even established forms of "traditional life" may collapse into a closed, that is to say a repetitive, pattern of secluded temporality.

Once creative, it looks at present as if "traditionalism" is not mindful enough of the "signs of the times" coming down to us through the mediation of *History* (this concept of *History* being essentially different from an uncritical, naive conception of "technological progress," another paradigm of secluded temporality). As one of the participants feelingly put it (and, significantly enough, it was a Californian, "a man without tradition" located at the extreme point of the West, facing the Far East) in an anxious interrogation arisen once again, "Who failed, we or tradition?" It would be, of course, naive to expect a simple, prefabricated answer. Nevertheless, evoking here some insights from modern currents of thought, we would say that "from the heart of our sedentary existence, a remembrance of our nomadic destiny comes forth" (Claude Lévi-Strauss); and it sets us in motion towards "the outside thought" (Michel Foucault), which is not exactly, or not only, that of other ethnic religious or spiritual traditions, not only that of so-called primitive cultures and arts interspersed with "old stones that cannot be deciphered" (T.S. Eliot), but which leads us beyond our too familiar space so that other forms of thought and language may arise within our own mind.

It has already been said that the Houston Colloquium was also inevitably an adventure in language. Would it be too pretentious or farfetched to summon here, at this precise point, the name of Plato? After all, is he not one of the most conspicuous forefathers of our Western tradition and of the "planetary" civilization based on it? By the virtues of the human *Logos* — the *Word* — he shaped and handed down to the following centuries the *dialogue*: supreme mold of human communication, a privileged way for meeting each other and for establishing teamwork; but also artifact and *techne* and, furthermore, foundation of the city, democracy, and the state. On the other hand, it has been gradually noticed that under the authority of its traditional form inherited from Plato, the dialogue remained essentially an "assertive" way of contemplating reality and acting on it so that the already existing order of ideas and values might be extended and consolidated and, though unconsciously, the strange(r), the troublesome, the unheard of, might be eliminated from the realm of language.

The Greeks would have called this type of language *cataphatic*, i.e., merely connoting the already positively established facts or those which are going to be established along the same lines, the already admitted ones or those about to be admitted. The language itself may then develop into another closed precinct, not always easy to penetrate by those who come from "outside." Notwithstanding this perennial tradition, another one, tracing back to some immemorial way of contemplation and action, points at another status of human mind and language where connotations express themselves under the form of "negation" (the *apophatic* way): words do not indicate "what is" — the solid, established appearances and their interrelations — but what beings are not; and by doing so the language criticizes itself and keeps open to any "surprise" that may occur from any point of the horizon of knowledge and reality.

And to begin with, the very first and last word, the most controversial and unavoidable one of our understanding — God — has to be approached accordingly. For, what is revealed (positively) refers to, and constantly derives its meaning from, the mystery it reveals. The "symbol" (in its all-encompassing sense as the fundamental process of the mind, correcting both the inaccuracy of language and its self-sufficiency) comes forth at this point. (And, characteristically enough, the most imaginative spirits in the contemporary sciences deal with it in order to transcend the inadequacy of our common concepts when deeper reality is contemplated.) Yet we would like to underscore that another equally creative challenge may very simply occur in this respect from the sheer fact of human beings "being there" with their unaccounted

13

share of struggle and distress, of quest and hope: not unlikely, an "unknown god" might try thus to cut through a path down to our language and recognition.

We are therefore compelled to single out another rather uncommon feature of this Colloquium. At no moment was it an elitist dialogue or a self-complacent meeting. Besides the active participation of many young scientists from various American universities and research centers, representative people from Africa as well as from Latin America were there with the urgent and burning problems of their countries fully reentering history and facing again, from the standpoint of their respective traditions, their own destiny. In this way the proceedings of the Colloquium, parallel to their cognitive value, constitute the sign of a still strenuous, complex, and nevertheless already imaginable co-respondence between the "traditional ways of contemplation and action" and the search for what is to come.

Finally, one cannot avoid facing the sign itself of this Colloquium's location, the Rothko Chapel. Etymology and semantics may provide in their own, often unimaginable way, the words for understanding through the understanding of words. Most probably, specialists alone would remember today the meaning and the origin of this term — chapel — present in all our modern languages. It simply coincides with a turning point in the history of Europe (the fourth century, the passage between antiquity and the Middle Ages) and expresses a certain basic ideal of the Western world. A young knight and military commander of that time, Martin of Tours, received the faith, and meeting a poor man on his way almost immediately afterwards, he cut his knightly mantle in half and shared it with him. Later on, after Martin's death, the place where the relics of his mantle (Latin: *cappa*) were kept as an abiding sign came to be named *cappella* (chapel). The conversion from military might to sainthood through the mediation of the "poor one" lays also (believe it or not) at the foundation of our Western civilization, and the very word chapel is there to echo it even if in a subdued way. And behold, here at the other "end," if we may say, of the Western itinerary stands the Rothko Chapel without any "trace" inside, neither material remnants nor figurative forms. The

14

"poverty" is fully there in the Chapel. The shape of the Chapel, consonant to one of the most enigmatic symbols of all traditions of knowledge, the Ogdoad — Octagon — cipher of the "consummation of all," leads to no definite end. The dark — or rather beyond any color — panels allow no "point of view" which would still mark a sedentary, restrictive attitude, engendering sooner or later petrified if not petrifying systems, ideologies, exclusivistic dogmatism. No dead end either: the mind recommences its forgotten pilgrimage under the spell of the (in)visible, formless presence into the space suddenly opened from beyond the obscure dark by a living fire akin to the dancing stars and vast breathing of beings.

And yet, for all the signs it endeavors to convey, here it stands, this volume, a transient, perishable object: a book. It seems that some years ago, a contemporary French poet, in an interview, was asked the classic question: If a fire broke out in your house, which object, which book would you rush to save? If there was a fire in my house? . . . I think I would save the fire, was the answer, thus letting the books perish.

Paradoxically enough, the authors of this book will not mind the same fate, providing the "fire" that they simply tried to relay at the Rothko Chapel will continue to burn.

*André Scrima*

15

# The Dual Aspect of Faith

SHOJUN BANDO

*Editor's Introduction:* Besides the crucial importance of "ultimacy" in religious faith, all the higher religions seem to have in common a factor of no less importance: *the simultaneous experience of life and death.* Not only are all deeper religious practices aimed at bringing about this experience, but their final fulfillment could never be realized without this central spiritual event.

The paper deals with some instances of this experience as manifested in various religious traditions, especially Buddhism and Christianity and the expressions given to it by sages and saints. It also points to the necessity of modifying Tillich's definition of religion as "ultimate concern," so as to embrace the ideas of "death-in-life," i.e., the death of the old self and the birth of the new Self: *metanoia.*

Although faith may be regarded as the core of religion, the history of religions has shown that, roughly divided, there are two types of faith: one in a personal God and the other in an ultimate principle such as the Dharma of Buddhism, for example. It is noteworthy, however, that even in the metaphysical traditions such as Taoism, for example, in which the ultimate principle is not a personal God, that image is often given both an abstract and a personified expression. In this paper, the term "faith" is used in its broadest sense so as to include the faiths of all the higher religions.

In the *Heart Sutra*[1] the following passage appears:

Form (*rûpa*) is no different from voidness (*śûnyatâ*),
Voidness is no different from form; } A

Form, as it is, is voidness,
Voidness, as it is, is form. } B

16

Nothing could be more revealing of the universal truth of religious faith than these statements. They are an indication of the profound insight of the ancient Buddhist sages into the core of metaphysical truth. These lines might be called the "equation of metaphysical truth."

Essentially, the first two lines which I shall call *(A)* and the last two lines which I shall call *(B)* are one, with the sole difference that *A* is still tinged with an interpretative color or a residue of the ultimate level of awareness.

We find a striking counterpart to the above sutra in the following passages from the *Meditation Sutra*[2];

> This mind becomes a Buddha;
> This mind in itself is a Buddha.

The universal contrast shown by the equation of *rûpa* with *śûnyatâ* represents all conceivable opposites:

| | | |
|---|---|---|
| profane | versus | sacred |
| man | " | God |
| death | " | life |
| suffering | " | comfort |
| body | " | mind |
| matter | " | spirit |
| illusion | " | Enlightenment |
| self | " | Self |
| poison | " | medicine |
| Adam | " | Christ |
| Saul | " | Paul |
| means | " | end |
| crucifixion | " | resurrection |
| many | " | one |
| particular | " | general |
| relative | " | absolute |
| dying | " | living |
| Atman | " | Brahman |

This list could, of course, be continued indefinitely. What would happen, then, if an unenlightened man was suddenly shown a *B*

17

formula — for example, "illusion, as it is, is Enlightenment"? He might react with doubt, wondering at the confused identification of two totally different things. Assertions of the *B* type are too drastic for the ordinary mentality. If proposed prematurely to a mind that has yet to experience Enlightenment, they appear to be nonsense. To the ordinary consciousness, illusion is illusion, and so the last thing to be identified with Enlightenment. To the totally ignorant mind, even *A,* or the discriminatory expression of *B,* may seem odd enough. For the ordinary mind to reach an insight into the *B* statement, a spiritual experience of considerable depth is the prerequisite. In other words, one needs, at least, to have glimpsed into the transcendent. Without coming in touch with an enlightened person, there could be no way for anybody to be spiritually enlightened. Such a person is known by various names: *guru* (spiritual guide), *âcârya* (religious master) or *kalyâna-mitra* (good friend of the Way). Of the three, there seems to be a slight difference in meaning between the first two and the last one. Ordinarily, the *guru* or *âcârya* is acknowledged to be in an authoritative position, qualified to teach disciples *(śishya* or *chela),* whereas the *kalyâna-mitra* may be anybody, even an avowed enemy whom one hates, or one's social inferior, as long as he or she as a person represents an occasion or influence through which spiritual awakening takes place. Compared with the *guru* or *âcârya,* the *kalyâna-mitra* is a highly subjective and personal concept.

"Non-ego" or "self-less-ness" seems to be unanimously regarded as the supreme virtue not only in Buddhism but in any authentic religious tradition. It is the dynamic state in which the *rûpa* element is reduced toward its minimum degree until finally it approaches naught. It is then that the *śûnyatâ* element reaches its maximum. When man becomes truly selfless, he comes to assume a divine quality. This is the final truth inherent in all religions. The problem, therefore, always remains — how to attain this state. This process was pointed to by St. John as follows: "He must increase, but I must decrease" (John 3:30), until the point at which he could declare: "I am in the Father, and the Father in me" (John 14:11).

In order to reach this state, one need not detach oneself completely from the flesh. In the soteriological teaching of any religion, the denial of the flesh in its physical sense does not prevail. The state of bliss without the rejection of the flesh was explicitly testified to by Paul: "I live; yet not I, but Christ liveth in me" (Gal. 2:20).

Primitive and even highly developed religious thought sometimes gives rise to complete denial of the material existence of the physical body, insisting that in order to attain a final emancipation one should be completely free from bondage to physical factors. The idea of a final emancipation without human form was thus born. We can find the concept of *nirupadhiśesha-nirvâna* (Nirvana without a remainder) in the Brahmanical as well as in the early Buddhist teachings. In contrast to this negativistic concept of Nirvana, a positive idea of it was later put forward — that is, the idea of *sopadhiśesha-nirvâna* (Nirvana with a residual karma yet to be exhausted). "Remainder" here no doubt refers to our physical existence with all its mental defilements.

Overcoming the fatal dichotomy of Nirvana "with and without" a remainder, the wonderful genius of the Mahayana thinkers arrived finally at the definition of Nirvana as "Non-abiding." According to them, a Bodhisattva does not abide in the defiled world because of his great wisdom *(prajñâ)*, nor does he abide in the realm of Enlightenment because of his great compassion *(karunâ)*, hence his being always "on the way," neither attached to *mâyâ* (illusory state) nor to *satori* (Enlightenment). The great Mahayana sages called this dynamic process, aptly enough, the "Non-abiding Nirvana." The basis of their attitude was the typical Buddhist principle of the Middle Way, which is dialectical and at the same time critical of all the extremes, extremes that it transcends with creative consequences. Here, attachment to Enlightenment is clearly rejected as much as attachment to illusion. The "Non-abiding Nirvana" is thus none other than Enlightenment in action.

Concerning Nirvana, we are reminded of a subtle distinction made by Christians between Heaven and Paradise, as well as by the Pure Land Buddhists between Nirvana and the Pure Land. Father Thomas Merton once remarked: "Paradise is not 'heaven.' Paradise is a state, or indeed a place, on earth. Paradise belongs more properly to the present than to the future life, though in some sense, it belongs to both. It is the state in which man was originally created to live on earth. It is also conceived as a kind of antechamber to heaven after death — as for instance, at the end of Dante's *Purgatorio*. Christ, dying on the cross, said to the good thief at His side: 'This day thou shalt be with me in Paradise,' and it was clear that this did not mean, and could not have meant, heaven."[3]

The development of the two concepts of Heaven and Paradise, of Nirvana and the Pure Land, was, in a sense, a prerequisite for man's understanding of the supramundane state of ultimate deliverance. The concepts of Heaven and Nirvana no doubt sound removed from our everyday consciousness. They not only transcend our relative human existence, but are also inherent in it: yet because of their implications of radical ultimacy, they appear to be very far removed from us. Hence Father Merton's significant remarks.

In his *Treatise on the Pure Land*, the great Buddhist Vasubandhu (ca. fifth century A.D.) states: "Contemplating the appearance of that realm (implying Nirvana) we find it to be above the three worlds,[4] infinite, vast, and boundless as space itself."[5]

On the other hand, "Paradise" and "Pure Land" sound rather this-worldly and more familiar to us because of their substantive connotations. These ideas are necessary to bring us into contact with Reality. Indeed, "Paradise" and "Pure Land" are perceived, at first sight, by us ordinary beings, as something like an "antechamber" to Heaven and Nirvana, but behind the scenes they are merged with the innermost sanctuary, that is, Heaven and Nirvana. Hence we find such meaningful statements as "Nobody cometh unto the Father, except through me" (John 14:6), or "He that hath seen me hath seen the Father" (John 14:9).[6] It has rightly been said that the ideas of "Paradise" and "Pure Land" are a kind of *upâya* (skillful means)[7] provided by the Enlightened One in order to guide the unenlightened in the right direction. T'an-luan (Jap.: Donran)[8] aptly called the way of "birth in the Pure Land" the supreme *upâya*.[9] It might therefore be said that Paradise and Pure Land are substantive expressions of the formless, dynamic Reality called Heaven or Nirvana.

An oft-quoted imaginative comparison in religious writings is that of "many paths leading to the same summit." At first this may seem to be a somewhat specious way of expressing the ultimate unity of all religions. But religion is closely related to actual life experience, and in that experience nothing could be less adequate to express religious truth. So long as one is an outsider discussing religions only in objective terms, they may well be likened to the many paths leading to the same summit. When it comes to the actual practice of the way of any religion, however, the situation changes. There are no longer many paths before one, but only a single path — that which is karmically closest to the individual and which requires a life commitment. Innumerable factors, direct or indirect, usually unseen, affect one's coming upon a true religious faith through which final deliverance may be attained. While a religion may be satisfying to one intellectually, emotionally it may be unacceptable, although the authenticity of faith never depends upon one's likes and dislikes. All this belongs to the mystery or unknowability *(acintyatâ)* of the encounter of man and the divine.

One pitfall in the interpretation of the above comparison, namely that of the many paths to the same summit, is that its higher religious dimension may be overlooked. While ethics or morality is naturally concerned with good and evil, the merits and demerits of man's conduct in a "horizontal perspective," religion is by its nature concerned rather with the degree of concentration or devotion with which deeds are performed, a "vertical perspective." If this "vertical perspective" is overlooked, the comparison in question remains relevant only on a superficial level, thus forfeiting its true religious significance. What matters most here is not the problem of *which* way to take, but *how* one's way is pursued. The "religious" question will not arise before and until the question of "how" is asked.

The "how" in question here is concerned with the degree of thoroughness with which the *ego* element is reduced, through contemplative practices, to the stage where one realizes one's true Self. Dôgen (1200-1253) said: "To know the Way of the Buddha is to know oneself. To know oneself is to forget oneself. To forget oneself is to be enlightened by all things. To be enlightened by all things is to allow one's body and mind, as well as those of others, to drop off."[10] Indeed, "the question of God and the question of myself are identical."[11] When one encounters his true Self, his deliverance is attained. At the crucial moment or *kairos* when this encounter takes place, he undergoes a drastic turnover that is the experience of conversion.

This experience cannot be caused by one's contrivances, but would be motivated by the transcendent. T'an-luan significantly called it the "Other Power." He states: "Action of no-action is called the practice in accordance with Suchness (Skt.: *tathatâ*)."[12] The philosopher Tanabe Hajime (1885-1962) used the term "nothingness being in action"[13] to denote the experience of conversion. When sitting in meditation culminates in the state of Self-awareness, the quality of the act of sitting itself has undergone a qualitative change. Man's act should now be called the act of the Buddha. Hence Dôgen's expression: "Sitting in meditation is none other than the Buddha's act. It is nonaction. It is one's true Self. In the Buddha dharma there is nothing other than this which should be sought for."[14] Shinran (1173-1262) applied the term *fuekô no gyo*[15] (the practice of non-merit-transference) to the *Nembutsu* practice in which there is no dichotomy between the utterer and the uttered.

When the "how" aspect is pursued, it is self-evident that it should be followed along the line of reducing the *rûpa* element. The *rûpa* represents the "ego" with regard to the person as well as "substance" with regard to things. In reducing the *rûpa* element, most religions usually resort to the practice of meditation *(dhyâna)*: e.g., yoga in Hinduism, *Nembutsu* in the Jôdo-shû school [established by Honen (1133-1212)] of Pure Land Buddhism, *dhikr* in Islam, *japa* in Hinduism, *shôdai* (reciting the formula of *Namu Myôhô Renge Kyô*) in Nichiren Buddhism, and the Jesus Prayer in the Orthodox Church. It might be said that all religions orient themselves in some manner to attain the state of *samâdhi*, which is so vital in religious practice because it unfailingly assures people of the transcendence of both the *rûpa* element and the *sûnyatâ* element. As D.T. Suzuki so aptly put it, "Zero equals infinity; infinity equals zero."[16] The core of all authentic religions thus lies in this truth.

So long as something of the *rûpa* element remains, the final deliverance falls short of being attained. The mind may be likened to a cup with some residue in it. If it is to be filled with the grace of God, it ought to be completely empty, for "to be full of things is to

22

be empty of God, while to be empty of things is to be full of God."[17] Thus Eckhart states: "Therefore if a heart is to be ready for Him, it must be emptied out to nothingness, the condition of its maximum capacity. So, too, a disinterested heart, reduced to nothingness, is the optimum, the condition of maximum sensitivity."[18] The religious truth here expressed so clearly is based on the "natural law" of the human mind. It is not only natural but necessary. Eckhart further says: "When free mind is really disinterested, God is compelled to come into it; and if it could get along without contingent forms, it would then have all the properties of God himself,"[19] and also "God necessarily gives himself to the disinterested heart."[20] As the *rûpa* element is reduced toward the zero point, the sphere of the mind's freedom increases accordingly. Hence, this state is called *moksha* (freedom or liberation), when all psychological knots and entanglements are dissolved. The Biblical expression "The truth will make you free" (John 8:32) could only be affirmed by the mind that has thus actually found deliverance. Augustine says to the same effect: "There is a heavenly door for the soul into the divine nature — where some things are reduced to nothingness."[21]

It is only natural that this simultaneous process of the decreasing of self and the increasing of Self should often be expressed in terms of death and birth. St. John says: "A man cannot see the Kingdom of God without being born anew."[22] In the words of Shan-tao (Jap.: Zendô, 613-681): "Life comes to an end at the previous thought; it is resuscitated at the subsequent thought."[23] One might compare these aspects of one *kshana* or thought-moment to the two pages printed on one leaf of a book.

The characteristics of this simultaneous experience of death and birth may be twofold: first, it is beyond man's self-will to have this experience, since the transcendent, which might also be called "God's Will" or "Holy Spirit," must be present as the primary efficient cause of its occurrence, man being merely an agent through which this ineffable, timeless event takes place. Second, more often than not, this experience is painful because it demands a cataclysmic annihilation and transformation of man's "ego," requiring that its powerful forces of resistance be overcome. Hence the admonition of

23

Jesus: "He who loves his life will lose it; he who is an enemy to his own life in this world will keep it so as to live eternally."[24]

In the *Nirvâna Sûtra*[25] we find a story of a Way-seeker who experienced a conversion deep in the woods of the Himalayas. One day a young Way-seeker happened to hear a *gâthâ* (verse) recited by somebody to a beautiful chant, and he started to follow the voice, for it contained the truth he had sought during long years of ascetic practice. The chant ran as follows:

> Even the most exquisite beauty
> Is doomed to disappear;
> How could this life be everlasting?

Presently, he met a ferocious-looking demon: it was he who had recited the verse. The Way-seeker entreated him to recite the latter half of the verse for him. The demon agreed, but told him that, being hungry, he would devour him after reciting it. The young Way-seeker readily accepted the terms offered by the demon. Then the demon recited:

> Crossing the deep mountains
> Of this phenomenal world,
> I am going to enter the realm
> Free from dreaming and self-deception.

Filled with inexplicable joy, the Way-seeker climbed a nearby tree, and faithful to his promise, threw himself into the yawning jaws of the demon. At that instant, heavenly music filled the air and he found himself serenely resting amid the petals of a lotus flower in the Pure Land.

This allegory vividly conveys the rigorous process of attaining Enlightenment. It demands staking one's entire being, mind and body. It will readily be seen that the admonition of Jesus quoted above is deeply expressive of the real nature of religious truth. We are reminded here of the Confucian saying: "One who has heard the Tao in the morning is ready to die gladly in the evening."[26] The truth expressed in the gospel of St. Matthew (23:12), "whosoever shall exhalt himself shall be abased, and he that shall humble himself shall be exalted" applies only to the level of morality, because there still remains a self to be humbled or exhalted.

Despite the meaning of the allegory of the Way-seeker, the

24

reduction of the *rûpa* element does not necessarily mean the disappearance of physical existence, but rather the existential death of man's ordinary self. Once this event takes place, however, the "zero" comes to equal "infinity," that is, the actual appearance of the True Self, or Enlightenment. The following Japanese haiku is a most concise and succinct poetic expression of such a religious truth:

> No sooner do the petals
> Of the lotus fall than
> They float on the water.

This points to the simultaneity of death and birth. Indeed, "except a man be born again, he cannot see the Kingdom of God [or Nirvana]" (John 3:3), i.e., except through experiencing existential death.

A person who has experienced this, even while living an ephemeral and phenomenal life on this earth, is really living in the eternal. In other words, since he has become the vessel of the eternal life, the eternal life is living in him. Such a person is beyond the world of morality, and yet his way of life, while being characterized by total freedom, is found to be in perfect accordance with moral principles. The meaning of the Zen phrase attributed to Yün-mên Wên-yen (864-949): "When the great working appears, there is no prescribed course,"[27] could only be applied to such a person.

The Zen master, Shidô Munan (1602-1676) declared: "While alive, be dead, thoroughly dead; and all you do is good." It might be said that a truly religious person is a man who appears to be living as if dead to this world, and yet in fact is living in the true sense, with naturalness, freedom, and innocence like that of a child. His way of life will be found to be in perfect resonance with St. Augustine's teaching: "Love God and do as you will."

In spite of the blissful qualities possessed by those who have had this religious experience, they are still fully aware of their own inevitable imperfections so long as they retain the human form. Paradoxically, religious persons are those who suffer most, perhaps due to the more refined nature of a heart more conscious of its deficiencies. Man cannot become entirely free from anguish and physical pain during his lifetime. Therefore it is only human that Jesus should have undergone excruciating agony on the cross, and that the Buddha should have suffered severe pain before the end of his earthly existence. That they were subject to bodily pain, fatigue, and death as long as they were embodied in mortal flesh, was only natural and should not detract from the attributes of divinity usually associated with them. Because of the Bodhisattva's compassion for all beings, he may consciously choose to take their sufferings upon himself. When the great Buddhist layman, Vimalakîrti, was asked why he was sick, he replied: "A Bodhisattva is ill because all beings are ill."[28] In this connection, there is another Japanese *haiku* which says:

> The darkness of the pine tree's shadow
> Reveals the brightness of the moon.

---

[1]The *Prajñâparamitâ-hridaya Sûtra,* one of the Mahayana sutras expounding the teaching of *śûnyatâ* (non-substantiality of all things), and the shortest of the *Prajñâparamitâ sûtras.*

[2]One of three basic Pure Land sutras. Cf. The *Amitâyur-dhyâna Sûtra* (Jap. *Kwan-muryôju-kyô*) tr. from Chinese by J. Takakusu in *Buddhist Mahayana Texts,* ed. by Cowell (New York: Dover, 1967).

[3]Thomas Merton, *Zen and the Birds of Appetite* (New York: The Abbey of Gethsemani, Inc., 1968), p. 116.

[4]Skt. *tri-loka,* the realms of desire, form, and formlessness.

[5]Taisho Tripitaka, 26-230c.

[6]Cf. Buddha's admonition: "Whoso sees Dhamma sees me; whoso sees me sees Dhamma. Seeing Dhamma, Vakkali, he sees me; seeing me, he sees Dhamma." *Buddhist Texts through the Ages* by E. Conze (New York: Philosophical Library, 1954), p. 103.

[7]Japanese: *zengyô hôben* (Skt.: *upâya-kauśalya)* or skill in means. The Buddha's insight into the individual needs of each being enables him to adopt skillful means, benevolent strategems, adjusted to leading the ignorant to Enlightenment.

[8]A.D. 476-542, a Chinese Pure Land master of the Wei dynasty.

[9]Taisho Tripitaka, 40-842b.

[10]*Shôbôgenzô,* the chapter on *Genjôkôan.* Cf. *The Eastern Buddhist,* Vol. V, No. 2, Oct. 1972, tr. by Masao Abe and N. A. Waddell.

[11]Rudolf Bultmann, *Jesus Christ and Mythology* (New York: Charles Scribner's Sons, 1958), p. 53.

[12]His *Commentary on Vasubandhu's Treatise on the Pure Land,* Taisho Tripitaka, 40-840c.

[13]*Sangedô to shite no Tetsugaku* (Philosophy as a Way of Metanoia), *Tanabe Hajime Zenshu*, Vol. 9, Chikuma Shobo, Tokyo, 1963, p. 22.

[14]*Shôbôgenzô-zuimonki,* 3, tr. by Yaoko Mizuno, Chikuma Shobo, Tokyo, 1963, p. 139.

[15]*Kyôgyôshinshô,* chapter on Practice. Cf. *The Kyôgyôshinshô* tr. by D.T. Suzuki, Sinshu Otaniha, Kyoto, 1973.

[16]*What is Zen?* (New York: Harper & Row, 1972), p. 33.

[17]*Meister Eckhart* tr. by Raymond Blakney (New York: Harper Torchbooks, 1957), p. 85.

[18]Ibid., p. 88.

[19]Ibid., p. 84.

[20]Ibid., p. 82.

[21]Ibid., p. 89, quoted.

[22]John 3:3.

[23]*Ôjô Raisan* (In praise of birth in the Pure Land), Taisho Tripitaka, 47-439c.

[24]John 12:25.

[25]The Mahayana *Nirvâna Sûtra,* Chapter on "Sacred Practice." Cf. *The Mahâpari nirvâna Sûtra* (Mahayana) 3 vols. tr. by Kosho Yamamoto, 1973-5, Karinbunko, Yamaguchi, Japan; vol. 1, p. 352 ff.

[26]Cf. *The Analects of Confucius,* tr. by Arthur Waley, (Random House: New York, 1938), p. 103.

[27]*Hekigan Roku* (The Blue Cliff Records), Case II, Taisho Tripitaka, 48-142c.

[28]*The Vimalakirti Nirdesa Sutra,* tr. and ed. by Charles Luk (Berkeley and London: Shambala, 1972), p. 50. Cf. Taisho Tripitaka, 14-544b.

# The Interdependence of Contemplation and Action in Tibetan Buddhism

LOBSANG P. LHALUNGPA

*Editor's Introduction:* Tibetan Buddhism knows two types of paths: one is rapid, the other is gradual. In the rapid or direct approach, the contemplative tackles the problem at its root; this approach is designed to wear away or eliminate any ego manifestation or ignorant delusion. In the gradual path the aspirant has opportunity to examine self and potential so that his life may be individually fulfilling.

There are stages in the pursuit of the gradual path; the teacher approaches each case, at each stage, with specific understanding. No restrictions are imposed on any of the esoteric techniques. To solve the problem of delusion, however, requires a number of esoteric interpretations that cannot be obtained in an uninitiated reading of the sacred texts.

Liberation is cessation of delusion. According to one teacher, the distinction between samsara and Nirvana is *the awareness of unawareness.* The nature of contemplation involved in the understanding of this and other paradoxical statements is such that it could not, without danger, withstand public disclosure. It depends upon the level of esoteric communication between master and disciple.

The deeper one goes into contemplation, the more one's daily modes of speech and action become nonviolent. In the final stages, the disciple realizes full human potential: the "eyes" contemplate Śûnyatâ — Ultimate Wisdom, whereas the "legs" run the path of action that is conform to it.[1]

Historically, Śâkyamuni Buddha discovered the inadequacies of both contemporary knowledge concerning man and of consequent ways of thinking and acting. And He, Buddha, began to unmask the truth hidden behind the mystery of knowledge. His teachings are centered around samsara, the cycle of existence, and Nirvana, the transcendent peace, and the principle of the interdependence of

28

cause and effect embodied in the Four Noble Truths and so on. Samsara and man's dissatisfaction are nothing but his own delusion and ignorance, described as "unawareness" of the true nature of all things: by practicing the Path he will find liberation.

Buddha further expounded His discovery of the "Essence of Gone-suchness" (Tathâgatagarbha) as being the root of human perfection and potentialities, popularly called the Buddha-nature. Buddha said that the Essence of Gone-suchness is innate in all sentient beings. This is precisely the ultimate nature of human awareness, the substratum of all things — phenomena and noumena, samsara and Nirvana. As such, it is the source of all possibilities in the cosmic realm of the potentialities in human consciousness. Varying degrees of manifest qualities such as compassion, aspiration for liberation, and the several levels of awakening, are effects of the progressive unveiling of the Buddha-nature in human awareness, brought about in proportion to the elimination of various defilements. It was for this reason that the Buddha indicated multiple approaches to human individuals in guiding them to their goal.

Thus, three broadly distinct and mixed types of spiritual aspirants were classified, and three successive ways of training emerged as the gradual way, in contradistinction to the rapid path.

The "lesser aspirant," who is a beginner, keeps in view the appropriate goal — the attainment of ennobled human birth in his next life. The "moderate aspirant" seeks liberation through the Middle Path. The "great aspirant" views sentient beings with compassion and seeks liberation for their sake through the Great Path.

The Middle Path of the Buddha deals comprehensively with doctrinal theory as well as the nature and method of practice comprised in meditation and action. The threefold practice is phased so as to meet the needs of the three types of aspirants. It is comprised of (1) right view, in its middle-of-the-road approach as distinct from the two polarized concepts, viz., eternalism and nihilism; (2) right contemplation, which (a) avoids total suppression of all sensory perceptions so as not to create a vacuum of heedlessness without possibility of gaining a true insight, and (b) refrains from pacifying mental disquiet by indulging in unceasing activities of mind; (3) right action, as harmonized behavior, conduct, and activities, involving not only all phases of active life, but also the contemplative side, avoiding (a) extreme indulgence in sensory gratification or stimulation and (b) a propensity to self-torment.

## THE PRIMARY PATH

The "lesser" aspirants are made aware of the relative importance of this path and its links with the higher path. They should equip themselves with an appropriate knowledge which produces the right view with regard to the values and purpose of human life and its potentialities for the development of virtues. Hearing discourses, studying the relevant texts, observing and examining with due reflection are essential parts of this training.

The salient principles governing such an aspirant's viewpoint are: that, generally, human existence is the fertile ground for spiritual uplift — even though human qualities and spiritual aspiration rarely are manifest; that the external world, the result of universal karma of the past, is where sentient beings continue to sow new seeds of action while still harvesting the crops sown in the past; that all intentional and consummate actions — physical, vocal, and mental — bring their inevitable and distinct results upon the actor, and that any such action will produce results with the mere passage of time. The social and universal implications of this path are to be viewed with utmost earnestness; hence it is described as the noble view of the mundane law.

*Contemplation.* Contemplation here begins with reflection, observation, and inquiry, and ends up in meditative concentration, with one's attention focused on the inferential knowledge acquired as a result of previous examination. This path is apt for every beginner, regardless of his or her (intellectual and spiritual) capacity, its objective being to lay an efficient foundation. Learned monks, nuns, and lay persons alike, can draw upon a rich fund of knowledge by their critical examination, without any pretense at having the

30

capacity yet to solve such abstruse questions as the link between present and past lives; as for the ignorant, they should follow the maxims of the Buddha on each topic in order to gain some definite understanding. The theory concerning the cycle of existence with its twelve constituent parts, known as the twelve links in the chain of cause and effect or dependent origination, deals in fact with the question of past and future.

In a daily program, the aspirant will meditate on the three principles for mind-training generally, and then on each in proper order. These are: (1) the true value and purpose of one's own human existence; (2) the impermanence of all things, the certainty of one's death whether sooner or later; (3) the inevitability of effect following every kind of action, with its correlative possibility of one's being born in some inferior sphere of existence. The immediate purpose of meditation, therefore, is to purge one's consciousness of all that is harmful and to instill in it the habit of moral consciousness.

In both the contemplative and the active life, mindfulness, alertness, and earnestness are constantly called into play. The most important concern of a true seeker is "the perfection of this moment," for in this immediacy alone lies the best assurance of achievement.

*Action.* Action is the application of ten positive precepts and the abandonment of and abstention from ten negative ones. For example, the first precept, "not to take life," the principle of nonviolence in action and nonhatred in attitude, implies compassion, coupled with an exhortation for one "to protect life." The purpose, needless to say, is to humanize man. The criterion of moral transformation is whether one has cultivated strength to live up to these ideals.

The daily program is meant for regulating one's life so that it is consistent with the positive precepts. This program begins each morning with self-observation, followed by purifying oneself of such gross feelings as hatred and craving, and with the resolution to reject harmful deeds, habits, and tendencies, while cultivating such particular qualities that have hitherto been lacking in oneself. Then, in the evening before retiring, one contemplates in retrospect the experiences one has had during the day, with a view toward rectifying mistakes and failures and consolidating one's spiritual achievement, so that the expansion of human qualities may continue to progress without impediment. Thus this humanization process confers in its wake a spiritual content on man's material life. Hence it is described as "the Human and Celestial Way."

Among the qualities generally appreciated by Tibetans are integrity, humility, and helpfulness. Kindness is universally valued. Respect for elders and superiors, compassion for the poor, and tolerance in the face of adversaries and adverse circumstances are qualities especially to be cultivated.

THE MIDDLE PATH

One who has completed his training in the Primary Path may embark upon the intermediate stages of the Way. It is a process which will continue until one attains true insight and transcendent awareness as its higher outcome. Initially, "right view" concerns itself with the intellectual understanding of who one is, why and how one can overcome the fundamental difficulties of one's life, and what are the real causes of these difficulties and by what means they can be removed. Aspirants are thus made aware of the relative value and importance of acquired knowledge which, nevertheless, is but an aid to awakening the inborn knowledge through the medium of meditation and action. Knowledge without meditation and vice versa is like a man without eyes or legs. The following saying of Nâgârjuna, the great master who renewed much of the Buddha's teachings in India, will illustrate the point at issue: "Without depending on the support of empirical knowledge, one will not understand the significance of the Sacred Truth. Without getting awakened to the significance of the Sacred Truth, one will not attain to Nirvana!"

An aspirant's views of life will be determined according to his understanding of relative truth and ultimate truth, which between them encompass the whole realm of knowledge. Relative truth accords with the appearances of things, which must not be confused with Truth as such; relative truth is the truth for man while he is still situated at a mundane level. Moreover, the perception of appearances and of various sensory data is the basis of conceptual designation, whereon rests the function of the cycle of existence. Ultimate truth deals with the intrinsic reality of things, the validity of which does not depend on the relative nature of things. The doctrinal standpoint concerning the ultimate nature of mind and matter represents a form of dualism, as will be shown in the passage

According to the Vaibhâshika school, one of the schools representing the early Therâvada tradition of Buddhism, relative truth consists of the empirical knowledge of conditioned things, the validity of which does not stand close scrutiny. For instance, the cognizance of a house rests on its appearance arising out of a composite whole and is relatively true to the perceiver insofar as his identification of the appearance with the conceptual designation is concerned. Ultimate truth is the only real knowledge — of both subject and object — which cannot be nullified by close scrutiny. For example, the subatomic particles are without any measurable volume — hence suggesting objective reality — while the split moment of the flux of consciousness is without any conceivable units — hence suggesting subjective reality. The root of the cycle of existence, according to the Vaibhâshika school, is the craving for pleasurable objects, while the sister school, the Sautrântika, identifies that root with a gross form of clinging to self. The unique concept of "no-selfhood" is the essence of this doctrine.

The aspirant who has gained understanding through his study of the Dharma, investigation, and reflection, uses such maxims as: (1) all compound things are subject to momentary change, which the deluded mind confuses with stability; (2) all sentient beings are bound in misery and unhappiness in various degrees alternating with happiness; (3) the impurities of the human body are confused with what is pure; (4) a state of no-selfhood is confused with intrinsic selfhood.

In the right view of the way, it is regarded as a noble means by which to eliminate one's own existential bondage. The way itself is summarized in the Eightfold Noble Path, given here under three categories which cover all the principal aspects of the practice:

| I. Morality | i. right speech |
| | ii. right action |
| | iii. right livelihood |
| II. Meditation | i. right mindfulness |
| | ii. right concentration |
| III. Wisdom | i. right understanding |
| | ii. right aspiration |
| | iii. right effort |

*Meditation.* The varieties of meditation are brought together under two main aspects: (1) one-pointed concentration, and (2) Superior Seeing. This division is not merely abstract but points to the most convenient and expedient means of training. At higher levels the two aspects become one. Just as there are two aspects in man — his apparent and his ultimate nature — so are there two levels in meditation, namely the mundane and supramundane. This distinction concerning levels is a necessary indication of the nature and content of meditation, comprising the stage of practice as well as the attainment itself.

One-pointedness and Superior Seeing at the mundane level may be employed in the four contemplations. The meditator focuses his attention on his own consciousness and examines its characteristics, achieving mental peace, physical tranquility, and equilibrium. Later, both conceptualized contemplation and examination are dropped, and concentration is enhanced through constant mindfulness and alertness guarding against the obstacles of both distraction and dullness. Joy and ecstasy are incidentally engendered. Finally, all the sensations of joy and other such experiences are dissolved as the meditative trance deepens. Consciousness of compassion, love, and equanimity are engendered.

The next four stages are formless; attention is focused here on the subtle nature of consciousness. They are: (1) deep consciousness of the infinity of space; (2) deep consciousness of the infinity of consciousness; (3) deep consciousness of the knowledge of nothingness; and (4) deep consciousness of neither cognizance nor noncognizance. The immediate effect of these meditations is not only to purify of all gross defilements such as ignorance of one's own cravings and hatreds, but also to subdue one's innate conditionings without, however, eliminating them.

A meditator is guided to use the simplified form of meditation in which he, according to his particular needs, may begin with Superior Seeing, which practically is a profound self-examination. One could compare this preliminary stage to the state of a sick traveler who cannot undertake his journey unless and until he has undergone medical treatment and been restored to health. A meditator examines his own mental ailment, and then proceeds to meditate on each particular passion, using an appropriate method to eliminate it. Examination of anger, for instance, is carried on in a number of ways, until one touches the very core of the problem, so as to expose its root cause, the delusion of ignorance.

The principal contemplative expedient commensurate with this path is the method by which one seeks to examine one's psychophysical habits in order to gain a deeper understanding of that deep-seated notion of "self." Is it a reality identifiable with any parts of one's being or even with one's finite existence as a whole? With diversified methods of examination and through the quality of one's concentration, understanding of one's own selfhood is bound to grow. Higher meditation will follow naturally from progress in this early phase.

For meditation to be truly effective, the meditator must have an integrated approach to all phases of his life. He will be discreet and discerning in his attitude to "post-trance reflection," the stage immediately following every meditation and deep trance, coinciding with the beginning of his active life.

At this stage the expansion of human qualities must receive equal attention. A dispassionate mind, endowed with discerning wisdom and loving-kindness, is the immediate objective of the aspirant at this stage, while liberation remains his or her main goal.

Nirvana, personal liberation, is achieved when the purging of mental defilements such as ignorance and delusion has been completed.

*Action.* Action is a conscious involvement of man's whole being in any active endeavour for a personal or social purpose. The Buddhist concept of the active life emphasizes the qualitative aspect of living specified as four modes, namely, (1) movement, (2) excursion, (3) eating and recreation, (4) sleep. In fact, action and living provide virtuous exercises for personal transformation, with the immediate aim of attaining the Three Excellences — at the beginning, in the middle, and at the end of action. Thus the active life calls for right motive and intention as a prelude to any action envisaged. Self-examination in this regard is to be enforced with a view to ensuring excellence at the beginning. Apart from physical and vocal actions, there are purely mental activities which affect man's attitude and action, mode and character.

During the entire period of contemplative or active life, the excellence in the middle is to be achieved with the discerning knowledge appropriate for each phase of activity. The various sets of precepts are to be observed. In doing so, one employs the three guards — mindfulness, alertness, and earnestness — which play a vital role in one's life. Consistent with the dispassionate state which he seeks to achieve, the chief quality that will characterize the noble trait of the average aspirant is that he is bound to apply the principle of nonviolence as a positive expression of nonattachment, of no ill will, and above all of compassion.

The excellence at the end is applicable to momentary and daily engagement. It is the instant awareness and action, recognizing any unwholesome attitudes or actions, revitalizing the ennobling practice, and so on. In short, the aspirant seeks to explore inwardly for his creative or destructive potentialities, with the prime purpose of bringing out the best in himself and removing the seeds of delusion and defilements — particularly ignorance — rather than trying to suppress their symptoms, since this does not remove the root of the problem. In an ultimate analysis, there is no reality attaching to action as such; even so, its relative validity and value must be understood, appreciated, and deliberately applied.

## THE GREAT PATH

*The Theory of Right View.* The cultivation of right view is the true

36

purpose of the development of wisdom. In fact, wisdom plays a vital part, and an ever-expanding one at that, throughout the practice and the stages of awakening. Its expansion with regard to the development of nondiscriminating compassion and love is precisely what produces the faultless view that is characteristic at this level. The intimate link between wisdom and liberation is evident as cause and effect. Wisdom as intellectual comprehension precedes right view, even though the interdependence and interaction of the two continue until the final goal is reached.

Right view in its formative stages centers around the theory of (1) the ground of existence and emancipation, (2) the nature of path and practice, and (3) the goal of universal liberation. The ground is so-called because of man's unawareness of ultimate truth, unawareness which is the condition of mundane existence, while awakened insight is the condition of future emancipation.

Functionally, right view is the natural way of looking at things as they truly are, and this does not come about without right understanding arising from an inborn or else an acquired knowledge. Good understanding attained on the two mundane levels, known as (1) the path of consummate action and (2) the path of true preparation, culminates on the supramundane level of direct insight — a transformation par excellence.

The doctrinal condition for cultivating right view is understanding that what is perceived as "reality" by a deluded mind is mere appearance, which has only a relative validity. In actual fact, there is no absolute and substantive self-created reality of anything thus perceived. Such a perception is the basis of conceptual verbalization and action. The implication is that the ground of perception, too, lacks the content of reality, for it is conditioned by cause and effect. Even an infinitesimal part of reality is the consequent production of interdependent cause and effect. Supreme Enlightenment itself is devoid of reality, because the conceptualizing of reality is itself a product of delusion. The absence of a conceivable reality is the true nature of all things: this is Sûnyatâ, "the Emptiness" — not to be confused with nothingness. This knowledge is considered to be all-encompassing, for it concerns the suchness of all nature that defies verbal definitions or intellectual predications, and is evidently beyond the comprehension of the "deluded mind."

Understanding concerning the unity of appearance and actuality — that is, the perception of an image and its emptiness — is the keynote to obtaining rapid or gradual insight into the depth and diversity of perception. The essential unity of samsara and Nirvana has to be viewed in that very light.

*The Theory of Right Way.* Right Way is often presented as twofold: Skillful Means and wisdom, *upâya* and *prajñâ.* Wisdom is understanding of knowledge and insight into its diverse forms, and marks at various stages the depth of one's spiritual endeavor and emancipation; this includes, for example, the ability of an awakened Bodhisattva to penetrate the levels of hidden potentialities in individuals. Skillful Means encompasses all aspects of attitude and action born out of an ever-expanding compassion, through which the aspirant proceeds to achieve his goal of universal enlightenment.

Of the ten principles of "Gone-Beyond," the six to be dealt with later are particularly applicable to ordinary aspirants until they attain their primary awakening. Wisdom, the last of the six, as guiding light, and Skillful Means as dynamic action, are to be employed conjointly, being indivisible in essence and function; they may be compared to the eyes and wings functioning jointly in a bird as it flies across trackless space. A lofty ideal such as this demands, quite obviously, a high personal standard and a boundless spirit of sacrifice.

*Contemplation.* Meditation in its ultimate sense means the natural way of looking at things as they truly are — this indeed is its real function. It is identical with right view and awakened insight, that which is the level an aspirant seeks to reach.

Ordinarily, meditation is both simple and complex: simple, because it is an introspective approach to the discovery of man himself and his environment by means of self-observation and exploration; complex, because man's delusions and conditioning are diverse and deep, requiring different forms and methods of meditation. Buddhism produced two principal forms of meditation with their varying methods at different levels of progress and attainment, leading up to Supreme Enlightenment.

The two principal forms are practiced one after another as a successive path, whichever part is chosen to be the first; at a higher level, they become fused into a single state. The true unity of the two can only be achieved at the primary stage of awakening. One state is *Shiné* — "Dwelling in Quietude" — which is one-pointed concentration; the other state is *Lhak-T'Hong* — "Superior Seeing" — leading to a higher insight into the ultimate nature of things. Normally one-pointed concentration is regarded as the stable support and protective shield for Superior Seeing. The former is an unshakable stand on which the second, as a mental telescope, can rest and function. One will attain a deep insight by means of the combined effect of the two.

The following analogy illustrates the point: if a lamp in the shelter of a cottage is undisturbed by any current of wind, the flame will be steady and tranquil, manifesting its own innate quality of illuminating clearly. Mental disquiet may be compared to the flicker of the lamp caused by a draft; the fixation of one's attention, to the steadiness of the flame; and Superior Seeing, to the resultant illumination. Dwelling in Quietude pacifies any active disquiet of mind, and purges and prevents all emotive and conceptual distractions; as such, it is a refuge for those tormented by inner conflicts and despair and is the harbinger of peace, bliss, and nonconceptual consciousness. Yet, by itself, it is incapable of eliminating the root of delusion, without which no enlightenment is possible. The latter role belongs to the meditation concerned with Superior Seeing. For those who are contented with the first form, there is always a great risk of becoming tempted to seek and crave after the tranquil peace and tranced bliss of body and mind, thus losing sight of the true purpose of meditation, namely, the gaining of an awakened insight as the prelude to final liberation. It is like a man who, in the process of releasing himself from a fetter of iron only succeeds in binding himself again with yet another fetter, though it be gold.

The true state of one-pointedness does not come about easily. It is intimately connected with, and eminently dependent on, the level of mindfulness, one's fixing the attention on the steady image of an object; and clearly and alertly detecting undoing by way of distraction, distortion, or dullness. The achievement of steadiness and clarity of the mental image is indeed a state of momentary freedom from the endless flux of discursive thoughts. The consolidation and expansion of this tranquility produces the meditative absorption and tranced interfusion between the perceived image and attentiveness, and thus one achieves equilibrium.

Contemplative perfection may be achieved through the nine successive stages of tranquility. Special instructions are always available for the specific purpose of overcoming obstacles in their diverse forms, and enhancing progress at all stages. Among inward obstacles, one that is too imperceptible to be instantly identified is called the "subtle slumber," wherein the freshness and vividness of one's mental image fades out, chiefly owing to the increase of tranquility and bliss brought about by the loosening of the steady grip of attention. Even advanced meditators cannot recognize it, let alone check it, without experienced guidance. Where such danger is imminent is a decisive stage.

As for the object of one-pointed meditation, the primary consideration should be in choosing one which not only suits the meditator temperamentally, but will also help to overcome immediate mental disquiet such as fear, desire, hatred, jealousy, conceit, and so on. Until one is well accustomed to a mental posture seeking to stabilize attention, as well as imperceptibly gaining control over the dynamic forces of the mental world, one may choose a concrete object, such as an image of the Buddha, or another subject to be visualized.

The other aspect, Superior Seeing, is initially a self-exploration, the aspirant observing inwardly and examining himself. Of the two most important concerns of personal investigation, the question of the deep-seated notion of "selfhood" as against the doctrine of "no-selfhood" normally precedes the second question, the reality of the phenomenal world as against the theory of no-reality.

Man's clinging to an empirical selfhood is the root of delusion and, therefore, the origin of samsara. The direct way to uproot and utterly do away with it is to develop the wisdom that enables comprehending the truth of selflessness. Apart from this main

40

practice, meditators expand the scope of their inquiry by including such other specific difficulties as personal hatred, fear, and so on, which are typical manifestations of personal clinging to selfhood and its attendant delusions.

Actual investigation begins with the identification of selfhood, not as an abstraction but as the object of deep-seated personal clinging which normally remains indistinct. This clinging to selfhood derives from the inborn belief that there is in man a central entity identified with "I" and "mine," which may be compared to imagining a snake when seeing a rope in semi-darkness.

In both types of personal investigation, meditators can draw upon the wealth of expositions by the Buddha as well as the special instructions received from great masters, whose own understanding, reflection, and logical methods of critical examination and personal experience are a great source of light. The direct knowledge thus gained about the cognition of selfhood is in itself a discovery, exposing the falsity of identity as hitherto conceived, just as the presence of a snake was read into the rope when only half-seen; in actual fact, both are pure illusions, subject and object being devoid of any reality whatsoever.

The true form of Superior Seeing will be achieved as the result of an integrated approach comprised as follows: understanding gained from discourses heard and scriptures studied under competent masters; the practice of purifying the mind of its defilements, and cultivating qualities such as great compassion; critical examination conducted in contemplation and action; and especially, as a result of all of these, awakened insight into the true nature of things (the Emptiness), their appearance being comparable to a scene conjured up by a magician. The emptiness of reality belongs to the level of ultimate truth, and all appearances, whose only validity lies in conceptual verbalization, belong to the relative level. The two aspects are mutually inclusive and interrelated. The relative aspect is conditioned, yet unfailingly effective in producing results, while the emptiness of reality in things both conditioned and unconditioned is beyond all predications, which is realized when the two aspects are perceived as an indivisible unity by an awakened adept.

After each exhaustive examination, the meditator gains a certain definite understanding. With such understanding he concentrates his attention on one-pointed meditation.

Besides eliminating the clinging to selfhood with all its attendant delusion and defilements, such a meditation is capable of opening what may be called "the Wisdom Eye." Mind training is a specialized course, and has been an indispensable feature of all Buddhist education. Its purpose is to engender in one an ever-expanding understanding of self and others, leading to awakened insight into the nondual emptiness of subject and object, not merely in tranced contemplation, but even by means of observing external and internal delusion.

These methods are designed to bring the quintessence of the instructions to the full focus of mindfulness. The development of an entirely fresh outlook rests solely on one's scope and speed in cultivating great compassion and love by means of a revolutionary self-transformation, aimed at eliminating any segment of personalized selfhood; this is called "mutual transference." Both in contemplation and in the active life, the potential Bodhisattva should devote himself to the practice in which he unleashes his wrathful attack on his personal clinging to selfhood and selfishness; he then mentally and meditatively receives the sorrows of all other sentient beings while, in return, transferring to them all his personal happiness and virtues.

This practice not only prepares him to face any circumstances, good or bad, but also transforms unfavorable ones into favorable ones by activating an attitude of equanimity. Emotional attitudes — likes and dislikes — are to be treated as illusory and childish; such attachments and aversions prevent us from looking at things and events calmly and with insight — and only in this way, and no other, can we appreciate every experience in fullness, an appreciation capable of effecting an illuminating moment.

*Action.* The aspirant equipped with knowledge of the Great Path embarks upon its practice under the twofold sign of contemplation and action. As a personal commitment to the Way of the Bodhisattva, he receives from his master the ordination of the Development of Enlightened Awareness, and the instructions concerning the observance of precepts designed to help regulate his life in fulfilling the unique goal — the liberation of all sentient beings, without regard for himself. The means employed are dual: (1) the consummation of compassion and love; and (2) the consummation of awakened awareness. The development of qualities such as compassion and love may be achieved through the expansion of right attitude and virtuous actions (exercising generosity, for example), while awakened awareness may be achieved through wisdom. Because the Way of the Bodhisattva seeks to transform man totally in his outlook and aim, his values, and the purpose of his life, it demands from him exceedingly great determination, fortitude, and spirit of sacrifice.

The superlative significance of such practice transcends all preceding paths. The development of virtues according to the lesser paths here constitutes a spiritual transgression, on account of the motivation towards personal happiness and self-liberation. Aspirants who are still at the mundane level are required to devote themselves to the inner transformation, described as the aspirational generation of Enlightened Awareness. Mindful of his sacred pledge to work for universal emancipation, the aspirant should strive in all earnestness to overcome and eliminate any residual clinging to selfhood, so as to develop a positive attitude of equanimity towards what one normally considers one's foes and friends; he then expands this compassion and love to all.

It is in action that wisdom and compassion must find their right role. The aspirant exercises his compassion and love actively through the six principles of Gone-Beyond. These principles are: (1) generosity, which includes the giving of spiritual gifts and the protecting of lives; (2) the morality of universal service; (3) toleration of adversaries and personal hardship; (4) striving, applicable to all other principles; contemplation and wisdom are the fifth and sixth principles of Gone-Beyond, which have already been dealt with earlier under "right view" and "right contemplation."

In practicing one of these principles in contemplation and action, aspirants should employ the method described as multiple-streams-through-a-single-channel, by synthesizing the remaining five. For instance, in the practice of giving, the Gone-Beyond stage is

43

achieved by the elimination of return or reward, and by the development of nonattachment and nondiscriminating, unceasing generosity. Giving with respect and humility represents in addition the morality Gone-Beyond; the forbearance of personal hardship in overcoming any obstacles and arranging gifts — material or spiritual in nature — the tolerance Gone-Beyond; the unrelenting efforts throughout the giving, the striving Gone-Beyond; the single-minded devotion, the contemplation Gone-Beyond; and the knowledge of the suchness of Emptiness, the no-selfhood with regard to subject, object, and action, the insight into conditioned things.

In keeping with the supreme excellence of the ideal of Universal Emancipation, all practices of contemplation and action should be carried out with the mindfulness of the Three Realms of Holiness. These are: (1) holiness at the beginning, represented by self-examination, followed by renewal of one's pledge with regard to Universal Emancipation; (2) holiness in the middle, being the awareness of the nonsubstantial or "not-self" character of things during the practice; and (3) holiness at the end, where the aspirant dwells in the state of natural clarity of mental consciousness, free from the concept of and clinging to the selfhood of subject, object, and action, and comprehending their intrinsic nature described as the Suchness of Emptiness. Returning from the state of tranced awareness, one reactivates the sentiment of great compassion for all sentient beings and dedicates all one's virtues to their liberation, while still being aware of their ultimate nature. Practice such as this demonstrates the indispensability of the joint application of wisdom as knowledge, and Skillful Means as contemplation and action.

*Buddhist Esotericism.* Buddhist esotericism aims at the universal emancipation of all beings, as an aspiration of the Great Path. The path itself is known as Vajrayâna, the Invincible Way. As the Way of Ultimate Awareness, Vajrayâna brings into one harmonious moment all of these three phases: (1) human existence; (2) the path; and (3) Enlightenment; for it is the "Enlightenment in momentary awareness," and excludes any previous expectation of emancipation. Its teachings come from the Buddhist Tantric scriptures. "Tantra"

44

means a stream or a flux, such as the stream of ultimate awareness, which has been continuing ever since an individual sentient being activated its consciousness, and will continue even after Enlightenment.

Its doctrinal view concerning things conditioned and unconditioned, the path of wisdom and compassion, the practice of consummate virtues and ultimate awareness, as well as the twin aspects of Enlightenment, are all generally the same as that of the Great Path. The approaches and methods differ: the scope and forms of meditation are much wider, embracing almost every conceivable object ranging from one's physical body to the abstract aspects of mental experiences (including such objects as music, dance, art, and other symbolic mediums).

Although it is a direct path in itself, the two trends, the instant and the gradual awakening, are traceable in the system and its approach. An initiate who has trained himself through the three ways or who possesses inborn qualities of sensitivity and compassion may experience the first flash of awakening as he or she receives the initiation from a master, opening up the channel of deeper vision with which to carry on his practice. Women have a special position by virtue of higher potentialities and sensitivities.

The Tantric view of potentiality in human individuals not only recognizes the innate seed of spiritual perfection, but also emphasizes strongly the higher potency of internal energy, the nervous system, and the creative forces as mediums for awakening. The uncontrolled and untrained internal energies and forces, thus trained and harnessed, can activate the subtle aspects which are indispensable in gaining deeper insight. This transmutation — inward, outward, physical and mental — as well as the unconventional approaches and modes of practice, are designed as Skillful Means to enact within and around oneself psychological and emotive conditions that are novel and inspiring, in order to offset the imperceptible but unending effects of illusory appearances and other sensory perceptions upon one's consciousness or subconscious.

The novel and unconventional approach of the esoteric tradition is evident in that aspirants are not required to — in fact, are not supposed to — resort to any form of ascetic practice aiming at control over their passions, but instead should transform those very passions into passionless awareness; hence, their delusion becomes transformed into wisdom, their attachment into detached joy, their anger into compassion, and so forth. By implication, the aspirant should not under any circumstances debase himself in the name of his practice. The key to such practice lies in the tremendous capacity of the initiate to truly transform any of his sensual or other experiences, without in any way allowing personal attachment and clinging to overcome him. The transformation of poison into elixir is bound to fail, resulting in the death of the chemist himself, if he succumbs to the demands of his flesh and indulges in any particle of attachment.

Thus, the alchemical model is applicable to various aspects of esoteric practice. Even the divine forms employed in visualized meditation, normally treated as discriminatory devotion, can be a golden fetter to chain the aspirant if he lacks the depth of awareness and is overcome by delusive forms or phantom figures. Yet the illusory form, if wisely appreciated, can be an effective means by which to comprehend the nonsubstantial and unreal character of all appearances, thus freeing the aspirant from yet another fetter of his own delusive attachment and discriminating judgment.

Of the many forms of esoteric meditation according to each of the Four Classes of the Tantric tradition of Buddhism, the two principal forms widely used are: (1) visualized meditation, and (2) consummate inward-transmutation. Visualized meditation begins and ends up with a formless one, followed by mental projection of a sacred letter and an image of a chosen *yidam*. A *yidam*, for lack of a suitable term in English, is ordinarily referred to as a tutelary deity. It is an embodiment of the transcendent nature and qualities of the Enlightened ones and also of the true nature of human consciousness as well as those of the good potentialities lying in dormant state. The sacred figures, conceived by the human mind, vary in their peaceful and wrathful aspects, and as singles, couples, and assemblies.

The psychology and methods lying behind the representative figures make them effective mediums for contemplative practice. Such transformation of man's creative power into more visually imaginative forms is definitely a counterweight to ordinary perceptions of appearance, or of sound, etc., which subtly but steadily influence the human mind. A male and female couple in the act of union is an example of the unconventional approach of the Tantric tradition. The linked couple embodies a sublime message for initiates, constantly reminding them of the essence of all practices, namely, the undivorceable unity of wisdom and compassion. This, in the esoteric sense, means the unceasing transmutation of all personal experiences into joyful and ecstatic sensations, and the gaining of a deeper insight into the state of the experiencer and his emotive exaltation by means of wisdom, so that one may realize the true nature of one's own mind and of all things.

The other aspects of visualized meditation primarily include: a transformation of one's psychophysical aggregates into a *yidam* of a size which may range from small to colossal (depending on the type of practice); subjectively transforming the external world into a mandala — the mental depiction of the universe in its consummate form; and transcending the subject-object distinction and all other discriminations, and thus unifying all harmoniously in a single contemplation. Other means include the recitation of mantras, sonorously or else without sound, and chanting. Music can also enter into an integrated meditation in visualized form.

The consummate inward transmutation, mainly formless, involves concentration on a subtle form, such as the visualization of the mandala in a tiny ring of light, the internal energies as self-voicing sacred letters; and also harnessing, harmonizing, and diffusing wisely the various internal forces such as the nervous system, the five vital energies, the creative elements, seminal flow, and blood, in order to activate those higher elements, particularly the subtle energy lying in latent form. In this way, all the residual delusions and defilements may be eliminated once and for all, and the direct awakening achieved.

Among popular Tantric practices, the two most worth mentioning are (1) the turning of the Contemplative Wheels by hand or by harnessing the currents of wind or water, and (2) the raising of the Sacred Banner; these are often called the "prayer wheel" and the "prayer flag" respectively. These practices are based on the concept that the air-energy of the physical body is identical with the sound produced through the vocal cords, for there can be no sound without air as its support or source. This is even more so at higher levels. Esoteric aspirants, therefore, activate the air-elements by various means such as recitation, turning the Contemplative Wheel, and so on, in their meditative transmutation of external phenomena, as an essential part of their practice of expanding their compassion and insight, and also indirectly activating the energies in other beings so as to evoke their sensitivity and spirituality.

The Dwelling in Enlightenment is the instant perfection in contemplation and action; hence it demands from aspirants an extraordinary capacity in all respects: they must be most earnest, attentive, warm, selfless, and compassionate. The faithful observance of the esoteric precepts is the key to one's progress in regeneration. Essentially, the initiate must develop true compassion and gain the deepest insight, while constantly striving to free himself from any remnant of clinging to selfhood and egotism, thus dwelling truly in the spirit of Enlightenment.

[1]Excerpted from author's own oral presentation and an interview with Francesco Pellizzi in June 1973.

# Meditation and Intellection in Japanese Zen Buddhism

## Toshihiko Izutsu

*Editor's Introduction:* Zen aims at reducing all the historical forms of Buddhism to the enlightenment experience of the Buddha himself, a purpose which requires a systematic elimination of the analytic function of the mind. But behind this avowed anti-intellectualism lies a fundamental vision — both metaphysical and psychological: insight into one's own "Self-nature." This realization of the Self-nature that permeates the supraindividual world, while lying hidden in the depth of the individual self, is hindered by differentiating thinking. It may be achieved in Zen by two different methods, that of *silent-illumination* and that of the *koan*. Both are intent upon bringing about a complete cessation of thinking in the ordinary sense.

Even though Zen uses words and expressions of a negative nature — void, nothingness, emptiness — its aim is neither passivity nor dullness. On the contrary, what is meant by "no mind" is in reality "mindfulness," a heightened activity of the deepest layers of our being.

Since the twelfth century there have been developed in Japan a number of practical disciplines which embody the spiritual principles of Zen: swordsmanship, the art of archery, calligraphy, flower arrangement, landscape gardening, tea-ceremony, etc. These arts are being cultivated as an alternative to the stricter training going on in the Zen monasteries.

The present paper purports to elucidate the peculiar relation observable at different levels and stages of Zen practice between meditation and intellection, the word "intellection" referring here to the act of cogitation or the discriminating function of the discursive intellect. For all those who have some knowledge of Zen, whether practical or theoretical, will no doubt agree that these two terms, meditation and intellection, are absolutely incompatible with each other.

In fact Zen abhors all forms of intellectualizing, verbalizing, and conceptualizing, not to speak of those random thoughts and ideas that constantly arise and dart about in the mind to perturb its serenity. Not that the masters, i.e., those who have already attained enlightenment, remain permanently in a state of mental void and silence. Quite the contrary, they are in complete possession of their thinking faculty, which they exercise freely and spontaneously. Their thinking, however, unfolds itself in a totally different form and at quite a different level of consciousness from that with which we are familiar in ordinary circumstances. We shall deal with this aspect of the matter later on. As for the disciples, i.e., those who have not yet attained enlightenment, they are strictly forbidden by their masters to think. They are told that the more seriously one thinks the more hopeless will it become for one to experience the final "breakthrough." The very first step in the Zen practice of meditation consists of the disciple's wiping out of his mind all the deep-rooted habitual patterns of thinking.

There is inherent in Zen a profound, ineradicable mistrust of ratiocination or thinking in general. In Zen, philosophy is regarded suspiciously, as typical of the discriminating function of the intellect. What counts primarily — or even exclusively — for Zen is a direct experience of reality in its primordial nondifferentiation, which in Zen terminology is often called "your original Face even before your parents were born." The purity of this "original Face" is often contaminated by the differentiating activity of the discursive intellect. Hence the abhorrence of all kinds of abstract and theoretical thinking, an abhorrence which also has an historical basis. Zen arose in China as a vigorous reaction against the development there and in India of the multitudinous systems of Mahayana Buddhism, which indulged in extremely complicated, often hairsplitting, abstract arguments. Holding the latter to be nothing but the futile entanglements of the discursive intellect, Zen started by shattering these grandiose philosophical systems and proposed to return Buddhism to its simplest and most original form, to what in the Zen view was the fundamental personal experience of the historical Buddha himself: the enlightenment experience which lies beyond the limits of intellect. It would be only natural that the man of Zen should in practice and on principle oppose any use of intellect in the understanding of the central part of Zen teaching. In the Lotus sutra we read: "This Dharma is not to be comprehended through thinking and intellection." For a man of Zen this is still an understatement. More positively, one must methodically and systematically eliminate all intellection. For as long as the intellect remains activated, in no matter how subtle a form, one could never hope to reexperience the original enlightenment experience of the Buddha. For this is considered to be primarily an awakening to a dimension of supraconsciousness, or an *ontological* awareness in its pure "suchness" prior to its being articulated into the myriads of things and events through the discriminating activity of the intellect.

In fact, ever since Zen arose in China, all the masters have unremittingly demanded of their disciples a drastic abandonment of thought: Absolutely no thinking! Do not try to comprehend anything, for there is properly nothing to be comprehended. Instead of thinking, what should the disciple do, then, in order to attain to enlightenment? He is to muster all of his inner force of concentration to fight against the ever-surging waves of thought and finally to sweep out of his consciousness all images, ideas, and concepts. Only then, he is told, will he be able to witness an entirely new realm of his psyche opening up.

The semilegendary first patriarch of Zen in China, Bodhidharma, remarked to his Chinese successor E-Ka (Ch.: Hui K'e) when asked by the latter as to how one could enter into the realm of absolute Reality (Tao):

> No more agitations in the external world,
> No more panting of the mind inwardly,
> When your mind is like a perpendicular wall,
> Then only can you enter into the realm of Reality.

This is nothing other than a strong exhortation to the practice of meditation. Bodhidharma is here urging upon his future successor the absolute necessity of disciplining the psyche through imperturbable meditation. Incidentally, Bodhidharma, so the legend goes, having retired to the Shorin (Ch.: Shao Lin) Temple in the province of Honan, sat in meditation there in a cave for nine consecutive years facing a high rock wall. Be that as it may, it is clear that Zen, from the beginning, has always been a religion based on meditation and nothing but meditation. Meditational discipline in Zen is called *zazen* (Ch.: *tso ch'an*), i.e., sitting in dhyana or meditation.

The primary, or even exclusive, concern of the man of Zen, in the words of Bodhidharma, is to "enter into the realm of absolute Reality," and entering into the realm of absolute Reality is actualizable only through sitting in meditation. From the point of view of Zen we must go a step further and say that sitting in meditation *is* entering into the realm of absolute Reality. The meaning of this will be clarified later when we shall discuss the position of Soto Zen in Japan as represented by its founder, Dogen, of the thirteenth century. Let us for the time being continue to devote our attention to the anti-intellectual aspect of Zen.

It will be interesting to notice that at the back of this anti-intellectualism of Zen there is a clearly delineated "philosophy," although the Zen people themselves would be loath to recognize it as philosophy of any kind. In any case, it is a fundamental idea which is both metaphysical and psychological, and which, though it is not in itself a philosophy in the ordinary understanding of the term, could very well be developed and elaborated into a grand-scale system of metaphysics and depth psychology. This fundamental idea or vision, which, as we shall see, underlies the whole structure of Zen practice and thought, was given its earliest explicit formulation in the celebrated stanza ascribed to the first patriarch, Bodhidharma, who is said to have made in this verse the first proclamation of the foundation of the school of Zen in China. The second half of this stanza runs: "Directly pointing to one's Mind/Attainment of Buddhahood by seeing into one's Self-nature." These two lines indicate that at the inmost existential depths of every human being there lies hidden a noumenon technically known as the Self-nature or Buddha-nature — the sudden realization of which is nothing other than the attainment of Buddhahood, that is to say, *satori* or enlightenment. It is the metaphysical depth of Being itself, the ultimate ground of all phenomena, the unity of all things, in the sense of primordial nondifferentiation.

We can speak of the Self-nature lying hidden in the existential depths of each of us only in metaphorical language. The Self-nature cannot be confined to any individual being; it permeates and runs through the entire world of Being; it is supraindividual. But the curious thing about this noumenon is that it can "exist" only in concrete individuals, and that it can be realized only in the consciousness of a person. Each individual is in this sense a double personality: individual and supraindividual at one and the same time; that is to say, he exists as an individual point into which is concentrated the universal existential energy infinitely surpassing its narrow personal confines. Ordinarily, however, man is not aware of this, the realization being impeded by thinking. Even the slightest activation of the discursive intellect renders the immediate grasp of the primordially Undifferentiated utterly impossible, because at the very moment the discursive intellect begins to function, the Undifferentiated necessarily becomes differentiated: the noumenon turns into a phenomenon; the "I," the empirical ego, becomes conscious of itself as a discrete entity standing against an external world, and the resulting dualism of "myself" and "not-myself" intrudes, contaminating the original nondifferentiation.

Nothing better illustrates this subtle transition, from the original nondifferentiation to differentiation through thinking, than a celebrated passage in the *Rinzai Record (Lin-Chi Lu)* in which Rinzai, the outstanding Zen master of the T'ang dynasty describes what he calls the "True-Man-without-any-rank," that is to say, without any delimitations. This is a typically Chinese expression for what Bodhidharma designated in the above-quoted stanza as Self-nature and Mind. The passage reads:

> One day the Master took his seat in the lecture hall and said: "Over the lump of your reddish flesh there is a True-Man-without-any-rank. He is constantly going in and coming out through the gates of your face (i.e., through your sense organs). If you have not yet encountered him, catch him, catch him here and now!"
>
> At that moment a monk came out and asked, "What kind of a fellow is this True-Man-without-any-rank?"
>
> The Master suddenly came down from the platform, grabbed at the monk, and urged him, "Speak, you speak!"
>
> The monk hesitated for an instant.
>
> The Master on the spot thrust him away, saying "Ah, what a useless

dirt-scraper this True-Man-without-any-rank of yours is!" And immediately he retired to his private quarters.

The monk hesitated for an instant, in order to give an adequate response to the violent urging of the Master. This was the moment when discursive thinking became activated. Note that at that very moment the True-Man-without-any-rank turned into a useless dirt-scraper.

Reasoning or thinking, in whatever form it may appear, always involves the "I" (the ego-entity) becoming conscious of something. It is in its basic structure "consciousness-of." The thinking ego and the object of thinking are separated and stand against one another: "consciousness-of" implies dualism. But what Zen is concerned with above everything else is the actualization of "consciousness" pure and simple, not "consciousness-of." Though they seem closely related, "consciousness" pure and simple and "consciousness-of" are worlds apart. For the former is an absolute, metaphysical Awareness without the thinking subject and without the object thought of. It is not *our* awareness of the external world. Rather, it is the whole world of being becoming aware of itself in us and through us. And it is to this metaphysical awareness of Being that Bodhidharma refers with the word Mind or Self-nature and Rinzai with his peculiar expression: the True-Man-without-any-rank.

The metaphysical state in question here may be interpreted either as pure subjectivity or as pure objectivity; in truth, it is above and beyond both, i.e., a state which is ready to realize itself at any moment in the form of an absolute Subject and simultaneously in that of phenomenal things. It becomes quite understandable now why Zen considers all forms of thinking as a deadly hindrance to the attainment of enlightenment. Even cherishing the idea of enlightenment in the mind works as a formidable obstacle in the way of the disciple. As Daie (Ch.: Ta Hui) remarks in one of his epistles, "If you are to make the slightest effort to attain enlightenment, you will never be able to get it. Such an effort is comparable to your trying to grasp limitless space with your hands — sheer waste of time!"

Shosan Suzuki, one of the famous Zen men of Japan in the seventeenth century, when asked about the attainment of Buddhahood, made the following remark:

> Attainment of Buddhahood properly means to "become empty." It
> means that you return to the primordial state (of nondifferentiation) in
> which there is not a speck of "I," "the other," the Truth, and the
> Buddha. It means that you thrust away everything, wash your hands of
> everything, and produce for yourself an infinite space of freedom. This
> cannot be actualized as long as there remains in your mind anything at
> all, even the thought of enlightenment.

This kind of emptying the mind is not an easy and simple task to accomplish because it is not merely a matter of suppressing arising thoughts. For trying consciously to prevent thoughts from arising is itself a thought; the very idea of abstaining from giving rise to a delusory thought is also a delusory thought.

The training method here in question is in reality far from aiming at inducing in the disciple a purely negative state of quietistic inaction or a total blankness of consciousness. Quite the contrary; what it aims at primarily is the cultivation of "mindfulness," a dynamic intensification of awareness, which allows — or forces — the mind to sustain itself taut and concentrated. There is thus a strongly positive aspect to this meditational discipline, and so realizing brings us immediately to the most crucial point in the understanding of Zen.

The elimination of discursive thinking (which by itself could lead to a negative state, i.e., a complete cessation of consciousness) is designed, in the actual practice of Zen meditation, to go hand in hand with a gradual unification of the mind, making it intensely one-pointed. This latter process cannot but lead to "mindfulness" instead of "mindlessness." This fact distinguishes *zazen* from a technique of passive introversion (exemplified in the West by the "prayer of quiet") by which one learns to sit in mental stillness, emptying the mind of all stirring thoughts and images, and gradually falling into a blank state of mindlessness. The difference between the two techniques of meditation will spring to the eye if we but observe the so-called "life-and-death struggle" involved in the traditional koan exercise in Zen. Koans are all precisely devised so as to keep the mind of the disciple unusually alert and active; in grappling with a given koan, the disciple is necessarily prevented from resting serene in a vacuum of thought. If he does experience such serenity, he must further brace himself and break through that state of mind itself.

Zen likes to use words and expressions of a negative nature, like "nothingness," "void," "emptiness," "no-mind," "from-the-beginning-nothing-was," etc. These negative expressions, if taken psychologically, are liable to suggest trance, unconsciousness and the like, if not to induce apathy and torpor. Rendering the mind thus passively inactive, however, is exactly the contrary of what Zen intends to achieve. What is meant by "no mind" is not a purely negative state in which the mind has just ceased to function. As we have indicated previously, "no-mind" is "mindfulness"; it is a peculiar state to be reached at the extreme limit of "mindfulness," a state of apparent inaction brought about by an unusually intensified activity of the mind. Paradoxical though it may sound, we might say that the complete cessation of thinking activates THINKING. That is to say, the cessation of thinking at the level of images and concepts activates another kind of "thinking," in the subliminal regions of the mind. Zen meditation in this sense is definitely of a noetic nature in that it involves an active awareness, a peculiar type of "thinking" (or THINKING) by which one achieves a metaphysical knowledge of Being in the supraconceptual dimension of consciousness.

It is important to observe that in the notoriously anti-intellectual context of Zen there is still a possibility of our talking about a peculiar kind of thinking, though, to be sure, it is of such nature that it would not ordinarily be recognized as thinking, because "thinking" — at least in the Cartesian tradition of the West — is a conscious manipulation of clear and distinct ideas.

Let us now turn to the inner structure of this THINKING. To begin with, it is not a newly invented concept. On the contrary, we find it well established in the history of Zen Buddhism, although here again Zen has preferred to use a negative expression: "not-thinking" (hi-shiryo) instead of "thinking." The locus classicus concerning this problem is the famous mondo (Zen dialogue) between Yakusan (Ch.: Yao Shan),[1] an outstanding Zen master of the T'ang dynasty, and a visiting monk.

Once Yakusan was sitting in meditation, when a monk came up to him and asked: "Solidly immovable as a rock, what are you thinking?"

*Master:* "Thinking of something which is absolutely unthinkable [*fu-shiryo,* 'not-to-be-thought-of']."

*Monk:* "How can one think of anything which is absolutely unthinkable?"

*Master:* "By not-thinking [*hi-shiryo,* 'thinking-which-is-not-thinking']."

Commenting upon the mondo, Dogen[2] observes that in the case of Master Yakusan there is no contradiction, as the monk thought there was, between "thinking" and "something absolutely unthinkable," for he says, "thinking" here does not mean ordinary thinking at the level of ideas and concepts, but a depth-thinking, a "depth-thinking going down to the very marrow of reality."

In its normal form, our thinking functionally requires an object to think about. The mind in this sense cannot work in the void. Thinking is always thinking-about or thinking-of; it needs something to hold onto. In the mondo which has just been quoted as well, Yakusan, in his first statement, speaks of THINKING as a thinking-of, that is, as if he meant the ordinary pattern of thinking having a definite object to which it is directed. Since, however, that "object" happens to be of such a nature that it is not-to-be-thought-of, the thinking in the case is left in the void, without any definitely delimited object. THINKING, as Yakusan gives us to understand, is *objectless.*

But a thinking which has no object is at the same time a thinking without a subject, i.e., a thinking subject. An absolutely "object"-less thinking is, according to Zen, impossible to actualize as long as there remains in the thinking subject the "subject"-consciousness, i.e., ego-consciousness. THINKING is objectless and subjectless, which is exactly what Yakusan means by the term "not-thinking."

From the viewpoint of Zen, THINKING, although objectless and subjectless, very importantly does not mean an act of thinking from which consciousness of both object and subject has been eliminated. If such were the case, THINKING would simply be a peculiar psychological event. In the Zen meaning it is rather a dynamic metaphysical awareness of Being-itself, or pure Existence, before it bifurcates itself into subject and object, the knower and the known — or we might also say, the "I" and the world. This point is best shown in another, equally famous mondo in which a Zen master replies to one of his disciples who has asked him how enlightenment could be attained. "Enlightenment can be attained," he says, "only by seeing into Nothingness." The mondo continues:

> *Disciple*: "You say: Nothingness. But is it not already 'something' to see (i.e., object of thought)?"
> *Master*: "There certainly is 'seeing', but its object does not constitute 'something'."
> *Disciple*: "If it does not constitute 'something', what is the 'seeing'?"
> *Master*: "Seeing where there is absolutely no object, that is true 'seeing'."

The reference is to the apparent absence of thought in samadhi. On the surface of consciousness there is no longer any thought-in-motion, because the bifurcating intellect has completely ceased to function. But the "mind" in such a state is no longer what that word ordinarily means; rather, it is the plenitude of Being spontaneously disclosing itself as an illuminated Awareness, which is here designated as "seeing where there is no object" — to which we must add "and no subject." "Where there is no object and no subject" can be nothing other than an absolute "emptiness." But the important point to note is that the "emptiness" here in question is not a psychological state of there being nothing in the consciousness. It is rather a metaphysical state of emptiness which, because it is not limited to any definite thing, whether subjective or objective, is the very plenitude of Being.

Thus THINKING (or the "not-thinking" form of thinking), which constitutes the crux of Zen meditation discipline, consists in man's plunging right into the existential depths of himself, even beyond the so-called unconscious. But by doing so man is no longer probing the depths of *his* being; he is in reality probing the depths of the metaphysical ground of Being itself, which remains eternally untouched by the stream of images and concepts that pass across the empirical plane of consciousness. What is actualized here is neither I-and-Thou nor I-and-it. For there is no longer I as a subjective entity nor Thou or it as an objective entity. There remains only IS, a self-illuminating "is," which is precisely THINKING.

In the earlier phases of Zen history there was no systematic method of meditational discipline, although from the very beginning meditation itself had always been practiced. Up until the end of the T'ang dynasty, each individual Zen man trained himself in his own way. In the course of history, however, special training methods were worked out for helping the disciple-aspirant activate in himself THINKING, or the "thinking which is a not-thinking" as explained in the preceding section. The training methods were comprised of two major varieties, known respectively as the *"zazen*-only" method and the koan method, the former characterizing the Soto (Ch.: Ts'ao Tung) school and the latter the Rinzai (Ch.: Lin Chi) school. Zen was introduced into Japan from China in the Kamakura period (twelfth to thirteenth centuries) through the channel of these two rival sects that were flourishing in China at that time, each providing a different method of spiritual discipline. These two schools have survived in Japan up to the present time, and the two training methods are still being practiced in thousands of places.

The Soto school, which was introduced to Japan by Dogen (1200-1253), goes back to two great Masters of the T'ang dynasty in China, Tozan Ryokai (Ch.: Tung Shan Liang Chieh, 807-869) and his disciple-successor Sozan Honjaku (Ch.: Ts'ao Shan Pen Chi, 840-901). As is clearly indicated by its popular name of "silent illumination (*moku sho,* Ch.: *mo chao*) Zen," under which this school has come to be known, the Soto emphasizes above everything else the importance of sitting in meditation. The underlying idea is that enlightenment can be achieved only through a total participation and transformation of the personality of the disciple. The attainment of enlightenment cannot happen suddenly nor should it; rather it must be a gradual process of spiritual maturation. Only at the end of, and as the result of, such a gradual process of quiet mind-illumination can the real nature of Self, i.e., the real nature of Being, be realized. Because of this position the Soto is known as the school of "gradual enlightenment" in contradistinction to the Rinzai, which is known as the school of "sudden enlightenment."

Against the static meditation of the Soto school, the Rinzai advocates dynamic meditation, that is, a particular type of meditation in which we observe a vigorous, dynamic activity of the mind. The koan is used for this particular purpose. The disciple is sternly ordered by his Master to solve a given koan through meditation; he is ordered to grapple with the problem "with body-and-mind" while sitting in meditation. Of necessity the meditation becomes a kind of spiritual battlefield. The koan grows into an "iron ball of doubt" and exhausts all the mental resources of the disciple. Suddenly the ball of doubt is broken to pieces, and the Self-nature is realized. The Rinzai school thus holds that enlightenment cannot come gradually, by degrees, but that it can come only as an abrupt and sudden spiritual event.

Now we turn to a more detailed examination of the inner structure of meditational practice as it is conceived by the Soto and Rinzai schools. As we have noted above, the Soto position concerning meditation is generally known as "*zazen*-only" or "silent-illumination." Historically it can be traced back to Jinshu (Ch.: Shen Hsiu, ?-706), the founder of the so-called Northern school of Zen, and is markedly colored with quietism; it emphasizes the importance of a serene, quietistic contemplation of the "original purity of the Mind." This position rests on a basic theoretical assumption that consciousness is broadly a two-level structure, consisting of a "surface level" and a "depth level." It goes without saying that this is in truth nothing but a figurative manner of speaking, for in the authentic view of Zen there are properly no real layers to be distinguished in consciousness; consciousness as Zen understands it is not an entity having a structure of any kind. But for the sake of practical explanation the two-level-structure theory is very convenient.

What is meant by the "surface level" is our ordinary waking consciousness, characterized by incessant agitation brought about by an uncontrollable proliferation of images, concepts, and thought forms, particularly by the activity of discursive thinking, which never ceases to chase after objects in the external world. The "depth level" refers to the same consciousness as it remains serene and undisturbed in spite of the constant turmoil observable at the surface level. Zen likes to represent this structure of consciousness by the image of an ocean whose surface is agitated with waves, but in whose depths there is a zone of eternal calmness.

With such an image in mind it will be easy to understand that the primary aim of *zazen* as understood in the Soto school is to bring the whole of the psychic energy into an intensely concentrated state of unity, so that the mind, now absolutely one-pointed, might immediately witness its own depth level, which under ordinary conditions remains invisible, being submerged under waves of thought forms.

The "*zazen*-only" type of meditation consists physically in one's sitting with stability and equanimity, "firmly immovable like a rock" in the full-lotus or half-lotus posture, cross-legged, keeping the back erect and straight, with rhythmically regulated breathing into and out of the depths of the lower region of the abdomen.

With the body thus massively planted, one must go on intensifying one-pointed inner concentration, the mind being kept alert and attentive. Yet curiously enough, this one-pointed awareness is to have nothing definite on which to focus. That is to say, no tangible object of concentration is actually provided. Having nothing to hold on to, the mind, as it were, is left in the void. Concentration is not supported, as it is in the Rinzai type of *zazen*, by an all-absorbing attention to the solving of a koan problem. Nor is it supported by the continued visualization of some shape or pattern, or by the act of holding some definite idea before the mental eye. There is not even recourse to the most elementary yogic technique of counting the breaths or following the in and out breaths. Only a heightened state of concentration is to be sustained; the mind, as it were, sinking deeper, ever deeper beyond the realm of ideas and concepts, then beyond the subliminal realm of visions into a purely one-pointed awareness of Being.

Such in brief is the fundamental idea underlying the meditational practice of the Soto school, the "*zazen*-only" school. This understanding of *zazen* reached its culmination in the view of Dogen, the Japanese founder of the Soto Zen, who saw in the practice of sitting in meditation the very actualization of the Buddha-nature itself, that is, the intrinsically undifferentiated oneness of Being. For Dogen, *zazen* is not an artificially devised technique for achieving enlightenment; in fact the highest principle of Zen established by Dogen is that enlightenment and practice are exactly one and the same thing. A man is enlightened by sitting in meditation, whether he be aware of it or not. For sitting in such a situation is not merely a bodily posture. Rather it is the most limpid awareness of the highest degree of existential plenitude. "He" is the sitting itself. And "He" is the awareness of Being. "He" is a living crystallization point of universal Life. Dogen says:

> *Zazen* consists solely of sitting in tranquility. It is not a means by which to seek something. Sitting itself is enlightenment. If, as ordinary people think, practice were different from enlightenment, the two would become conscious of one another (i.e., one would become conscious of enlightenment while engaged in *zazen*, and one would remain conscious of the process of self-discipline after one has attained to the state of enlightenment). An enlightenment contaminated by this kind of consciousness is not genuine enlightenment.

Evidently the "silent-illumination" type of meditation is essentially of a static nature and is liable to lead to pure quietism. The Rinzai school vigorously protests against this tendency, saying that quietism goes against the spirit of Zen. In so doing, the Rinzai school upholds the dynamism of the teaching of Eno (Hui Neng).

Master Nangaku (Ch.: Nan Yueh) who succeeded Eno in the transmission of the teachings of the Southern school is said to have admonished one of his disciples in the following way:

> Do you want to be master of *zazen*, or do you intend to attain Buddhahood! If your intention is to study Zen itself, [you must know that] Zen does not consist in sitting or in lying. Do you want to attain Buddhahood by the cross-legged sitting posture? But the Buddha has no specific form.... Trying to attain Buddhahood by merely sitting cross-legged in meditation is nothing other than murdering the Buddha. As long as you remain attached to such a sitting posture you will never be able to reach the Mind.

The Rinzai school, which faithfully follows the teaching of the sixth patriarch in this respect, takes a very strong stand against the meditational method of the Soto school. Thus Daie (Ch.: Ta Hui), the above-mentioned master of the Rinzai school, says:

> When you are talking with your guest, just concentrate your energies on talking with him. When you feel like sitting quietly in meditation, go

and sit concentrating your energies on the act of sitting quietly. But never, while sitting, regard sitting as something supreme. In these days there are a number of false Zen masters who are leading their disciples astray by teaching that quiet sitting in "silent illumination" is the ultimate thing in Zen.[3]

It is quite clear that by the expression "false Zen masters" Daie means the masters of the Soto school.

Nevertheless, the Rinzai school does not dispense with meditation. Quite the contrary: for the Rinzai people, too, sitting in meditation is the pivotal point of the process by which one advances toward enlightenment. However, the inner structure of Rinzai meditation is totally different from that of the Soto variety: it consists in making consciousness concerned exclusively with a vital existential problem or thought so much so that the mind wholly becomes that problem, that thought; the "I," losing itself, becomes, totally converted, so to speak, into the thought. And this existential transformation is effectuated by means of koans.

The koan (Ch.: *kung an*) originated in the T'ang dynasty, as a legal term denoting a case establishing a precedent to be relied upon in decisions of a similar nature. It came to be used as a Zen technical term in the later Sung dynasty, meaning a special problem or theme for meditation.[4]

These koans are all intended to be meditation themes synthesized from (1) some of the classic mondos between disciples and masters of the T'ang and early Sung periods, (2) fragments of the Buddhist sutras, (3) significant portions of the masters' discourses, and (4) anecdotes relating various attributes of the masters.

The koans, no matter how varied their contents, are all of one and the same structure insofar as they are considered meditation themes. Each of them is an expression in paradoxical, shocking, or baffling language, of ultimate Reality as Zen understands it. It is meant to be a direct, vigorous presentation, in verbal form, of Being — a naked, individual crystallization of the original Undifferentiated. As a problem to be given by the master to his disciples it is, in the majority of cases, deliberately meaningless;[5] it is designed in such a way as to confound discursive thinking at the very outset. It aims at awakening in the disciple a special level of existential understanding involving the whole of his personality, body and mind, far beyond the reach of the intellect.

However, it is a mistake to think that a koan is only disconcertingly irrational or meaningless. Keeping in mind the way the koans were originally constructed from earlier mondos, anecdotes, etc., it is easy to see that each koan yields a certain meaning in the realm of intellectual understanding as well, if only we can return it to its historical context, whether fictitious or real, and approach it from that angle. In other words, there is a particular sense in which each koan can be regarded as an epitome of Zen philosophy.

The koan is in principle a two-dimensional construct, and each of its dimensions may be handled differently. This observation is very important because the two dimensions have often been confused with one another.

In the first dimension, a koan is to be treated as a meaningful utterance or anecdote, no matter how nonsensical it might look at first sight. In this dimension the koan does have a solid philosophical meaning perfectly graspable by the intellect. Every koan in this sense is a kind of "historical" document allowing for an intellectual interpretation. At first it may seem to offer an insurmountable barrier to any intellectual approach, but the barrier is such that it can ultimately be broken down.

In the second dimension, the koan, on the contrary, is not a meaningful utterance or anecdote in any sense; at least it is not supposed to be taken as such, but rather as a totally irrational problem, calculated from the beginning to bring the mind to a dead end. By closing off, one after another, all possible avenues to the habitual pattern of thinking, it forces the mind into a state of formidable tension verging on psychosis, and thus leads it to a final "breakthrough." Each koan in this aspect is a kind of artificially devised means for giving a psychological shock to the disciple. But the remarkable thing about this is that our mind is so firmly habituated to working on the level of intellectual understanding and never to stand still until it finds a "meaning" in any utterance or statement, that it seems to be almost an impossibility for it to begin to grapple with a koan as a violent, drastic psychological shock.

Hence the stringent admonition of all Zen masters against "thinking," against any attempt on the part of the disciple to "understand" the meaning of koans.

Now to illustrate the two different dimensions of the koan, which have just been outlined. Take, for example, the following famous koan, the Cypress tree of Joshu.[6]

> Once a monk asked Joshu, "What is the significance of the first patriarch's coming from India (i.e., What is the ultimate truth of Zen Buddhism)?"
> Joshu replied, "The cypress tree in the courtyard!"[7]

What relation is there between a cypress tree in the courtyard and the real, living essence of Buddhism that was brought to China from India by Bodhidharma? In ordinary circumstances Joshu's answer would sound nonsensical, completely devoid of meaning. However, from the point of view of Zen philosophy (i.e., in the "first dimension") Joshu's words do make sense as an answer to the monk's question. Briefly stated, the Cypress Tree of Joshu points to exactly the same thing as the above-mentioned True-Man-without-any-rank. The only difference between the two is that in the latter the primordial Undifferentiated is presented as pure subjectivity, while in the former the same Undifferentiated manifests itself as pure objectivity. As we have observed earlier, the primordial Undifferentiated as envisioned by Zen is in itself beyond subjectivity and objectivity, but it is at the same time of such a nature that it can freely manifest itself as either or both absolute Subject and absolute Object.

The whole world is the Cypress Tree. Joshu is the Cypress Tree. The monk also is the Cypress Tree. There is in short nothing other than the Awareness of the Cypress Tree, because at this metaphysical zero-point, Being itself in its very nondifferentiation is illuminating itself as the Cypress Tree, unique and universal at the same time. Let us try to interpret (of course, in the "first dimension" again) another koan illustrating in a somewhat different form the same aspect of Zen metaphysics. The koan is this single sentence: "Listen to the sound of one hand clapping!" Unlike the majority of koans ordinarily discussed in Zen textbooks, which are of Chinese origin and which relate to the sayings and doings of the T'ang dynasty masters, this short koan is an original meditation theme newly devised in the eighteenth century by Hakuin, who was by far the greatest of all Rinzai masters in Japan.[8] The koan, widely known as *Sekishu* (One Hand) of Master Hakuin, proved to be so effective in actual Zen training that it has come to acquire in Japan a popularity nearly as great as Joshu's *Mu* (No!).[9]

Now Hakuin demands that his disciple listen to the sound of one hand clapping. If we clap both hands a sound is naturally produced. What is the sound of the clap of one hand? In ordinary circumstances this would simply be a nonsensical question. As in the case of the Cypress Tree, however, the koan conceals a hidden metaphysical meaning, which will be disclosed to the intellect in the "first dimension."

The "sound-nature," which is represented in this case as the "sound of one hand clapping," is everywhere present, ready to actualize itself at any moment as an empirically audible sound whenever and wherever one chooses to strike both hands together. Zen goes further and says that the Mind is sensible of the sound even before it is empirically actualized, even at the stage of "one-hand clapping." Zen in this case consists of "seeing into" the "sound-nature" at the precise moment when the latter begins to stir and discloses its intrinsic impetus towards articulation. This is what is meant by the sound of one hand clapping. Note that when the two hands are actually clapped, the articulation has already taken place, and the "sound-nature" conceals itself behind the physically audible sound.

It is in reference to this situation that another eminent Japanese master, Bankei, makes the following remark about hearing the sound of a temple bell before it is heard:

Listen, a bell is now ringing; you hear the sound. [Properly speaking] you are all permanently and unceasingly aware of the sound of the bell even before the bell is struck and before the sound is actually heard. The transparent awareness of the sound of the bell before the tolling of the bell — that awareness is what I call the unborn Buddha Mind. Becoming aware of the bell only after it has rung is merely following up a trace left by something that has actually taken place. There you have already fallen into the secondary position, tertiary position (i.e., you are no longer in the primary position of the Undifferentiated).

The pure, absolute Subject — the "unborn Buddha Mind" of Bankei — remains awake always and hears incessantly the sound of the bell. This is why, when a bell is struck, we become immediately aware, i.e., without an instant's delay, of the sound as the sound of a bell. There is no room here for reflection. And in the view of Zen, the absolute Subject in such a context is totally identified with the sound (or "sound-nature"); it *is* the sound. These and all other similar interpretations, however, are matters pertaining strictly to the "first dimension" of koan. That is to say, they are secondary matters. From the methodological viewpoint of the Zen masters, i.e., in terms of the above-mentioned "second dimension" of koan, all intellectual interpretations must categorically be rejected as something unnecessary, futile, and even noxious.

From the Zen point of view, *any* understanding of koan by the intellect, no matter how profound and exact it may be, creates only hindrances in the way of one who is undergoing Zen discipline.

It is to be noted that the rejection of all intellectual understanding of koan in Zen is thoroughgoing. One may succeed in elaborating a system of profound philosophy on the basis of an intellectual interpretation of koans; one still remains on the plane of the discriminating intellect; nothing has been achieved by way of a total transformation of man toward an *immediate* grasp of the Undifferentiated, which is what Zen is exclusively interested in.

In its "second dimension," koan is to be treated as a technique specially devised for the purpose of pushing the Zen student almost by force into an existential situation in which he has absolutely no way to allow his thought processes to function. In accordance with the principle, the student is told to sit in meditation, concentrating day and night on a given koan, not to think about it or try to understand its meaning, but simply to *solve* it totally and completely. But how can he hope to solve a problem which is calculated from the beginning to be unsolvable? That is the question he must confront at the very outset. The only authentic way to solve a koan, in the traditional view of the Rinzai Zen, is by *becoming the koan*. The solution of the Cypress Tree of Joshu, for instance, consists in one's *becoming* the Cypress Tree. The solution of Hakuin's One Hand consists in one's *becoming* the "sound of one hand clapping." But what is, more concretely, the meaning of man's "becoming a koan"? "Becoming a koan" would seem to imply an existential process. What, then, is the inner mechanism of this process?

Nothing provides a better answer to this basic question than our considering the way in which the famous koan of Joshu's *Mu* (No or Nothing) has traditionally been employed in the Rinzai sect as the best possible means for disciplining students. The koan itself, which is widely known as "Joshu's Dog" or "Joshu's *Mu*-Word," reads as follows:

> A monk once asked Master Joshu: "Has the dog the Buddha-nature?"
> The Master replied: "*Mu* (Ch.: *Wu*)!"[10]

The "first dimension" understanding of this koan, that is, the philosophical "meaning" of this koan, will now be clear without a lengthy explanation. Against the background of Mahayana metaphysics upholding the view that the Buddha-nature (i.e., the Absolute) is universally inherent in all things, the monk asks Joshu whether even an animal like the dog has the Buddha-nature or not, trying thereby to fathom the depth of Joshu's grasp of Zen. As usual, the master shatters the conceptual level on which the monk stands in his question, by presenting to him directly the Mu, the supraconceptual reality itself.

There is another, more elementary — or more primitive — dimension to this anecdote in its prekoan status, before it was given the form of a koan and began to be used as such. It had been a longer anecdote of a more doctrinal nature, in which Joshu alternately gives the contradictory answers yes and no to exactly the same question asked on two occasions by different monks. The first part of the original version, in which Joshu takes the negative position, shows this character well:

> A monk asked Joshu: "Has the dog the Buddha-nature or not?"
> *Joshu:* "No!"
> *Monk:* "[According to a Buddhist sutra], all sentient beings are endowed with the Buddha-nature. How, then, is it possible that the dog has no share in the Buddha-nature?"
> *Joshu:* "It is because the dog exists by its own karma."[11]

The last statement of Joshu may be explicated as follows. The

Buddha-nature — which is omnipresent — is nullified in that through the ontological proclivity of the canine karma it has assumed the form of an individual dog. As long as we have the awareness of an individually differentiated dog, there is no trace of the supratemporal and supraspatial Awareness of the Undifferentiated. Whether this interpretation is right or not, it is certain that the whole anecdote touches upon an aspect of Buddhist doctrine, and that Joshu's *Mu* in this particular setting is to be taken as an ordinary denial of the existence of the Buddha-nature in the individual dog, meaning, as Dogen remarks, that the Buddha-nature, being in itself an absolute undelimited, does *not* and can *not* exist in its original purity as something delimited. Thus the prekoan anecdote already clearly points to what will constitute in the koan the above-mentioned "first dimension."

As we have repeatedly pointed out, however, such an understanding is nothing but an unnecessary intellectual entanglement from the point of view of the "second dimension." In this latter dimension, the *Mu* must fulfill an entirely different function. The koan must work as a psychic technique, and the *Mu* as a driving force inducing a total transformation of the psychic mechanism of the Zen student.

Instead of trying to work out the meaning of the koan, the student is strictly commanded to go on contemplating the *Mu* until his subjectivity becomes entirely dissolved and transformed into the *Mu*. What he has to do is to face the ungraspable *Mu* without thinking about it. Master Mumon,[12] the celebrated compiler of the *Mumonkan*, admonishes: "Do not mistake the *Mu* for absolute emptiness or nothingness. Do not conceive it in terms of 'is', or 'is not' either." The problem is above and beyond the existence or nonexistence of anything whatsoever. In an entirely different dimension of the mind the problem must be transformed into "something like a red-hot iron ball which you have swallowed and which you cannot disgorge no matter how hard you may try."[13]

Settling into a state of deep, one-pointed concentration, the student must continue gazing at the *Mu* tenaciously and intensely, at the same time repeating the word *Mu* to himself silently or loudly, until finally his whole body-and-mind, losing itself, arrives at a particular state indicated by the word *Mu*; that is to say, until he attains the same level of consciousness at which Joshu himself exclaimed "*Mu!*" ("No!"), beyond the bifurcation of consciousness into subject and object. It cannot be doubted that intoning the word *Mu* in such a state of intense concentration produces almost the same psychological effect as the recitation of a mantram. But the particular meaning of the word *Mu* ("nothing") also contributes a great deal toward inducing in the student a special psychological state in which the subject and the object have coalesced into an absolute unity of pure Awareness. The student may have started by objectifying the *Mu*, setting it up before him as "something" to be gazed at; he must sooner or later realize that by its very meaning the *Mu* cannot be grasped as an object. Rather it opens up an entirely new metaphysical reality, in its "suchness," as NOTHING in the sense of the absolutely undifferentiated plenitude of Being. He will then realize that "he" is no longer there, that there is neither "I" nor "not-I," but *Mu*, just *Mu*, without a speck of duality.

Such is in broad outline the instrumental ("second dimension") aspect of the koan. Even such a brief account will have clarified how differently one and the same koan appears as we consider it in terms of its two different dimensions. In the "first dimension" the *Mu* is the noumenal, the metaphysical, the actualization of which is properly Zen metaphysics. In the "second dimension," on the contrary, the *Mu* is a method, something by means of which the Zen student disciplines himself toward unveiling what we have earlier called the "depth level" of his consciousness. This brings to light at the same time a close tie connecting these two "dimensions" of the koan with one another. For it is only in the very "depth level" of consciousness which thus becomes unveiled by the methodology of using the *Mu* that the *Mu* as the noumenal becomes actualized here and now.

Our principal aim so far has been to shed light on the fact that *zazen*, or sitting in meditation, is not a technique for emptying the mind in the sense of inducing a total mental blankness; that, on the contrary, it involves the activation of a most intense and concentrated working of the mind on a certain level of consciousness where the subject and object are not differentiated from each other;

and finally, that such a working of the mind deserves to be regarded as a very peculiar type of "thinking." This is most obvious in the Rinzai use of the koan method, but in the *"zazen*-only" method of the Soto school too, what we have earlier described as "depth-thinking" is, albeit in a less obvious form, unmistakably at work.

[1]Yakusan Igen (Ch.: Yao Shan Wei Yen), 751-834.

[2]Dogen: *Shobogenzo*. Iwanami Series of Japanese Thought, XII-XIII (Tokyo: 1970-1972), 1:127.

[3]*Daie Sho, Epistles of Daie*, ed. K. Araki (Tokyo: 1969), pp. 71-2.

[4]The koan exercise was standardized by Daie in the eleventh century and has since then remained popular in the Rinzai school in China and Japan throughout the past eight centuries. Many koan collections have been compiled: the *Hekiganroku* (Ch.: *Pi Yen Lu*, compiled in 1125), which contains 1125 koans; and the *Mumonkan* (Ch.: *Wu Men Kuan*, compiled in 1228), which contains 48 koans, being among the most celebrated of all.

[5]On the problem of the "meaninglessness" of Zen sayings see my Eranos Lecture 1970: *Sense and Nonsense in Zen Buddhism*, Eranos-Jahrbuch XXXIX (Zurich: Rhein-Verlag AG, 1970), pp. 183-215.

[6]Joshu Jushin (Ch.: Chao Chou Tsung Shen, 778-897), an outstanding master of the T'ang dynasty.

[7]*Mumonkan*, Case No. XXXVII.

[8]Hakuin Ekaku (1686-1769). A remarkable Zen master, calligrapher, and painter, Hakuin systematically rearranged the principal koans that had come down to his time and revived the koan method in Zen discipline. He is admired as the founder of the so-called modern Rinzai school of Zen.

[9]See p. 68.

[10]*Mumonkan* Case No. I.

[11]This part of the anecdote is reproduced here as it is quoted by Dogen in his *Shobogenzo* (op. cit.) Vol. I, p. 31. The full original anecdote is found in the *Sayings of Joshu*.

[12]Mumon Ekai (Ch.: Wu Men Hui K'ai), 1183-1260. The quotation here is from his commentary on the koan in question.

[13]Ibid.

# Vedantic Meditation
# and Its Relation to Action

### T. M. P. MAHADEVAN

*Editor's Introduction:* There are two traditions in Hinduism, one theistic and the other supra- or transtheistic. Theistic schools in Vedanta include *Viśishtâdvaita* and *Dvaita*. The *Viśishtâdvaita* believes that the soul is a part of God, and that in samsara it has broken away; thus spiritual discipline is designed to restore the whole: the soul has to again become part of God. *Dvaita*, the pluralistic school, believes that the soul is related to God as servant to master. Through devotion the soul has to become the servant of God and thereby regain its right relation to Him. Here again "becoming" is relevant. In the *Advaita* school of Vedanta, which is supra- or transtheistic, the soul is a reflection of the Absolute, only apparently conditioned by the body-mind complex. Here we do not speak of becoming, i.e., the reflection becoming the prototype, but rather of recognizing what one already is.

The tradition of *Advaita* Vedanta is presented in this paper with a particular reference to the theme of this colloquium, contemplation and action. What place do action, meditation, and contemplation have in guiding the soul to its goal of freedom and liberation? According to *Advaita*, release or *moksha* is the eternal nature of the self, the natural state of the nondual self. Situated as we are in the temporal process, ignorance prevents us from realizing that our true nature is the eternal nondual Brahman or Atman. Realization in *Advaita* is the removal of this ignorance, so it is the direct means to release. Action cannot be the direct means, for karma or action, born of ignorance, does not merely mean the movement of the body or the operation of the mind; it implies the false identification of the self with the ego. Meditation is mental action, and meditation and contemplation too are not the direct means of release. Do action and meditation have no place at all in the discipline that leads to release? They do indeed have a place, but a distinction is made between direct means and auxiliaries, and among auxiliaries a distinction is made between the remote auxiliary and the proximate one. Action is a remote auxiliary and meditation is a proximate one, but knowledge alone is the means of release.

The Vedanta is not only a view of reality but also a way of life. The Upanishads which constitute Vedanta (literally, the Veda-end) not only teach about the ultimate reality which is referred to by such terms as *Brahman* and *Atman*, they also detail the methods by means of which the reality is to be realized. Here, the expression "realized" does not mean "to be made real," but "to be experienced as the sole reality." According to the Upanishads, as expounded by Śankara (the outstanding philosopher of *Advaita* Vedanta, ca. 788-820), "the Absolute Spirit is the sole reality; the world of phenomena is an illusion; the so-called individual soul is the Absolute itself, and no other." The world appears to be real, and the soul as different from the Absolute, because of nescience or ignorance. It is ignorance that causes the bondage of the soul which consists in its involvement in the recurring cycle of birth and death. What can remove ignorance is knowledge — knowledge of the nondual Self; knowledge effects the release of the soul by removing ignorance. When ignorance is removed, there is release (*moksha*). Release is only another name for the eternal Self (Brahman, Atman). The Self which is to be realized is not the object of an act. It is ever existent, or is existence per se; it does not depend on human activity. This is the position of Vedanta, according to Śankara: knowledge (*jñāna*) is the means to release, and not action.

The goal of Vedanta as taught in the Upanishads is release, which is *not* what-is-to-be-accomplished. It is rather the eternal nature of the Self. Release is not a new acquisition; it is the realization of what eternally is. Anything that is caused by action is bound to perish. Through action one of four results may be obtained: origination, attainment, purification, and modification. Of these, origination, attainment, and modification are not possible in respect to the eternally attained, unchanging Absolute. Nor may we suppose the possibility of purification (removing unrighteousness, etc.), for the Absolute is ever pure, flawless, and undefiled. In reaching a place or in curing a disease, there is required action in the form of movement or taking medicine. But, in the case of the Absolute Self which is "attained" from eternity (the word "attained" is used only figuratively), what need is there for activity? What should be removed is ignorance; and for the removal of ignorance knowledge alone is potent. A person not knowing what is already attained, such as the gold ornament round his neck, wants to attain it again, and not knowing that what is perceived as a snake in near-darkness is only a rope, wants to avoid it. What he desires is accomplished, however, not by any act, but by mere knowledge. Similarly, in the attainment of the eternally attained Self and in the remedying of eternal transmigration, the means is the knowledge of truth.

That the attainment of the Self (Brahman) is figurative becomes evident from such scriptural texts as "and being (already) released, he is released,"[1] "being (already) Brahman, he attains Brahman."[2] Release has neither a beginning nor an end. If release had a beginning, it would also have an end. And if it had an end, it would be a misnomer to call it release. Further, if release be attainable by an act, then its relation to body, senses, etc., would have to be predicated, and there would be for it the capacity to increase and decrease. And that which is subject to growth and decay is not imperishable. There is no embodiment for the self in release. Release, as we have noted, is the natural and eternal state of the self. It comes to be clouded by nescience, and as a consequence, the nonembodied appears as if embodied, the pure appears as if impure, the eternally attained appears as if unattained. When ignorance is removed by knowledge, Brahman, as it were, is attained.

Action which is a product of ignorance cannot destroy its parent. The delusive cognition of the rope-snake is not removed by the darkness which is its cause. Pain is the result of being embodied; the body has its root in the previously acquired merit and demerit; merit and demerit are the fruit of prescribed and prohibited acts; these acts are dependent on appetition and aversion; appetition and aversion are conditioned by attractiveness and unattractiveness which are superimposed on sense objects; superimposition is caused by the world of duality which appears to be real on account of noninquiry; the world of duality, however, is illusory, like nacre-silver, and it is the result of this ignorance which obscures the nondual self. Hence ignorance of the self is the sole cause of all evil; and it is only knowledge that can remove ignorance. Delusion which is brought about by nescience is dispelled by the cognition of the true. Darkness is destroyed by light alone. The removal of nescience can be by knowledge alone, not by any act.

Is not knowledge, it may be asked, an act of the mind? The reply is that knowledge is not an act. Action is dependent on the will of the agent; knowledge should conform to the nature of reality. To go to a distant town, for instance, action is necessary. The action of going, however, is determined by the will of the agent. One may go, or not go, or go by alternative modes of transport. But the case of knowledge is otherwise. In the matter of perceiving a green parrot perching on a tree, for example, the perceiver has no option. He cannot "will" to perceive it as a leaf. Knowledge must conform to the object. It is true that action may precede knowledge but knowledge itself is not an act.

In order to understand what knowledge is, we should contrast it with action. Although both action and knowledge relate to the mind, action is what the agent does and is dependent on his will, as we have seen, whereas knowledge must be conditioned by its object. Action is *kartri-tantra;* it depends on the agent. Knowledge is *vastu-tantra;* it depends on the content of its object. For instance, it is within the sphere of a man's will to decide to go to a place or not to go, and if to go how to get there. Such is not the case with knowledge. If what is in front of me is a post and I mistake it for a ghost, that would not be knowledge. Knowledge should conform to its object; it cannot be arbitrarily constituted by an act of will. Will is not Idea. Opinion and belief, in so far as they are conditioned by will, do not constitute knowledge. If one worships an image believing it to be Vishnu, one may obtain the appropriate meritorious results; but this is not a case of knowledge. Acts may precede knowledge such as, in visual perception, the act of turning the face in the direction of the object and opening the eyes, etc. But perception itself consists in the revelation of its content.

If knowledge is the means to release, and not action, it may be asked if there is no place at all for action in the scheme of Vedantic discipline. The answer is that there is indeed a place. The competence to tread the path of knowledge is gained only when one's mind has become pure. For the purification of the mind, the means is karma-yoga, the performance of one's duties without attachment to results.

It is not action that binds us so much as our attachment to the fruit of action. So, desirelessness or freedom from attachment is what we should first achieve. By mere inaction it is not possible to achieve this. We may be inactive outside, but intensely active inside. Action does not mean mere bodily movement. Action is conditioned by the soul's sense of agency through the wrong identification with its body, etc. Freedom from the sense of agency cannot be gained by making the body motionless. The desire for inactivity is as much harmful as that for the fruit of action. So, the principle of karma-yoga is this: Let not the desire for fruit be the motive for your actions, and, too, let not there be a longing for inaction.

Is is possible to act without motive? It is true that there cannot be endeavor without motive. But instead of having a different motive for each action, one should have one and the same motive for all actions. That motive should be inner purification, which is essential for following the path of knowledge that leads to Brahman-realization. Unless the mind is thoroughly cleansed, it will not receive the ray of wisdom, that illumination which reveals the nondual Self.

The path of knowledge consists of three phases: study or "hearing" *(sravana)*, reflection *(manana)*, and contemplation *(nididhyâsana)*. Study stands for the proper understanding of the Vedantic texts. The texts fall into two categories: intermediary and major. The intermediary texts relate to the nature of the world, the nature of the individual soul, the nature of the nondual Self, etc. The major texts impart the supreme knowledge of identity. From the intermediary texts, only mediate knowledge of the truth is gained. From the major texts, the direct experience of the plenary reality may be obtained. In the case of the eminently competent seeker, even a single hearing of the major text "that thou art" *(tat tvam asi)* will be enough to effect release. But for others, impediments arise in the form of long-established false beliefs, the belief that the Vedanta teaches what is impossible *(asambhâvanâ)*, and the belief in what is contrary to the truth *(viparîtabhâvanâ)*. The first of these beliefs should be countermanded through rational reflection (*manana*); and the second should be removed through the practice of contemplation (*nididhyâsana*). When the impediments have been destroyed, there arises the intuitive experience of the nondual Self. The intuition which is the final mental mode is technically called *akhandâkâra-vrtti,* the mode which has taken the form of the impartite Self. Although it is a mode of the mind, it is not like the other modes. It destroys the other modes and finally destroys itself, with the result that the self-luminous nondual Brahman alone remains. The final mental mode destroys ignorance or nescience; when nescience is destroyed, bondage disappears, and there is gained self-realization which is release.

To follow the path of knowledge which is the path of inquiry, Sankara lays down certain qualifications as being necessary: the discrimination of the eternal from the noneternal phenomena; nonattachment to the enjoyment of fruit here or in a hereafter; the possession in abundance of virtues such as calmness, equanimity; and the longing for release. Of these four qualifications, each that is earlier than another is the cause for acquiring the subsequent one. He who is endowed with these qualifications is the one who is eligible for pursuing the path of knowledge.

It should be obvious that the qualifications of eligibility are difficult to obtain. What one should basically achieve is perfect mind control. The method of mind control through concentration and meditation, which is known as raja-yoga, is an auxiliary discipline to the path of knowledge. This method which is generally referred to as yoga is very ancient. In the Upanishads and the Bhagavadgîtâ, the yogic technique of controlling the mind is taught. The basic text of the classical Yoga school, however, is the *Yoga-sutra* of Patañjali. The most important concept of the Yoga school is that of *citta* (mind). By itself the *citta* is all-pervading and is called the *kârana-citta* (the cause-mind). But when it is associated with a body it contracts and is called the *kârya-citta* (the effect-mind). The object of yoga is to make the *citta* assume its original, pure, unmodified status and thus release the *purusha* (soul) from its travail.

It is through the functioning of the *citta* that the *purusha* acts, enjoys, and suffers. The functionings produce also latent tendencies which, in turn, give rise to other tendencies; and thus the cycle of samsara revolves. Tossed by the surge of desires and passions, the individual ego is restless and knows no peace; it is subject to the five afflictions of *avidyâ* (ignorance), *asmitâ* (erroneous identification of the self with the mind, body, etc.), *râga* (attachment), *dvesha* (aversions), and *abhiniveśa* (the instinctive clinging to life and dread of death). In order to free the self from the stranglehold of *prakriti* (primal nature), the modifications of the mind must be quelled. The modifications are *pramâna* (valid knowledge), *viparyaya* (false knowledge), *vikalpa* (verbal knowledge), *nidrâ* (sleep and dream), and *smriti* (memory). These must be abolished by removing the afflictions.

How are the afflictions to be removed and the mental modifications suppressed? Through continued endeavor *(abhyâsa)* and dispassion *(vairâgya).* It is only by long practice that a person acquires the habit of detachment which will impart to him the discriminative knowledge of the self and the not-self. The details of this practice are set forth in the form of eight steps which are called the limbs of yoga *(ashtânga-yoga).* The eight steps are: *yama* (abstentions), *niyama* (observances), *âsana* (posture), *prânâyama* (control of breath), *pratyâhâra* (withdrawal of senses from their objects), *dhâranâ* (fixed attention), *dhyâna* (meditation), and *samâdhi* (concentration).

The first two, *yama* and *niyama,* constitute the ethical basis of yoga. The third, fourth, and fifth members of yoga, viz., *âsana, prânâyama,* and *pratyâhâra,* govern respectively the disciplining of body, vital force, and sense organs, and are necessary to mind control. The last three limbs of yoga, viz., *dhâranâ, dhyâna,* and *samâdhi,* mark the different stages of concentration. As such they constitute yoga proper and together they are called *samyama* (constraint). A perfectly controlled and concentrated mind is essential for a fruitful inquiry into the nature of Brahman.

Meditation, however, should be distinguished from inquiry, which is the path of knowledge. Meditation is a mental act which is different from knowledge. It is prescribed for those who are not fit for the path of knowledge. It arrests the current of the mind which courses its way to objects of sense, and causes it to contemplate Brahman. Meditation on Brahman may be compared to a delusion that becomes fruitful. A delusion which yields a fruitful result is called *samvâdi-brahma*. *Visamvâdi-brahma*, its opposite, is a delusion which does not lead to any fruitful consequence. Both the light of a lamp and the light of a gem may be mistaken for a gem. Both are cases of delusion. But the man who mistakes the lamplight for a gem and approaches it gains nothing, whereas the man who mistakes the light of a gem for the gem itself gets the gem. Meditation on Brahman is like the latter. There is meditation on Brahman with attributes *(saguna);* there is also meditation on Brahman without attributes, without qualifications *(nirguna)*. It is the same reality as endowed with attributes *(saguna)* that is called God when viewed in relation to the empirical world and the empirical souls. Brahman is the same as *nirguna* (attributeless) and as *saguna* (with attributes). There are not two Brahmans, as wrongly alleged by some critics. Even when God is referred to as the lower *(apara)* Brahman, what is meant is not that Brahman has become lower in status as God, but that God is Brahman looked at from the lower level of relative experience. These are two forms *(dvirûpa)* of Brahman and not two Brahmans: Brahman as-it-is-in-itself, and Brahman as-it-is-in-relation-to-the-world. The former is the unconditioned Brahman; the latter is Brahman conditioned by nomenclature, configuration, and change.

Meditation on Brahman with attributes is the same as the worship of God. The object of being devoted to God is to gain His grace and to achieve one-pointedness of mind. It is to be noted that Hinduism in general — and Vedanta in particular — does not take any narrow view of devotion to God. Foremost among the particular characteristics of Indian theism is that it is not fanatical in its outlook and provides for a variety of conceptions regarding the Godhead. No one has a right to claim that his view of God is the only view. As early as the time of the Rig-veda it was discovered that, though the Truth is one, it is variously given by different sages. According to the *Mahâbhârata*, there is no *muni* (sage) without a view of his own. This is as it should be. As no two minds are identical, the form of faith that suits one may not suit another. Śrī Krishna expressly declares that there are different ways to God, and that even those who worship other gods reach Him alone. What one finds in Hinduism is, thus, a philosophical theism, which is often mistaken for polytheism. The Hindu is prepared to bow before many gods, because he knows that the principle of Divinity is the same in all.

Devotion to any of the forms of God is called *bhakti*. The external accessories of worship are not important. What is essential is that we should offer ourselves to Him. The offering of a flower or a fruit is only symbolic. The ideal devotee is one who leads a dedicated life. "Whatever you do, whatever you eat, whatever obligation you place in the sacred fire, whatever you bestow as a gift, whatever you do by way of penance, offer it to Me,"[3] says the Lord. When one's love of God becomes constant and complete, one attains wisdom through His grace, the wisdom which liberates the soul from the bonds.

Superior to meditation on Brahman with attributes is meditation on Brahman without attributes. The criterion by which the superiority of a particular method is determined is its relative proximity to Brahman-knowledge. Judged by this standard, meditation on the attributeless Brahman is superior to the remoter methods such as the performance of rites and rituals and formal worship. Just as a delusion that turns out to be fruitful becomes very much like valid knowledge at the time of yielding fruit, meditation on Brahman, when it matures, becomes like knowledge at the time of release.

Meditation on the attributeless Brahman usually takes the form of meditation on the sacred syllable *Om,* referred to as the *pranava.* Gaudapâda, an illustrious predecessor of Śankara, explains the method of meditating on the significance of *Om,* in his verse commentary on one of the Upanishads, the *Mândûkya. Om* is the sound which is indicative of Brahman. It is inclusive of all sounds and hence it is the foundation of the world of speech (*vâk-prapañca*). And of all that is denoted by sound, the ground is Brahman. So, for the purposes of meditation, the sound *Om* is made to stand for the Self or Brahman. Of all the symbols, the sound *Om* has come to be regarded as the most important and fruitful. The *Katha Upanishad* says, "The word (or goal) which all the Vedas declare, that which all

80

penances proclaim, and desiring which people lead an austere life, that word (or goal) I tell thee in brief: It is *Om.*"[4] The *Mundaka Upanishad* compares the *pranava* (the syllable *Om*) to the bow, the individual soul to the arrow, and Brahman to the target, and says the target is to be unerringly hit: thus is union with Brahman attained.[5] The fifth question of the *Praśna Upanishad* relates to the meditation on *Om* as a means to the realization of the higher and lower Brahman, i.e., the unconditioned Brahman and Brahman as conditioned. It is stated there that by means of *Omkâra* the wise one arrives at the Highest, which is quiescent and free from decay, death, and fear.[6]

Thus, the use of *Pranava-dhyâna* or meditation on *Om* is well-recognized in the Upanishads. In fact, the *Mândûkya* starts by saying that its object is to expound the significance of *Omkâra,* and sketches the method of identifying the components of the sound *Om* with the aspects of the Self, and thereby realizing the truth of nonduality. There are four matras or morae of *Om* corresponding to the four phases of the Self. The four matras are *a, u, m,* and a fourth, which is really amatra or moraless, represented by the point *(bindu)* of the *anusvâra.* The phases of the Self are Viśva, Taijasa, Prâjña, and the Turîya; the first three stand for the self in waking, dream, and sleep, respectively, and the fourth is the self per se. The principle of the meditation on *Om* is to equate the matras with the phases. Gaudapâda calls the knowledge of equation *mâtrâsam-pratipatti* (i.e., knowing the matras to be identical with the phases) and *omkârasya-pâdaśo-vidyâ* (knowledge of the morae of *Om* as the phases of the Self ). Now, if two things are to be identified or compared, there must be some similarity between them. The *Mândûkya* and, following it, the *Kârikâ,* give reasons in each case for the identification of the phases of the Self with the matras. And it is well to remember that the reasons are intended only for helping concentration on the significance of *Om.*

The first of the matras is *a* and the first of the phases is Viśva. These two are to be regarded as identical because of the common quality of being the first *(âdi)* as well as that of pervading *(âpti).* Of the sound-components of *Om, a* is the first; so also of the aspects of the Self, Viśva is the first. And just as *a* is pervasive of all speech,

Viśva is pervasive of the universe. In the case of the second matra *u,* and the second phase of the Self, Taijasa, the common qualities are exaltation *(utkarsha)* and intermediateness *(ubhayatva).* The exaltation of *u* is due to its being subsequent to *a.* Similarly, Taijasa is exalted over Viśva, because of its superior order. *U* is intermediate between *a* and *m,* as Taijasa is between Viśva and Prâjña. The common features that constitute the basis for the identification of *m* and Prâjña are being the measure *(miti* or *mâna)* and the locus of mergence *(apîti* or *laya).* In pronouncing *Om* repeatedly, *a* and *u* merge into and emerge from *m,* as it were. Hence *m* is said to be the measure of the other two matras. Prâjña is the measure of Viśva and Taijasa because these two evolve out of it in creation and enter into it in dissolution; the worlds of waking and dream get resolved in sleep, and from sleep they emerge again. The second common quality is *laya* or disappearance; just as *a* and *u* end in *m,* Viśva and Taijasa disappear in Prâjña. It will be clear that the letters, *a, u,* and *m* are employed in this meditation as mnemonics. Each letter stands for the first letter of the words signifying certain features of the Self in its manifestations as Viśva, Taijasa and Prâjña. The second quality of Prâjña is the only exception. Thus *a* stands for *âdi* and *âpti; u* for *utkarsha* and *ubhayatva; m* for *miti* or *mâna.*

The fourth matra is, as we said, really amatra. It is the silence into which the sound *Om* culminates. It is the *Om* without the distinction of parts. It has not even a name, and therefore it does not come under the purview of empirical usage. It is the Tuîiya Self or pure consciousness which transcends the distinctions involved in the forms of Viśva and Taijasa, and the seed of plurality implicit in Prâjña.

The *Mândûkya Upanishad* eulogizes the meditation on the identity of the matras and the phases of the Self by specifying the fruit which each stage in the meditation yields. He who knows Vaiśvânara (i.e., Viśva) as *a,* says the Upanishad, obtains all desires and becomes first among the great. He who knows the identity of Taijasa with *u* exalts or increases the continuity of knowledge and becomes equal in or of the same attitude towards all, and in his family none who does not know Brahman is born. He who knows the oneness of Prâjña and *m* measures the whole world (i.e., knows its true nature) and becomes the place of its mergence (i.e., he becomes the self which is the cause of the universe). He who knows the moraless *Omkâra* in its fullness as signifying the Turîya realizes the Self and does not return to empirical life.

Meditation of *Upâsanâ* is defined thus by Śankara: the process of taking hold of some stay or *âlambana,* established as such in the sacred texts, and directing a continuous flow of even modes of the mind towards it, without the intervention of any other cognition contrary to it. There must be some point of attention for concentration. This is the *âlambana* (support), which serves in steadying the thought-current and making it flow in one direction. The *pratîka* or images are useful in this way. The centrifugal tendency of the mind is arrested, and it becomes unflickering and one-pointed like the flame of the lamp kept in a still place. The images which are miscalled idols have a place in spiritual discipline because they help to turn the mind of the aspirant Godward.

We shall end this essay by summarizing a short composition ascribed to Śankara, which consists of five verses. In this composition, *Sâdhana-pañcaka,* the disciplines required for gaining release are set forth in an ascending order. The traditional account regarding its composition is that on the eve of Śankara's departure from this world, his disciples gathered round him and begged him for his final instruction. In response Śankara composed this quintad known as *Upadeśa-pañcaka* (the Five Verses of Instruction): "(1) Let the Veda be studied everyday; let the karma taught there be performed well; through such performance let God be worshipped; let one reject all thought of desire-prompted action; let the stream of sin be shaken off; let one reflect on the defects in empirical pleasures; let one endeavor in the direction of inquiring into the nature of the Self; let one go out of one's home quickly; (2) let there be association with the good; let there be cultivated firm devotion to God; let virtues like calmness, etc., be practised; let karma with its stranglehold be given up soon; let a good teacher be approached; let everyday his *pâdukâs* (sandals) be worshipped; let him be entreated to teach the one-lettered Brahman, i.e., *Omkâra;* let the major texts of the Upanishads be listened to; (3) let the sense of the major texts be inquired into; let the view of the Upanishads be well adopted; let one retire from bad logic; let logic that is in conformity with scripture be explored; let there be meditation of the form "I am Brahman"; let day after day pride be eschewed; let debate with the wise be abandoned; (4) let hunger, as a disease, be treated; let everyday alms be eaten as medicine; let one not beg for delicious food; let there be contentment with what one is destined to obtain; let one bear with cold, heat, etc.; let no futile words be uttered; let the attitude of indifference be cultivated; let favoritism and cruelty to people be discarded; (5) let one remain comfortably in solitude; let the mind be concentrated in what is superior; let the plenary self be easily intuited; let this world be seen as sublated thereby; let past karma be allowed to get destroyed; let the karma that has begun to fructify be enjoyed here; and then let one stay as the supreme Brahman-Atman."

[1]*Katha Upanishad*, v, 1.
[2]*Brihadâranyaka Upanishad*, IV, iv, 6.
[3]*Bhagavadgîta*, ix, 27.
[4]*Katha Upanishad*, I, ii, 15.
[5]*Mundaka Upanishad*, II, ii, 3.
[6]*Praśna Upanishad*, v, 7.

# Action and Contemplation as Categories of Religious Understanding

### RAIMUNDO PANIKKAR

*Editor's Introduction:* We cannot be satisfied any longer with any *one* world view, thinking that it will embrace the range of human experience universally. We are insufficient unto ourselves, and this confession of insufficiency is an exercise in humility and also in adoration. Without providing the ultimate clue, the contemplative aspect has historically played a great role in the encounter of religions. One must not be blind to the achievement of the *active* element, which has positively added to the meeting, understanding, and cross-fertilization of religions. The vision from within implies experience and conversion. The perspective from without implies the critical approach, and the healthy skepticism that is equally needed.

While the active approach brings us to our own traditional point of departure, the approach from contemplation, at the transcendental level, pursues a dialogical understanding often neglected to a great extent. Given as an example are two fundamental tenets of two different traditions between which an unsurmountable gap was believed to exist: the conception of karma in some traditions and the person of Jesus in the Christian one.

> It is not understood by those who understand; it is understood by those who do not understand.
>
> *Kena Upanishad 2:3*

> I shall destroy the wisdom of the wise, and nullify the understanding of the understander.
>
> *I Cor. 1:19*

Action and contemplation have since time immemorial and under one name or another been invariant religious categories designating two fundamental human attitudes, the centrifugal and the centripetal: the first, predominantly material, exterior, "realistic"

85

and temporal in contrast with the second, predominantly spiritual, internal, "idealistic," archetypal and atemporal. *Poiesis* and *theoria* or *karma* and *jñâna* could perhaps be equivalent words, whereas *praxis* and *bhakti* would have a role of mediating between them. The active mood checks, interferes, experiments, reasons; it is mostly pragmatic and tests an idea by its fruits. The contemplative mood observes, experiences, intuits; it is mostly theoretical and accepts an idea by its own radiance and power. The former is mainly existential — truth is conquered (in the making of it). The latter is mainly essential — truth is discovered (in the *simplex intuitus*).

Our purpose here will be threefold: 1) to uncover the paradoxical fact that though contemplation, by and large, has been considered within the respective traditions to be a superior form of religious life, it has hardly played its incumbent role in the interreligious dialogue; 2) to demonstrate the indispensable use of the contemplative approach in the religious encounter, by means of two central examples from the Hindu and Christian traditions; 3) to suggest that both approaches are: a) necessary but insufficient, if taken in isolation, b) complementary, if rightly understood, and c) leading to a cross-religious fertilization which may be one of the major hopes for mankind today.

## I. THE PRIMACY OF ACTION

> As one acts, as one behaves, so does one become.
> *Brihadâranyaka Upanishad 4:5*

> Except you be circumcised . . . you cannot be saved.
> *Acts 15:1*

A) *The Active Approach and Recent History.* In our present tortured time there is a positive aspiration for a truly human culture, one which would also make room for an almost indefinite number of subcultures. We breathe in everywhere a desire for tolerance, mutual respect, and freedom, at least theoretically, and when a different attitude is defended, it has to clothe itself in the same values it really denies. We no longer justify excommunications, holy wars, wholesale condemnations, and elitist positions. To be sure, we are certainly far from an ideal situation, but the collective conscience of mankind is moving generally in a positive direction.

Yet most of these results are, by and large, almost compelled by a certain historical dynamism. In fact, scholars, thinkers, writers, as well as men of religion are in the wake of men of action in politics and business, simply following the trend of the times. The scholars are busy explaining the astonishing changes taking place (sociology has become the Queen of the sciences) and hardly have time for anything else, let alone to steer the course of events and much less to bring a contemplative and creative view to bear on them. Most of the modern prophets in all fields are men of action.

Action and the active mood dominate the modern scene. It is certainly true that within particular groups, and even in the world at large, many are prepared to accept the contemplative attitude as the superior one; but contemplation, generally reserved for the elect few, will hardly be noticeable within the decision-making agencies which seem to steer the events of the world on many different levels. One is not likely to find many theoreticians, "saints," monks, and contemplatives in these agencies; they prefer calm and solitude, and disdain or even despise the strains and stresses of the active man. In the encounter of cultures and religions, the dominating force belongs to the events brought about by active men.

B) *Shortcomings of the Active Approach.* There seems to be a built-in double standard in self-judging and judging others — not only because of self-centeredness or moral cowardice, but also, and probably mainly — because we have not the contemplative or even theoretical point of view.

To begin with, we judge our own group (of whatever kind) from within, from the standpoint of a concerned participant with insight — a contemplative vision — its sources of inspiration. In contrast we judge other groups from outside, by their mixed fruits and without the same discrimination. We adopt the "active" approach in evaluating others by inferring what they are from what they do, always according, of course, to our own particular criteria of judgment. We then attribute what we find this way to their particular group, culture, or religion. We reserve for our own group or tradition an opposite approach: we consider its positive values as the decisive criterion for interpretation, so that we judge what we are not from what we do, but from what we are supposed to be and from our intentions. Are those who speak of the dignity of Christianity and the indignity of Christians ready to accept the dignity of Marxism and the indignity of Marxists? When Christians persecute, then they are bad Christians, but when Marxists do so they are consistent — so Christians tend to think. When a Christian is tolerant or broadminded, this is because of some Indian or at least Asian influence — a Hindu tends to think. And if a Christian is concerned with social justice a Marxist will feel that this is due to Marxist influence. Can we compare the Dhammapada with the Crusades or the Sermon on the Mount with Turkish conquests?

But the misunderstanding goes deeper than just judging acts by different standards; it concerns also the very doctrines. Can a Muslim be convinced that the Christian trinity is not tritheism? Can a Christian agree that Hindu *advaita* is not monism? Can a humanist accept that Islam is more than just a theocratic form or can a Buddhist acknowledge that the Jewish idea of an elect people is more than another form of religious caste-ism? Is the Hindu ready to recognize that his idea of tolerance may be a very intolerant one?

We are only signaling the enormous task ahead and pointing out that the problem transcends the realm of good will, the desire to understand, mutual respect, and sympathy. As important and necessary as these factors are, they are not sufficient.

Commitment to truth as one sees it, irrespective of the consequence, loyalty to one's community, fidelity to one's own destiny, karma, duty, historical mission, etc., fear of anarchic eclecticism and of barren syncretisms, mistrust of generalizations, abhorrence of abstract and lifeless statements, avoidance of the deleterious effects of indiscriminate permissiveness, etc. — all this represents the other side of the issue which in no way should be minimized. Not all problems are solved, indeed.

C) *Advantages of the Active Approach.* It would be a distortion of the true perspective if we were only to criticize the active approach or to underline its deficiencies. Were it not for the active thrust, in spite of the many aggressions, the world would still be living in compartmentalized and narcissistically self-satisfied little boxes, each one thinking itself to be the whole universe and to have a hold on the whole truth. Were it not for the pressures of history and the active spirit in man, brahmins, pandits, scribes, priests, and professors of all kinds, races, and creeds would still be convinced that they have the keys to any human problem and the property rights over any lasting and transcendent value. Only the incursions of one group into another have brought about eclectic and syncretistic attitudes, which were the starting points for more permanent and even natural symbioses and syntheses among different cultural worlds and religions.

## II. THE PRIMACY OF CONTEMPLATION

> One becomes that which one meditates upon.
> *Śatapatha Brâhmana 10:5,2,20*

> What shall a man give in exchange for his soul?
> *Matt. 16:26*

A) *The Contemplative Approach.* Understanding the other as other is not sufficient, for the other does not understand himself as "other," but as self. In other words, I shall not really understand the other until I am able to perform on the intellectual-spiritual plane a comparable feat to that required by the moral injunction: Love your neighbor as yourself, i.e., not *as* your neighbor but as *your own self.* Is this love possible? By traditional Christian morals it is only possible under the influence of divine grace, for man's "natural" disposition is incapable of such a transcendence. As to the comparable feat of understanding on the intellectual plane, we may add that it is only possible if we transcend the field of mere reason and, without denying it, reach the realm of true contemplation.

If contemplation has here any function, it is, of course, in meeting this challenge without having to subscribe to any particular theory or theological school.

In order to understand the other as he understands himself I have

89

to become the other, viz., to share in his experience, to participate in his particular world. How can a Christian understand a Hindu if he does not become a Hindu? A Christian may perhaps understand — from the outside — a kind of objectified "Hinduism," but this need not tally with what the Hindu accepts and believes as *his* Hinduism. Living Hinduism is constitutively linked up with the Hindu understanding of it, including the Hindu's self-understanding.

And conversely, how can a Hindu enter the world of Christian belief if he does not hold as true that same belief? I may perhaps understand you *better* than yourself, but certainly not *as* yourself if I do not share your self-understanding. Or, to put it in philosophical terms, the belief of the believer belongs essentially to the religious phenomenon, so that the *noema* of religion is not an objectified *creditum* or an hypothetical *credendum,* but entails an unbreakable link with the *credens.* The belief of the believer remains opaque for the observer until in one way or another it also becomes the belief of the observer.

Within the categories of action this enterprise is impossible. I cannot be in your place just as my body cannot occupy the place your body occupies. If I am an active member of a particular religious group and that community embodies for me the concrete way towards my own ultimate fulfillment, I cannot belong to a parallel group. We may meet, like parallels, in the infinite; we may share in the same mystical body, but we should not blur all distinctions between the concrete human groups to which we belong. You can be a member of two different clubs, but you cannot belong to two churches; so it would seem from an active point of view.

Now, contemplation means precisely the overcoming of the spatio-temporal categories which limit the possible ways of being consciously in the world and of participating in the ongoing process of existence. Contemplation does not mean comprehending by mere mental effort or developing a rational understanding of what, say, a Hindu believes if one is a Christian, or vice versa; contemplation is not an act of the imagination or a product of fantasy; it is actual participation in the reality one contemplates, the real sharing in the things one "sees," the factual identification with the truth one realizes. Contemplation is not merely a pointing at the object one contemplates or a sheer intentional identification with it by virtue of a mental (or epistemic) process. Contemplation is a dynamic identification with, the actual becoming of the reality one contemplates; it is the real building of the temple of reality in which the onlooker is part and parcel of the whole construction. This may be the reason why concentration — i.e., the ontic condensation of reality, the functional crystallization of what is, the construction of a center of reality, the overcoming of mere psychological state and fluctuations thereof is in all traditions one of the most important features of contemplative activity. Contemplation implies the vision of the totality in which the contemplator becomes in fact part of the contemplated reality. It obviously does not depend exclusively on the will of man or the nature of things, but rather requires a higher harmony as an integrating force. Contemplation is an ontological category.

If there is any bridge possible between the different religious traditions it is through the contemplative who can be in two or more such traditions, but not in a schizophrenic manner, and thus perform a mediating and integrating role.

Needless to say, true contemplation is an experience and not an experiment. It dawns upon one and is not a product of mere willpower. Not all men can have or are even called upon to have such an experience between radically different religious traditions. But we cannot deny the possibility of such an experience, nor even that almost everyone is at least to a small extent called upon to transcend his own limitations by an experience of conversion into "something else," or rather "somebody else," which would keep alive his constitutive human openness. Assimilation is essential to life.

The contemplative approach is not, properly speaking, an approach; neither can it be used as a tool for anything else. The contemplative insight cannot be manipulated in favor of any cause, however good it may be.

B) *The Nature of Karma.* There is hardly any term more central, more universal, and more expressive in the cluster of religious traditions originating in India than karma: all forms of Hinduism, Buddhism and Jainism, Sikhism and also many forms of Parsi and animistic religions, all, in one way or another, recognize the law of karma and its power.

A certain idea of karma links it with so-called reincarnation, and thus seems to flatly deny the unrepeatable dignity of the individual and the uniqueness of man's personal life on earth. As such it seems radically opposed to and thus incompatible with any Christian interpretation of man and reality. Scores of popularizing writings have propagated this notion, now expanded to the East as well as in the West. Does it not seem to be today the stumbling block of a dialogue between Christianity and Indian religions, perhaps even more than the "personal" character of God?

One of the reasons for this impasse is the predominantly active approach to the whole question. You cannot owe allegiance at the same time to the "immortality of the soul" and to the "reincarnation of the individual." A contemplative approach to the problem may yield unexpected possibilities for a cross-religious understanding and even for a mutual fecundation.

To begin with, the contemplative approach finds no difficulty in disentangling the karmic intuition from its different expressions. It will not identify that mysterious force or reality which the concept of karma points to, with a particular doctrine expounding it. If one has had the contemplative insight into the meaning of karma and the law it expresses, one will forego any given explanation or doctrine, and remain fully aware that concepts are meaningful only within the particular context that has given birth to them.

This being the case, we may certainly discuss doctrines regarding karma, we may indeed think that our partner's explanation is wrong and that his integration of that concept in an overall, more or less coherent world-view is weak, but the discussion is only possible at all precisely because we both claim to see into that ultimate reality, which gives us the right to speak with the strength of our convictions.

This attitude certainly does not imply that there is a mysterious "thing in itself" independent of our access to it, but neither does it imply that a mere subjective opinion is all there is. It implies that my conception of a "thing" belongs to reality and even to the "thing." But precisely because this is also the case with you, it follows that neither my vision nor your vision is the total reality. But we should go back to our example.

An important disentanglement which a contemplative insight will immediately effect is the separation of the karma idea from the idea of reincarnation. Reincarnation, under a set of assumptions not necessarily connected with the idea of karma, may be a way of explaining it or rather of exemplifying it, but by no means are they equivalent. Just as the Christian idea of the beatific vision does not entail a mandatory idea of heaven as a beautiful garden or hall on some celestial planet where God entertains his loyal servants, the Hindu idea of karma need not be linked up with an imaginary lingering of the past personality in the new bearer of the past karma. If there is anything karma excludes it is the private owning of one's life, so that to consider the next life still as one's own amounts to the very negation of karma.

The central idea of karma relates to the cosmic solidarity of the whole creation, it relates to the unrepeatable and unique value of every act, which never falls prey to the void or remains barren and without effect. It relates to the ultimate community of all beings, and it expresses, at the same time, the idea of finiteness and contingency, for no being can escape the law of karma, i.e., no being can escape interrelatedness with and responsibility to the whole universe.

The contemplative mood is not one of satisfaction with the mere exegesis or simply interpretation of texts. It certainly entails a high regard for what others have thought, and especially seen, but not the demeaning role of a mere scribe or translator. It will have to prove eventually that everybody is referring to the same reality, but that very clearly reality itself has something to do with the *vision* one has of it.

Expressing it for our times, in our particular context and with our contemporary language, we may venture to say that karma is that word which stands for the vision of the *unity* and yet *contingency* of all empirical — or created — reality.

Karma is that unitary link which connects us with every speck of reality and makes us sense our unity with the whole universe, for all beings without exception are governed by the same cosmic law of karma. The law of karma should not be rendered as a mere causal chain, for there are forms of dependence which belong to karma and are not necessarily causal, unless we expand the concept of cause to any process of interdependence.

Essential in this view is the universality of such a law, not the specific nature of this dependence. It stresses, however, that all that is, precisely because *it is,* has a relatedness to everything else. The chain of being is not exactly a chain — for it also liberates; it is karma. The communion of all existence is not exactly communion — for there is also strife; it is karma. The unity of the universe is not precisely unity — for it is also disunity; it is karma. To discover how karma works, how it acts, is the acme of wisdom; it is realization.

Karma is, at the same time, acknowledging the *contingency* of all beings; it expresses their interrelatedness, and thus their unity, precisely because none of the individual beings populating the universe — and the entire universe in its entirety — is complete, full, perfect, achieved, finished. The entire universe is unfinished and, in this sense, infinite. It is this infinitude which accounts for freedom and the unforeseeable movement of all that is. Karma stands not only for unity, but for the freedom of the contingent creature. It is an ultimate freedom, for there is nothing beyond, behind, or more fundamental than karma. Karma is, as it were, the very coefficient of creatureliness. Karma vouches for freedom and makes it possible — a real freedom which goes so far as to allow us to jump "outside" the realm of Being, and reach the "other shore" which is neither "other" nor, certainly, a "shore." Here the freedom is so absolute that it may be converted into a freedom from Being itself: Nirvana, the Buddhists would say.

Karma is, then, the ultimate expression of contingency. It can be burnt, it can be transcended — at this price: the creature, or rather being itself, is volatilized in the jump "outside" existence so that only nothing reaches Nothingness. Karma is coextensive with existence.

All there is submits to karma, because the karmic structure of the universe is the ultimate pattern. The "Lord of karma," inasmuch as it is the Lord of karma, is also within the embrace of karma. If it were "outside" karma it would no longer be its Lord — for there must be a link between the Lord and his world. This link, by definition, cannot but be karma. What could it be otherwise? If it were something else, this "else" would be the real karma.

Significantly enough, it is in speaking about karma that the otherwise sober and concise Upanishads seem to open up not only to esoteric meanings but also to a more cordial and holistic approach to the mystery of life and death. It is in point of fact the subject matter of the public dialogue between Jâratkârava Ârtabhâga and the famous sage Yâjñavalkya. Five questions are put to the latter by the former: 1) what are the different organs of reality and how is reality modified by them; 2) what is the death of death, if all is mortal; 3) what is the destiny of prâna, the vital breath, when a man dies; 4) what is the only thing which does not abandon a man when he dies; and finally 5) what becomes of the person, i.e., what is the mystery of life. It is at this moment, when speaking about the cosmic law connecting all the elements of the universe, that they both went away hand in hand and in secret began to discuss and to praise karma. The whole context helps us to realize that it is not a philosophical subtlety but a fundamental query concerning the very nature of the whole universe. The nature of karma is not disclosed in an open polemical discussion nor is it accessible to mere dialectics, but is revealed in the ultimate dialogical intercourse with the master, in the personal meditation about the mystery of temporal existence.

There remain, indeed, very many doctrinal problems, and Indian philosophies and the theologies have tried to articulate them precisely, but the primacy here belongs to a certain intuition of ultimate mystery.

The Western contemplative will perhaps not speak the same language; he may not have access to the same symbols, but once this language is heard he will be in tune with it. It is for him, then, in collaboration with the philosopher or theologian, to propound a language which will reveal that aspect of the mystery of life and reality.

Seen in this perspective, the nature of karma may even help to explain such fundamental Christian concepts as the connection of Adam and Adam's sin with the whole of mankind, as well as the relation of Christ and Christ's Death and Resurrection to the entire humanity.

C) *The Identity of Jesus.* A stumbling block from the other side, not minor, is the exclusive claim Christians lay upon Jesus as being the unique savior, the only name, the single way.

If we try to answer the question, already put by Jesus himself, of who is this Jesus about whom such claims are made, we discover that the active approach, based mainly on the spatio-temporal and thus also logical categories, has tried finding the personality of Jesus in his geographical and historical identification: he was that young Jew born of Mary, who lived in Palestine twenty centuries ago, died under Pontius Pilate, and who still has historical and sociological significance. Now, how is that man one of the Trinity, how was he before Abraham, how was he the Messiah, the Redeemer of the whole world, the alpha and omega, and thus the only Savior, Way and Name?

The contemplative approach will not minimize those problems, but will stress another starting point: it will not be satisfied by finding out the *identification* of *what* Jesus did or is, but will seek the *identity* of *who* he actually is. Now the *who* of Jesus may or may not be separable from his *what,* but it is certainly not identifiable with it. The *who* of Jesus is only disclosed in the personal encounter of faith, in the interpersonal relationship of finding a *thou* answering to the call — prayer — of the *I,* and it will be found when the *meta-noia,* the change of perspective and of roles takes place so that Jesus becomes the *I* and the seeker the *thou,* so that the Master's *I am* becomes something more than a metaphysical or a psychological statement.

The *who*  discovered by the Christian may have been revealed to him in and through the *what* that tradition has handed down to him, but he will not confuse the two, and in the central Christian mystery, the Eucharist, for example, he will recognize Christ's *Real Presence,* and yet he will not believe that he is eating the proteins or drinking the hemoglobin of Jesus of Nazareth. Communion is with the real *who* and not with the *what.*

Furthermore, the mystery of the *who* cannot be reduced to the coordinates of the *what*. We will not say that *what* the Buddhist believes in is *what* the Christian worships, but we may be inclined to admit that the *who* beneath the Buddhist's compassion or behind the Muslim's surrender is none other than the *who* of Christian agape.

In the dialogue with the Hindu or the Buddhist the question of the *who* needs also an immediate qualification. Obviously, the *what* of Jesus, his identification, is not the *what* of Krishna, his identification, despite the many resemblances which we may find in favor of a merely psychological or archetypal theory regarding the origins of religious cults (which is not our problem now). But we do not need to entertain a "personalistic" or anthropormorphic view of the personal relation either. A personal relationship is any free and conscious mutual relationship which totally or partially constitutes the existence of the persons who emerge, totally or partially, by this very act. We have used the personal pronouns, which happen to be the most universal linguistic symbols, but we do not assume necessarily a particular conception of a person. The *I-thou* relationship, for instance, does not need to be seen from the angle of two separate beings exchanging the overflow of their own lives. We could equally consider the personal relationship in a more radical way so that nothing of the *I* would be there if the *thou* were not there and vice versa.

The burden of our tale, however, is not to say that there is no language without its implications and limitations, but rather to show the possibilities of an approach from contemplation in the encounter of religions.

Just as we have quoted Yâjñavalkya speaking about karma, let us quote here the Evangelist's witnessing to the angel's words about Jesus: "He is not here, for he is risen," said the angel, explaining with real insight what the Resurrection is all about to the courageous women, bewildered at the sight of the empty tomb; or in a more forceful and shorter way: "He is risen, he is not here."

I beg not to be misunderstood. We do not offer a whole theology of the Resurrection but a contemplative insight into one of its dimensions. Comparable with John 16:7 and Matthew 24:23-27 is the following: It is good, convenient, or rather it is necessary that he go, that he disappears from your eyes, otherwise the Spirit will not come; otherwise we will make of him an idol; we will pinpoint him in spite of his repeatedly saying that when the Son of man comes he will not be here or there, but will be like the lightning which appears in the east and in the west alike.

Over against this background as well as the whole eucharistic discourses of John we may be allowed to understand the quoted passage as saying: "He is risen; he is not here," or, again, "He is risen, i.e., he is not here," as if the angel were saying that the true resurrection is his absence, his not being here or there, his not being limited to one point or to one idea and interpretation. He is not here, he cannot be located and surely not by geographical categories or with merely historical parameters. He is risen, risen above the limited human horizons, above the theological and philosophical speculations, well above any kind of worship, and yet he is present in his absence; we do not need to discover him in order for him to receive our acts, since anything we do to the little ones we do unto him.

But, at the same time, as the Christian liturgy stresses at Easter quoting from a rather free though traditional version of the Psalms of the Old Testament: "I am risen, and I am still with you." Precisely because I am risen I am not here, and precisely because I am risen I can be with you. The presence of the living Christ is not the encroaching upon us of a guardian or a vigilant eye, not even the ultimately alienating presence of an "Other," but the intimately liberating presence of an absence which allows us to grow, to become, and which at the very moment of revealing the Lord manifests him in his disappearance: only when left with the bread alone did the disciples recognize him.

This Christ certainly is the living Jesus, and yet in no way does this prevent *him* from being recognized, from being present and active under as many different *whats* as there are religious traditions. Not all problems are answered, but a breakthrough may be in sight if the contemplative joins mind and heart with the active approach.


III. RELIGIOUS UNDERSTANDING

In this world a twofold foundation was proclaimed by me of old — O blameless one: the discipline of wisdom for men of reason, the discipline of action for active men.

*Bhagavadgîtâ 3:3-5*

Not everyone who calls me "Lord, Lord"
will enter the Kingdom of Heaven, but
only those who do the will of my Father. . . .

*Matt. 7:21*

*A) Necessary but Insufficient Categories.* The contemplative sees, he intuits the truth, he attains a certain immediacy which makes him a mystic; but the mystic ceases to be such the moment he speaks. Speech irradiates his experience, but also dissipates it. The Word is the Firstborn of the Father, the Firstborn of the Universal Order, but words are only broken pieces of that Word and each human language is only one channel to a given system of words incarnating a particular cultural and religious world.

How is the contemplative going to express himself if he can do it only in the language of his time and his place? Each word he utters will sound to him as a lie the moment that people take his speech literally. No living word is ever literal. The active method is as insufficient as it is necessary. Without it there would hardly be any interaction. With it alone, however, understanding cannot take place except at the heavy price of the practical surrender of one of the partners in the encounter, when one of them so totally submits to the rules of the encounter proposed by the other that its role is thereby reduced to stimulating and serving the interests of the other.

*B) Complementary Methods.* What is needed today is a double task. On the one hand, we need the contemplative steeped in more than one religious world, having achieved the experience of more than one religious tradition not as an interesting experiment, but as an excruciating and yet liberating personal experience in which he is naturally and existentially involved and, at the same time, with the necessary skill and intellectual acumen to be able to express himself in more than one theological and religious system.

We need the contemplative, further, for a very important corrective in the encounter of religions and cultures, since harmony

99

does not imply uniformity, and metaphysical oneness does not imply administrative union. Precisely because the contemplative insight discovers the underlying oneness beneath the multiformity of things and appearances, it does not lead to rendering them uniform, or to considering that an external union on the levels of geography, history, administration, and the like is essential for the recognition of the deeper unity. The example of Christian ecumenism could be revealing here. The contemplative will not push for having a single administrative ecclesiastical body, but will emphasize ecclesiastic and sacramental unity.

Furthermore, the contemplative will offer a salutary corrective to the haste and the desire for tangible results of the active approach. Many frustrations on all levels appear because we tend, on the one hand, to overlook the factor of time and, on the other, to overvalue it. Peace, harmony, and understanding cannot be brought about overnight. What is the result of millenia cannot be solved without reckoning with the factor of time and the proper rhythms of history. On the other hand, if the total results are not achieved the contemplative insight will prevent us from being discouraged or frustrated. It is only natural that the spiritual realization of an internal oneness is closer at hand than its external manifestations. Moreover, in the heart and mind of the truly contemplative person something happens which is more than a private dream: it is an anticipation of a real state of affairs. The contemplative has here a priestly-prophetic role: he mediates between issues irreconcilable until now, and he anticipates an age by realizing in his inner being what one day may also have an historical repercussion. The mind and heart of the contemplative are a kind of cosmic and historical laboratory. Once the experience happens there it may well spark on a greater scale when the time is ripe.

But, on the other hand, more is involved than pure skill on the part of the contemplative approach. The contemplative alone will easily overlook or neglect other dimensions of reality which are equally important; for man is more than a pure contemplative and needs systems of thought, structures for action, and institutions to live in. The man of action is equally needed, and all have to be involved in dialogical, and not merely dialectical, communication in order to let the different contributions play their part in the growth of man into the fullness of his own being — or vocation, as some may prefer to call it.

And again appears the problem of the criterion to coordinate the active and the contemplative approaches. How is the mere understanding going to affect actual life and how is active interference going to modify the contemplative insight? I may be convinced that Muslims are right to worship in the way they do and to believe the tenets they hold, I may further share in their belief from my point of view, but this may not be sufficient nor make it desirable for me to join the Muslim religion in a formal way. In other words, acknowledging a certain transcendental unity of all creeds or the relative validity of all religions, as important a step as it may be, does not solve the problem of a divided mankind, for the ideological aspects of the different traditions may be at variance and even in mutual conflict.

The two methods are complementary, but the complementarity cannot be articulated in any strategic or programmatic way lest it become subservient to some of the parties. Here we could apply the saying not to be anxious about tomorrow and to have the confidence that tomorrow will look after itself.

C) *An Ongoing Process.* Action and contemplation have to join hands in an act of cosmic or human or divine trust. No man, no religion, no theology, no action or contemplation has the right to set the rules of this ultimate game of the human encounter in depth. From all sides we have to recognize our insufficiency, and this humble but true recognition may put us on the right path towards a new step in human growth.

To recognize that we are in an ongoing process of which we are not the masters amounts to the awareness of the radical relativity of our human situation, from which we can in no way escape so as to justify any absolute standpoint.

What we can do is become more and more aware of our situation and thus of our insufficiency, hence welcoming any contribution from whatever corner it may come and maintaining ourselves in an attitude of hope, which is here represented by a mood of expectancy.

This attitude makes the interreligious dialogue and the common search for truth one of the purest religious acts today. It entails not only confidence in my neighbor, impossible without love (and thus also understanding), but also faith in something which transcends us both, whatever name or no-name we may use for it.

By way of summing up this complex problematic, we may comment upon the two mottos of this study.

Reality, truth, brahman, the mystery of life, existence, human nature, God and, in a word, any ultimate problem, is certainly "not understood by those who understand," for they only understand what they understand and with it their own understanding of the mystery is reduced to their particular capacity for understanding. Those who understand do not completely understand really; they understand only from their particular angle or from their own understanding. They only understand what they are capable of understanding — and no man or human group can pretend to have exhausted the understanding of truth. Brahman or any ultimate which by this very fact would also encompass the subject cannot be an object of anything and thus cannot be the object of any understanding. How can you know the knower? It would be the "known" if you happened to know it. You can only know along with the knower, but you cannot know it.

Moreover, "it is understood by those who do not understand." And here we should take the message again literally. The true and authentic nonunderstanding is the real understanding, the true "standing under" reality and, in a way, being its foundation. The text does not say that it is understood by those who understand that they do not understand. Those are the intellectuals, the more or less conceited if intelligent people who play with the knowledge of their ignorance. They play at being humble, they certainly do not understand anything, those who are conscious of their own ignorance. If they understand that they do not understand, they certainly understand it, i.e., their nonunderstanding. Those who really understand do not know that they do not understand, which is already a form of understanding. Real ignorance or true knowledge cannot be feigned. There is no possible pretense here. All that we know, we know; but this is not the ultimate knowledge. The ultimate knowledge is the innocent ultimate knowledge that does not know that it does not know. It knows without knowing *it*. "Blessed are the poor in spirit" could be another way of saying it.

The second text echoes the collection of Upanishadic texts and is orchestrated by another series of sayings of the New Testament. It has the same purport. The two greatest values of man, wisdom and prudence, or intellect and acuteness, all are shattered without escape. The wisdom of the wise and the intelligence of the intellect, He, the Lord, will destroy. He will apparently make no use of any human value, nor will He build where others have built. It is again a new creation — out of nothing. It is the foolishness of the Cross, the weakness according to the world, the stupidity of men that He will extol. It is obvious that the moment that we want to understand or to defend those words we contradict ourselves, for if we succeed in letting them make sense, we have then overcome foolishness and we begin to manipulate with the foolishness of the Cross as if it were only for others and not for us. If we fall into the scum of the world and we begin to feel comfortable there, remembering the words of Paul, then we become the worst of hypocrites, playing the publican and choosing the last places with the secret desire to be praised or asked to come up higher. There is no escape. We have no right to judge others, not even ourselves.

What does it ultimately mean? What do we know? We know perhaps that our knowledge is broken, fragmentary, and distorted; we know also that the refractions of my angle may be corrected by the diffractions of my brother and that those whom I may be inclined to consider valueless and of no interest may also contribute efficaciously to the web of the multicolored tunic of mankind. It means that we have no right to despise anything or to discard anybody, that we have to renounce that pronouncement of ultimate sentences and final affirmations, including these very ones, so as not to reject those who make them.

I am not pleading for an undifferentiated irenism or for the elimination of the criteria of truth or consistency. We have to stick to them precisely because we cannot do without them. I am probably addressing myself against any kind of idolatry, to put the same idea in traditional terms. I am trying to make room for the contemplative approach, but not by saying that the contemplative has to be received with full honors, as if he were better off than the others. I am only reflecting on those powerful words, because to put them into practice requires the highest power of powerlessness: "Blessed are those of gentle spirit, for they shall inherit the earth."

# Traditional Methods
# of Contemplation and Action

## Elémire Zolla

*Editor's Introduction: Method* and inspiration are respectively the female and male parts in a whole; method is the thunderbolt, wisdom is the handbow, and their eternal alliance is religious life.

Modern man is constantly tempted to seek spiritual life in sheer method, or else in some kind of blind rapture ringing with spontaneity and rich in creativity. *Contemplation* needs both. Method in itself leads only to disputation and quarrels. On the other hand, inspiration in itself, without the help of method, will lead to vain strivings toward creativity for its own sake.

The gnostic meaning of *tradition* implies that we do not seek for novelty; tradition does not need novelty because it is constantly new. Following the Epistle to the Hebrews, tradition may be a person; in the Bible this person is called Melchizedek, King of Peace, "Without father, mother or descent, having neither beginning of days nor end of life; but made like unto the Son of God."

*Contemplation* soars above the archetypes and from these back up to the point from which everything arises.

*Action* is linked to the Greek *agonia,* which led to "agony": action in itself is always sacrifice. When we leave the paradise of contemplation and descend to the earth of action, everything, including mystical action, becomes sacrificial. But *agonia* signifies "struggle," "contest," as well as "anguish," and esoterically speaking, an unseen warfare. It may well be that the point of failure in contemporary civilization was precisely the failure to realize the necessity of constantly fighting against evil.


Method means pathway, from the Greek *hodos.*

According to a common Sanskrit metaphor, speaking is like walking along a path. Also in Latin one is said to walk *(percurrere)* along an argument. A method is a direction and the words that point toward it.

But there is a root in Indo-European languages that means both pathway and womb: *yeu-,* from which comes the Sanskrit *yoni,* "womb." The womb is the pathway of life, along which proceeds the seed or word of life. It is also the measurer, the matrix that forms living bodies according to their right proportions, nourishing them and bringing them into the world.

A method is like a matrix or a womb.

The method is the female, passive principle of artifacts or of actions. The rules to be followed in order to achieve a contemplative state, which form its method, are its female or passive cause. Their male principle, or seed or spark or word of life, is what causes the rules to operate and bear fruit. It is the inspiration, the urge from above to reach above the common human condition.

No spiritual birth can take place, no contemplative state may be reached unless a traditional method is inseminated, ignited, inspired. A hermetic metaphor says: unless the moon mates with the sun. Otherwise a method not only remains sterile but turns into a source of infection: of hysteria — which etymologically means an ailing womb. On the other hand, the seed, or inspiration, or urge to thrust oneself beyond the limits of ordinary human life, when left to itself becomes rabid, and turns into a destructive force: "Lilies that fester smell far worse than weeds" (*Shaks.*).

If one wishes to expand upon the hermetic simile, one may add that when the fiery sun of inspiration is absent, lunacy sets in, and when a cool, lunar method is lacking, one raves as if sunstruck.

Contemplation needs both method and inspiration. Method by itself is just an occasion for endless arguments. There is hardly anything as damaging to contemplation as disputation. St. Paul in the Epistle to Titus (3:9) warns: "But avoid foolish questions, and genealogies, and contentions, and strivings about the law; for they are unprofitable and vain."

But contemplation has even less, if possible, in common with charismata that drugs can buy. Seekers for free creativity and for experiments in expanded consciousness should not delude themselves that what they have or strive for has anything to do with contemplation. For those who seek solutions in drugs, the words of the Epistle to the Ephesians (5:18-19) still hold true: "And be not drunk with wine wherein is excess; but be filled with the Spirit;

Speaking to yourselves in psalms and hymns and spiritual songs, singing and making melody in your heart to the Lord."

Many traditions teach men to achieve spiritual awareness even through the use of drugs, but all such paths imply a sacrifice of one's ego as a general premise. This rules out all modern drug cultures.

There is a sure sign when a discussion or a stimulation is born of the marriage between method and inspiration, and is not just aggressiveness or emptiness in disguise. If the discussion gives a sense of peace and leads to greater insight and inspiration, or if thanks to the stimulation, a better understanding of the method is gained, then the marriage of method and inspiration holds good. The slightest touch of casuistry, on the one hand, and any willful seeking for something beyond the simple quietude of sinlessness, on the other, should be banned from the mind.

What is meant by a traditional method?

Traditional is what is handed down or transmitted *(tradere)* by more than three or four generations. We seek here for more than a lasting need: we look for a principle transcending time, whether or not it can prove its antiquity. A method of contemplation of a fully traditional nature, yet hitherto unknown, can be acquired through a theophany, a revelation of and by God. On the other hand, the acceptance for a long stretch of time of an untraditional method cannot turn it into something traditional.

A method is traditional, rather than just habitual or customary, if it is consistent with the traditional aim, which is to help man to transcend his bodily, psychic, and merely rational life, going beyond his sensations, feelings, and reasonings, in order to attain by an intellectual intuition the idea and the presence of the absolute Being, of Being in its absolute perfection, which is the cause of all being.

Clement of Alexandria used the expression "gnostic tradition" in this sense, and this use of the word "tradition" goes back to St. Paul, who in the second Epistle to the Thessalonians exhorts: "Stand fast, and hold the traditions which ye have been taught, whether by word or our epistle" (2 Thess. 2:15), and he explains the basis of tradition to Timothy (2 Tim. 3:14): "Continue thou in the things which thou hast learned and hast been assured of, knowing of whom thou hast learned them."

Tradition is the implantation of the seed, the starting point of a contemplative life. However, being perpetual newness, it shuns novelty. In fact the wish to keep abreast of the evolving times goes against the grain of contemplative life. In the Orthodox Church novelty (*neoterismos*) is an offense.

A traditional contemplative method is one that has always been — more or less implicitly — known, and has reappeared periodically through the ages among all peoples because it is inherent to the archetypal structure of contemplative life. It is timeless rather than ancient; it is therefore always intrinsically new.[1] If it seems to emerge as a novelty at a given moment, it is only because there happens to be no immediately available proof of its previous historical emersions. Paul recalls Melchizedek, who blessed Abraham, as belonging to the same tradition that reemerged with Christ: to a tradition that is Tradition itself, and has always been present, so to speak, behind the curtain of time (and even behind the veil of the Temple). Melchizedek, King of peace, is Tradition incarnate, "without father, without mother, without descent, having neither beginning of days, nor end of life; but made like unto the Son of God . . ." (Heb. 7:3).

What is contemplation?

The word derives from the root *tem* 'to cut.' To what severance, to what separation does the word allude?

In order to understand the allusion, we should try to relive an experience half-forgotten, something most precious lying hidden beneath the psychic rubbish that modern man heaps upon his heart. If we want to call that experience back to life, we should recall the sense of awe and wonder we feel in certain strangely meaningful places.

On a mound in the desert at sunrise.

Or at the edge of a somber swamp in an autumn evening. Or under a huge tree, its leaves singing in the breeze, in the midst of a vast plain. Or before a gaping, icy chasm in the mountains.

In such places at such moments, a kind of reverence and fear even today finds access to the dulled senses of modern men.

But what was such a feeling to a seer, to a priest-astronomer of, say, 7000 B.C.?

His fierce imagination was swayed and enthralled by the splendor of the revolving planets and of the constant stars upon the black vault of night. Those same essences that burned in the sky, he perceived when he hit upon some awesome, majestic spot. When in the outline of a rock, or of a tree, or of an animal he detected a luminous quality, full of freshness and grace, a swift delicate rhythm, he recognized the essence of silvery Venus up in the sky. And thus in all the qualities of earthly things, he perceived the manifestation of some star.

In fact the same essence was in turn a star, a mineral, a plant, an animal; especially, certain arresting spots in the landscape were hallowed by it. They possessed that power stunningly and gloriously. The seer in such places felt the holy essence beckoning to him. Something from the depths of his being delicately leapt out towards it and communed with it.

Our shabby modern language still reminds us of the intensity of those archaic events when it calls certain places "genial": inhabited by an unworldly being, a genie.

On such land the seer would feel called, impelled to perform a ritual, the natural response to a nod from above (the Latin word *numen* 'a nod' has that meaning metaphorically). Even today awe and wonder stir in man a strange need for solemn, eloquent gestures.

In some Orthodox and Catholic countries people still face experiences of great moment at least with a sign of the cross, ritually connecting the heaven and the earth of the microcosm and then, symmetrically, its west and death to its orient and dawn, imparting a ritual order to chaos when facing something momentous and arresting.

In the ancient worlds one was trained in the various complex patterns of holy gesticulation which acknowledged and praised the manifestation of otherworldly powers. The response was articulate and heart-raising. One knew the convenient ritual, one felt thankful, at home in the cosmos. Such gestures sometimes described the moment of the year, the relationship to the zodiac in sign language. The various Buddhas, the Christs of the holy icons, allude to solstices or equinoxes and to various forms of blessing.

A ritual is thus born, separating a space from space, a moment from time. The holy spot should be cut off from the everyday time of ordinary space: set apart, sacrificed, tabooed. There space shall cease to close in on man; it shall be absorbed into time, into the heartbeat of wonderment that clothes and outlines utter silence.

The ancient seer traced a circle on the spot that had "all Room within," to use the words of Traherne's poem, and that had granted him a revelation of silent awe.

On the circle he marked four points: the cross of the four moments of time, from the east — the beginning — the dawn, to the west — the end — the darkening of everything which comes into the world.

The seer would draw other patterns on the ground until he stood over an emblem and map of the cosmos. He was at its center.

He would then turn towards the star whose power had manifested itself, inspiring him to accomplish the rite. He might place a pebble, or a twig, or a flower on the point of the circle where the line from the star to himself intersected it.

In that direction he would steady his gaze.

Whatever crossed that line was a word from the star to him. He would bet that it was an omen.

In awe and wonderment he had marked off that space and time; now he staked that awe and wonderment on the omen that was born of it.

He was wrapt in contemplation, and contemplation showed him the sign, the commandment that would turn contemplation into action.

The flight of a bird, a gust of wind, a rumbling of thunder were words in the god's sign language, located in the structure of the universe into which they fitted, which he had drawn on the ground, feeling quiet, attentive, starlike.

Something of all this persisted through the ages. But the various elements fell apart.

The stargazing was preserved to some extent by the Kabbalists in the West. Something vaguely akin to the seer's experience is delicately described in the *Zohar* (II: 130 b):

"In the vast spaces of the sky, whose dome surrounds our world, there are forms and signs that may reveal the profoundest secrets. They are the constellations and the stars which to the initiate are an object of contemplation and a source of mysterious joy. He who sets forth on a journey early in the morning, needs but to rise at dawn and look at the eastern sky; he will, so to speak, see the letters written on the sky and the earth. They spell out his mysterious name."

As for the omens that appeared and portended the future, they became the "signs" that believers awaited before committing themselves to a course of action. The cult of signs was perpetuated in Puritanism, Quakerism, and Pietism; the journals of the followers of these doctrines, their substitute for confession, record the slightest and even the most trivial signs from above.

As for the drawing on the ground, it became the outline for the sacred buildings and the fundamental pattern of iconic art. It became also the plan of sacred cities and an object of contemplation in itself: in Sanskrit it was called *mandala*, from the same root as the Latin *mundus*, which means "world" and "beautiful, pure" (also the Greek *kosmos* bears out the connection of "world" and "beautiful").

Man still feels attracted by such regular patterns; their proportions still soothe his soul. The ancient seer drew them, prompted by a starry essence upon a holy spot. They encircled him in a ring of unity and simplicity, cutting him off from the world of multiplicity. Contemplation is what goes on in the heart and mind of the seer on the possible site of a temple.

In our everyday usage, to contemplate means to gaze joyfully at something. But as tradition in the highest sense is the handing down of a method of contemplation, contemplation in its mystic sense applies to the act of looking upon visible things as signs of what lies beyond them and causes them to be: looking beyond them at the essence, at the star they symbolize.

Contemplation implies meditation and is, as a rule, preceded by it. But meditation ponders over things, whereas contemplation grasps them directly. Patient meditation may lead up to contemplation, which takes place in a suspension of the ordinary consciousness of time. The aim of both meditation and contemplation is the same, to unveil the hidden workings of reality, the essences that cause the substances to become visible and tangible; but meditation rows towards them, contemplation sails into them.

Contemplation seeks the hidden workings, the formal and the material, the final and the efficient causes behind things. In this light, things are seen as though they were in the act of emerging out of their cause, in the process of being created.

Contemplation knows that creation did not happen in the past more than it takes place here and now, for it is perpetual. It is at the root of every instant. It hovers over and hides inside things; it does not only belong to days long gone.

Contemplation beholds things arising out of nothingness and meaninglessness, being created from nothing.

We behold rocks, roses, butterflies. They each have a look of their own, a shape that identifies them for what they are, that forms their essential character. Things and beings all belong to species and the species is what first strikes our eye when we hit on a thing or meet a being.

We instinctively place things within their species. We apprehend them as belonging to it, but contemplation does not stop here. It proceeds beyond the mere act of identification; it perceives the idea of the rock, or of the rose, or of the butterfly, gathering into its form and pattern the raw stuff of existence, molding it, organizing it into the shape of a rock, or of a rose, or of a butterfly, giving it its essence and name, its species, its specific mineral or vegetable or animal form of existence.

Contemplation sees the life-giving form or idea or soul of a butterfly animating the small body, the same idea or soul that extracted the fresh, moist flesh out of the dry cocoon, that trimmed the emerging being into its slender figure, and that now holds it together and renews it according to the archetype of the butterfly. Of every archetype or idea of a species the same can be said as of the idea or archetype or head of the Church, Christ, in St. Paul's words (Eph. 4:16), "from whom the whole body fitly joined together and compacted by that which supplieth, according to the effectual working of the measure of every part, maketh increase of the body into the edifying of itself in love."

Archetypes or ideas impart order and meaning, life to chaos, sorting it out in distinct species, each species obeying a call of its own.

Things never achieve their archetypal, ideal perfection; they can only suggest and represent or symbolize it. Contemplation perceives the ideal behind, above, and within things. It senses ideas at work, organizing undifferentiated matter according to specific, perfect forms; it admires how they keep each thing in due order according to its seed.

Up to this point contemplation was a rather common feature in ancient civilizations. To the so-called primitive, this first stage of contemplation in fact appears to be natural and self-evident. He directs his prayerful thought to the archetype or spirit of the fish and begs that it take pity on his need before he sets his net; he bows to the spirit of the craft residing in and symbolized by the potter's wheel when about to use some well-wrought earthenware; he feels the archetype, the idea of his people prompting them to war or to peace, that is, he feels eventful public decisions arising out of the depths of their being, from the very species that they belong to.

But even more important to him than all these ideas that he feels at work behind visible things, is his own archetype or guardian angel, his inmost, secret, life-giving self, which may be imagined as a female angelic being, or a familiar animal, or a sparkling gem, or as thunder or lightning. He craves its visitation and subjects himself to painful ordeals in order to receive it, for it caused him to be born, may assist him or abandon him, and might even recast him into the personality of a holy seer.

Even now men think in these terms, but hazily, muddleheadedly. They still feel the spirit of their party or nation molding their ways; they still wave its flag, and also think it wholesome to offer up human sacrifices to it. And if, on an ethnological spree, one should choose to inquire about the meaning they attach to their party or class or national or scientific spirit, they would answer that it gives scope and shape to their lives, though their world of drab ghouls is not as rationally articulate as the spiritual world of the primitives.

Order is made of interconnected proportions which acoustically correspond to rhythms.

Contemplation feels the rhythmic molds of all forms. The primitive drummer is a master of precise contemplation; he seizes the rhythmic essence of each reality.

But deep contemplation goes beyond the realm of archetypes or ideas, beyond the patterns of order. It goes to the source of all rhythms, the fundamental beat one-two, male-female throbbing against the final, ultimate silence, the source of everything.

Contemplation soars above the archetypes to the archetype of archetypes, and hence descends to the world of things and from these back up to the point from which everything issues.

Fountains are emblems of contemplation and have always been an essential element in shrines. Contemplation admires creation unfolding from its center of unfathomable silence to the periphery of visible things, and back to the eternal center and fountainhead, like a pendulum running from eternity to time and back, to the metronomic beat of the heart. Henry Vaughan explained:

I saw Eternity the other night
like a great ring of pure and endless light,
all calm, as it was bright,
and round beneath it; Time in hours, days, years
driv'n by the spheres
like a vast shadow mov'd, in which the world
and all her train were hurl'd.

The contemplative mind that admires the beauty of worldly things beyond words is the only mind that is not ensnared by the attractions of the world. It admires wholeheartedly and yet remains self-possessed. Contemplation proceeds from the beauty and glamour of things and creatures to the ideal beauty of which they are a reflection; and from archetypal beauty to the source of everything.

The magic power of things and creatures, their glamour that catches the eye and captures the will, is referred back to the archetype of power, and this is traced back to the Word that called everything into existence, to God who is constantly "upholding all things by the word of his power" *(Heb. 1:3)*. Contemplation is liberation. Only the contemplative escapes the fate of common man, who is hypnotized by material things and creatures.

The Orthodox mystic Nicetas Stethatos teaches us to look on a beautiful body admiringly, but also to wonder how such magic power can issue from a mere sack of filthy bowels, transmuting it into a thing of beauty in our eyes, an intoxicating semblance of its source.

He who views a body and its magic in this light is not enslaved. As St. John of the Cross said (*The Ascent of Mount Carmel* III, 24-4): "When delight is arrested by the will at the stage of sensual perception, it is nothing but mere vanity. It is instead an excellent thing if it is stopped before, as soon as one feels a delight in what one sees, hears or deals with, and that delight is made use of, and strength is derived from it in order to elevate oneself to the delight in God."

Contemplation disengages man's innermost self from all the teasing fancies, from all the treacherous roaming thoughts, from the moon-dominated ebb and flow of sentimentality. Contemplation undoes or cuts the magic knots that tie man to wordly powers.

Once having gained the upper hand in one's mind, one is free to decide what one shall indulge in: "Whatsoever things are true, whatsoever things are honest, whatsoever things are pure, whatsoever things are lovely, whatsoever things are of good report; if there be any virtue, and if there be any praise, think on these things" (*Phil.* 4:8).

Thanks to contemplation one forgets one's outer self, one sheds one's personality and identifies with one's faculty of detachment, of disengaged contemplation. A transfer of loyalties is effected from one's own personality to truthfulness.

The falsehood of self-righteousness and of self-praise is the radical evil, the source of all evils. And all save those immersed in contemplation are steeped in their falsehoods: "If we say that we have no sin, we deceive ourselves and the truth is not in us" (St. John, I, 1:8-9). Truth is not in us: the gaze of contemplation is not directed to the inner workings of our psyche.

In order to avoid self-deceit it is not enough to devote our skill in falsification to the service of our community, our race, or humanity as a whole. The falsity remains, however huge the number of

115

fellow-beings in whose favor it is practiced.

Only contemplation eschews self-deceit.

Who can truly say that truth is his aim? What has truth to offer? Falsehood is useful, not truth.

Modern man, who is a utilitarian at heart, rarely pretends to seek for truth. He can be amusing in his shameless frankness when he calls worldly hope and trust virtues, or when he values a judgment not for its truthfulness but for its optimism.

You will hear him openly urge that one give mankind something worldly to believe in and to hope for; this is the first commandment of the Archfiend and Confidence Man.

Contemplation offers only truth.

Cordelia's gift.

Rarely do the powerful of the world favor contemplation. They tend in fact to uproot it, or to distort it into some kind — their kind — of social service, of servitude, possibly to themselves.

St. Paul teaches that truth will make us free.


Contemplation is simplification. It relates everything to its archetype and archetypes to God: multiplicity to Onenness.

When contemplation is well advanced, reasoning ceases, having reached its goal; feelings are transcended, and only the recollection of the origin and of the end of everything persists.

The first and the last day of the world, the birth and passing away of everything are objects of meditation that easily lead to contemplation. The poets in the banquet halls of ancient times sang of the genesis; the minstrel of the Trojans in the Aeneid, like the bard of King Hrothar's retinue in Beowulf, drew the minds of their listeners back to the time when time was not. The idea of the all-consuming fire of the last days is equally heart-lifting, since it breaks the hold of the world on man's mind, and early Christians were trained in the expectation of the end, a feeling most useful to contemplation.

The origin and the end of everything bring us in contact with what precedes and survives the multiplicity of things: Oneness itself, without which the many cannot be conceived, which contains the possibility of the many.

If one contemplates Oneness, not only thinking out its concept but immersing oneself into it, one ceases to strive and settles into a blissful quietude.

Even though in *Endymion* he paid such a heavy toll to many banal ideals of the time, Keats felt this supreme possibility and wrote of it beautifully:

Wherein his happiness? In that which becks
Our ready minds to fellowship divine,
A fellowship with essence, till we shine
Full alchemized, and free of space.

Oneness is to be found in one's mind in the same core where the quiet apprehension of truth takes place.

An archaic traditional creation myth recounts that God, the One, was sacrificed and dismembered by demons or that he offered himself up as a victim to himself. From his dead limbs sprang up the various parts of the visible world. The visible world is his dead body.

The word *world* bears witness to the myth; it comes from the Old English *weorold,* which probably stems from *wer* 'man' (still found in *werewolf* 'man-wolf') and *ald* 'full-grown,' 'big' (hence *old*). The world is a dead giant or god.

We live in a carcass, among the vestiges of real life, amid the moldering limbs of what was the living Godhead, and yet we remember the lost purity and incorruption.

Within us we rediscover the life-giving Oneness, which lies fragmented and scattered abroad in the world. If we gaze inwards we approach life-giving life and freedom. If we stare at the world we surrender to what has lived or is living its life unto death.

We may also put this twofold possibility in other terms: we reach within us the Godhead as it eternally is before, after, beneath, above, beyond its sacrifice and death.

We reach before — after — beneath — above — beyond time-consciousness. We encounter the Godhead as it was before it created the world, after it resurrected from sacrifice, beyond the end of the world. These are all expressions of the near-inexpressible movement out of time and space for which the words before, after, beyond, above, are all inadequate. The movement that makes of a man a sheer, inarticulate, but clear recollection of God, a simple, unvarying attentiveness to the source of being, is the peak of acquired or self-willed contemplation, also known as prayer of simplicity or of simple presence or committal to God or of abandonment. One attains by its means the subtle point, or inmost depth of the selfless self, where there is a notion of God's silent presence, but no image, no emotion, no reasoning. "The dull brain perplexes and retards," wrote Henry Vaughan, and he described what is left after the tricks of reason, the play of fancy, and the incantation of external realities have been discarded, as nothing "but a white Celestial thought."

There is another possible description of contemplation, as the transcending of the soul in order to live in the spirit.

The distinction of the soul that feels and thinks and imagines from the spirit that blissfully perceives through an intellectual intuition the archetypes and God, is not always drawn, but it is traditional. We find it in the Virgin's prayer: "My soul doth magnify the Lord; and my spirit hath rejoiced in God my Saviour." The soul has felt devotion and has meditated; the spirit has perceived the object of devotion and meditation and has experienced bliss.

Contemplation is of the spirit.

St. Paul distinguishes between the psychic and the spiritual. Clement of Alexandria (in Stromata VII) defined the spiritual gnostics as "we who all our life make feast, being convinced that God is present on every side, who cultivate our fields praising and sail the wide seas singing hymns . . . . The gnostic is closely allied to God, being both grave and cheerful in all things, grave because his soul is turned towards the Godhead and cheerful because of God's blessings lavished on mankind. He always traces up to God the grave enjoyment of all things."

A great text on the distinction between the psychic and the spiritual is the *Dialogue about the Soul and the Passions of Men,* by John the Solitary, of about 500 A.D. It teaches that the psychic has to labor in order to gather his mind in prayer, and cannot maintain it in that condition for long. It wanders from one image to another because he fails to conceive of God as beyond man's understanding, a notion that is only clear to the spiritual.

The tears of the psychic are due to painful reflections, those of the spiritual to his wonder at God's majesty, to his marvel at God's wisdom. His are mainly tears of joy, though sometimes the confusion of men's minds may bring tears of sorrow to his eyes.

The psychic feels complacent because of his righteousness and wisdom, and the reason for his weakness is his failure to perceive the inexpressible. Even if he eliminates his passions, he cannot succeed in ridding himself of his opinions. The spiritual abolishes all remembrance of things evil and offers up in prayer thoughts of pure, admiring praise.

St. Augustine spoke of the two Churches, of Peter and of John, of the laboring and of the glorious, of those who strive and of those who rest on God's bosom: of meditation, which is of the psyche, and of contemplation, which is of the spirit.

One more word remains to be explained: "action." It comes from the same root (*ag* 'to push') as *agony*, which derives from the Latin *ago*, the priest who slew the victim at the sacrifice or *agonium*.

Sacrifice is the highest form of action. The act of creation and incarnation is symbolized by offering up, giving back to God His most precious gift. Life is thereby surrendered to its origin, from the periphery of visible things it exhales towards the center of all. A choice victim is placed as a wager on the benevolent presence of the divinity; jubilation and horror are knit together in the sacrificer's heart; his knife cuts off his rapt spirit from his overwhelmed, silenced soul as it slits the victim's throat. A tragic, ecstatic identification with the victim and with the Godhead takes place. The spilt blood cleanses all sins by the terrible renewing of the soul in the throes of pity and in the joyful knowledge that everything is offered as a due tribute to God, to whom the whole world is due back.

A small sacrifice may simply imply the pleasures that go with the bestowing of gifts, the intoxication of generosity. But when love becomes an unbearable flame, the greatest pain endured for the beloved one becomes adorable. The love of God may impel one to terrible sacrifices, to the point of identifying oneself with God's most terrible aspects, death and horror. There are moments when He cannot be looked at without one feeling one's heart shrink away from Him: "The roaring of the lion, the howling of wolves, the raging of the stormy sea, and the destructive sword are portions of eternity too great for the heart of man," said Blake. Bloody sacrifices, if they are felt as something horrifying, are also an identification with the unbearable portion of eternity. Mystics sacrifice their own soul and body; what Richard Crashaw wrote about St. Teresa may be applied to holy sacrificers:

O how oft shalt thou complain
Of a sweet and subtle pain
Of intolerable joys!
Of a death, in which who dies
Loves his death, and dies again
And would for ever so be slain
And lives and dies, and knows not why
To live, but that he still may die!
. . . . . . . . . . . . . . . . . . . . . . . . . . . .
When all thy deaths so numerous,
Shall all at last die into one,
And melt thy soul's sweet mansion;
Like a soft lump of incense, hasted
By too hot a fire, and wasted,
Into perfuming clouds.

But the shedding of blood repels. Many will not approve of the sacrifice of cherished living creatures. Many traditions in fact abhor bloody offerings, like the ancient Egyptian religion or the Christian — because God's own sacrifice replaces them, and is relived and reenacted by them. The sacrifice of Osiris who said "I am the Life, the Light and the Way" and that of the second Person of the Trinity are vicarious. These traditions feel above bloody rituals. One should remember, however, that whoever sees the splinter in his brother's eye fails to notice the beam in his own eye. Modern man is the least entitled to pass judgment. How can he pretend that the horrors of the slaughterhouse or of the vivisection ward are preferable to the measured dance of pious sacrificers who make a holy use of a dire necessity, turning mere butchery into an action leading to contemplation?

While the butchery of animals and the giving up of human lives for political or industrial issues are approved of, nobody should feel entitled to despise the animal and even human sacrifices of the various creeds. This is the kind of simple truth that minds unused to contemplative detachment cannot face. The sacrificial action is a tragedy. The word tragedy means the song *(odos)* of the sacrificed goat *(tragos)*. Sacrifice is the primordial, sacred action. The profane theater is a reminiscence of the holy sacrifice. There are as many arts as there were participants in the tragic event. There was the stager; the poet and the singer; the man who heaped up the stones or the clods of earth to form an altar, the first builder; the man who perfumed, painted, and wreathed the victim; the one who drew the symbols corresponding to the musician's strain; the man who observed and interpreted the fatal signs that marked the event, and was the first prophet, priest, leader, and historian; and some of the throng that advanced with a dancing gait up to the altar. All stories repeat the pattern of a victim facing an ordeal and laying claim on our pity and horror.

Sacrifice endeavors to act out the same process that meditation thinks out and contemplation identifies with: the return of the One, the surrender of multiplicity to simplicity. Infused contemplation in which God purges the soul with unbearable pain and makes it giddy with unutterable joy is a sacrifice in which the mystic's body and soul are the victim. God is the priest that kills it, the mystic's spirit is the helper, the singer, the decorator, the interpreter of the pangs and jubilations of his body and soul.

Pain, misery, horror are the unavoidable lot of man. The only hope of bearing them and turning them to some use is sacrifice: the offering of them up to God. Infused contemplation is a God-sent sacrifice of one's soul, in which supernatural joy and pain are experienced.

Our inmost self is by nature drawn to contemplation and truth. The necessity of returning to the world of action is a painful, heavy yoke. Torment and temptation are the fatal accompaniment of action. All who, after having known contemplation, are obliged to revert to the world, lament like Keats's Endymion:

> There, when new wonders ceased to float before,
> And thoughts of self came on, how crude and sore
> The journey homeward to habitual self.
> A mad pursuing of the fog-born elf,

Whose flitting lantern, through rude nettle-brier
Cheats us into a swamp, into a fire,
Into the bosom of a hated thing.

After having known the truth we have to retrace our steps, play a part again among the shadows and the delusions of active life. Like aged men compelled to revert to childish games, we are beckoned back to the nightmare of action, back to its unavoidable unreality. If we accept it as a sacrifice, we might overcome it; it might prove to be a blessing; we might earn through it and indeed in it our access back to heaven and contemplation. This is the promise made us and the method for facing action given us by Christ.

He announced that the various kinds of painful action, if accepted as welcome sacrifices, turn into the single progressive stages of contemplative bliss.

The Middle Ages juxtaposed seven kinds of sin, seven petitions of the Lord's prayer, and seven gifts of the Holy Ghost row by row, forming a fabric of sevens, an interconnected structure. The seven sins that would weigh down the seven gifts are overcome by the seven petitions and by the sacrifices that lead up to bliss like seven ribs of a gothic vault arching towards the cornerstone of sevenfold bliss. This was the structure built by a Durand de Mende with stones quarried from the Gospel.

It is the greatest method both of contemplation and action bequeathed to us by Medieval Christianity.[2]

In this world contemplation is doomed to be interrupted by action. The elation of an admiring gaze has to alternate with the contraction of a sacrificial act, and the tighter the contraction, the wider the elation.

Action should be consecrated. In fact no contemplation is possible without a life of consecrated, sacrificial action.

Only through the seven virtues is the sevenfold bliss obtained: by transcending self-centeredness or pride we place ourselves in the presence of God; by overcoming wrath through meekness we acquire mastery over our soul; by subduing envy through mourning we receive guidance; by discarding sloth, thanks to fortitude and a love of order, we are granted the nourishment of the soul, a holy festal spirit; by suppressing greed with our mind concentrated on the misery of everything worldly and with a sense of mercy filling our heart, the stain of sin is removed; by quenching gluttony with the constant search for spiritual meanings lurking behind everyday events, one attains a clear sight of God; by burning out the roots of lust with the fire of contemplative joy, a sense of peace radiates through us into the surrounding world.

The rule is that only through a sacrificial and consecrated life does one attain contemplation; however, exceptions are possible. St. Teresa mentions the case of habitual sinners who are for a short time possessed by God and may experience ineffable love and divine revelations.

A consecrated action should precede contemplation; contemplation should direct action along the right path. Without contemplation action is blind and cannot know its ultimate goal. Without a notion of the supreme end, there can be no certain knowledge of minor finalities and of their rightful hierarchy.

Man pays for not attending to contemplation by not knowing why he lives. Issues of great moment that might impart meaning to his life, he will not notice, and for miserable, degrading causes he will squander everything.

He speaks with other people's words, performs other people's actions, lives in order to impress others. He is therefore, however clever and ruthless, somebody else's plaything. In the midst of power and wealth he fails to see truth and to experience freedom.

The only way to define a clear scale of human values is to place at their head glorification through contemplation. Glorification in its highest phase becomes not only a praise of God but transforms the glorifier into a glorified being, with what was called a glorious or glorified body, which is technically a body that has become a mere tool, or to use another metaphor, a transparent veil of the spirit.

Nearly everybody has some vague, slight trace of divine quietude at the center of himself, even if he has never heard of a definition of God and even if he believes that he rejects God.

But that point of peace cannot be detected and appreciated unless its most majestic manifestations are reverenced and scrutinized.

What is the highest form of glorification?

Hebrew mysticism often uses the metaphor of the lamp. Its flame is the spirit that feeds on the wick which is the soul. It burns brightly when it is well trimmed. The oil is the body on whose sacrifice soul and spirit thrive. The flame strains to detach itself from the wick. Its life is all in the urge to soar above its wick. Its aim is to lose itself, to be dissolved. It eats away at the wick and slakes its thirst for oil but its true aim is suicide.

Why does it live dying to die?

Because such is its nature, one is tempted to reply.

But this is the answer reason gives when it knows no answer. Revelation answers instead, saying that wisdom moves it to do so. And that wisdom is the mystery that reason feeds upon. Wisdom is the source of life, says the Scripture.

So the man who wants to live a life-giving life wishes to cease being himself, wishes to be dissolved. So much man wishes to be dissolved that when he does not strive to dissolve in God, he tries to absent himself in the swoon that lust, drink, raving crowds, or absorbing spectacles may provide.

Without fainting away periodically in some way or other, man cannot live. Presence of mind, consciousness of his selfhood is not endurable to him without some intermission. Any price will be paid for it. Pain becomes irrelevant when it carries the promise of a loss of consciousness. Appreciation, mild self-conscious pleasure cannot replace a periodic intoxicating contact with nothingness.

The intoxication, the ecstasy of contemplation is unique because it transcends human nature. It achieves an awareness of truth that the endeavors of reason cannot hope to attain. At the same time it unclasps the grip of selfhood, and, according to character, to circumstance, and to Providence's design, either confers with a most delicate touch a sweet abandonment and quietude or exalts and intoxicates beyond the bounds of nature. Maybe the right description would be that sometimes the whole of man is immersed in a state of quietude, while at other times, it persists in the inmost core of man, while his soul and eventually even his body become supernaturally intoxicated.

Philo defined contemplative ecstasy as a sober drunkenness. The violent raptures that we find so often in the Catholic tradition are always, however, strangely attuned to a clear, continuous intellectual intuition — they are neatly explained in Crashaw's address to Saint Teresa (in *Upon the Book and Picture of the Seraphical Saint Teresa*):

> By all thy lives and deaths in love;
> By thy large draughts of intellectual day;
> And by thy thirsts of love more large than they
> By all thy brim-fill'd bowls of fierce desire.
> By thy last morning's draught of liquid fire.

Such fiery descriptions of love and tenderness have favored the idea that Western Christian mysticism is a path of sentimental devotion and not of metaphysical knowledge. This is due to a strange misunderstanding: even a great traditional thinker like René Guénon fell victim to it.

Royo Marin, one of the current authorities on Catholic mysticism, whose treatise is still the most quoted in the legal cases of beatification and sanctification, states that: "All theologians agree that infused contemplation is produced by the intellectual gifts, especially wisdom and understanding, and not by the sentimental ones." The treatise of Dom Cuthbert Butler gives a series of canonical definitions of mysticism drawn from the fundamental Christian texts: an intellectual intuition of a transcendent reality, whose nature is direct and objective; a stabilized conscious relationship with the absolute; a union with the absolute as far as this is possible during life; an experience of the presence and of the being of God; a union with God of an ontological and not of a psychic nature, as between two spirits. Even when the most conspicuous aspect of a mystical experience is the force of the sentiments involved, these are of a supernaturally incandescent quality and cannot be considered as ordinary psychically conditioned feelings, but rather as a symbolic text etched by a transcendent being in the soul and on the body of the mystic. Transverberations and stigmatizations are a nonmetaphorical writing of the Godhead.

If the supreme identity of man is his identification with God, all other possible states shall be measured by their distance from that summit, down to the lowest possible point, the complete identification with the hatred of that supreme possibility.

It may seem strange that so rare a state should be the cornerstone of the whole structure of human values, that in order to judge properly everyday events one should relate to this essential criterion, but it was taken for granted in the Christian West from the foundation of Constantinople to the eighteenth century. It was acknowledged in the ancient world up to the spread of unbelief in Greek city states and in Rome up to the class struggles, when a worldly-minded orientation prevailed, of the same sort as has been with us since the eighteenth century. The fatal consequences of this secular attitude are a cult of political power, a secular state-absolutism, a surrender to unchecked economic and erotic obsessions. Such evils Christianity reacted against in the ancient world.

As a whole, humanity has always been oriented towards the primacy of contemplation with the exception of the very few secularized centuries at the setting of civilizations.

To one of these grey patches our declining cycle belongs.

Periods like the present cannot extend for more than a few centuries because they violate truth. Not only the supreme truth is violated but, as a consequence, also the small everyday truths. Among the violated truths is the fact that man stands in a relation to nature that may be described metaphorically as between son and mother (as is usual in most creeds) or between brother and sister (as was usual among Christians). Modern man considers nature as something hostile that stands in the way of what he calls the Spirit. The consequence of the irreverence towards what was traditionally considered God's handiwork — in which the Scriptures of the West see a manifestation of Wisdom — is becoming clear, even to the metaphysically blind, in the form of the truth-sent overcrowding and pollution of skies and waters.

The gigantic machinery of industrial civilization will become unworkable. The few who knew the truth had spoken up in vain. From Blake to Dostoyevsky, from Hawthorne to Melville, there is hardly a sensitive and thinking man in the last two hundred years who has not told the truth against the dominant, secular lies.

The house built on sand is crumbling. The untruth stands revealed. But the truth is not yet generally perceived.

The house of modernity, divided against itself, stands at the threshold of its downfall. But the victims living within its walls can hardly imagine the truth and take for granted the most extravagant modern tenets.

They do not perceive the lying treachery of such slogans as "the root of man is man," or "the world must become exclusively human."

They fail to understand that God is not a projection of man's ideals, that nature should be admired and respected instead of being exploited. Exploitation leaves no room for gratitude and praise, and therefore deprives man of joy.

The only toil that brings happiness is consecrated work, performed in order to please and praise God.

What is meant by consecration of work?

Robert Graves wrote a beautiful essay "Harp, Anvil, Oar" (in *The Crowning Privilege*) about poetic meter and primordial smithcraft. The smith of old used charcoal made at a festal time of the year, reciting spells over the timber of holy trees; he fanned his holy fire with bellows from the skin of an animal ritually slaughtered, and worked according to the meter suited to the various stages of the art. He beat out hymns, charming the archetype of the red-hot iron, to the hammer-and-anvil rhythm: "A knight there was and that a worthy man."

Thanks to devotion and rhythm the master of the craft performs his work-and-ritual with the keenest attention and, at the same time, lost in a trance.

Happiness does not lie in the abolition of work, which would leave a gap in life that none save those initiated into a spiritual pathway could fill with any meaningful activity. Nor can happiness be bought with the payroll or by greater involvement in shared management. These measures can only help to smother the natural protest of the soul and of the body against labor unrelieved by contemplation and magic.

Industrial labor can only be redeemed by considering it something to be offered up in sacrifice. This idea would in the long run change the nature of society. Labor can only be made use of spiritually if considered an expiation, a form of punishment or an ordeal of purification. A traditional society made every activity holy,

127

not only labor, and even what now is gambling was originally an oracular procedure; our games originated as liturgies, our tours as pilgrimages, our vehicles as portable tabernacles, our cities and homes as shrines, our marriages as hierogamies, our jokes as sacred clowning, our laws as taboos, our languages and mathematics as prayers, our dresses as vestments, our medicine as propitiation, our jobs as symbolical worship. Christian zeal caused many of these sacred institutions to be reborn in the Middle Ages. Not the sporting activities, but certainly city-planning and cathedral-building were remade holy.

Medieval fraternities often taught a system of meditation on the tools of the craft, and labor thereby took on a symbolical meaning and became a pathway to contemplation.

This was most easy in the case of the higher arts. Icon painting even today in Orthodox traditional monasteries is preceded by fasting and prayer, and not one element in the picture is without a symbolic import. This is perhaps the last holy craft that is in itself a mystical pathway, a method of contemplation.

The craft of the bell-founder in the Catholic countries was not long ago of the same character, at least in its last phase, when over the liquid bronze the Mass was said and litanies to the Virgin were sung while the bell was cast.

Apart from such cases the West did not develop a neat counterpoint of work and contemplation such as Simone Weil suggested was possible from a Pythagorean point of view. When the Industrial Revolution set in, there were few attempts at making an ascetic use of it apart from the habit of hymn singing among the Calvinist spinners mentioned by Goethe or the introduction of the rosary in certain French factories during the nineteenth century.

In any case nothing could remotely be attempted unless certain conditions were granted: 1) that the working-team be unanimous in their common spiritual pursuit; 2) that the work be of a stable nature; 3) that the commodities produced answer a real need that might be humanly shared by the worker.

Meanwhile truth must be cherished in near-secrecy by the few; among them, all aspects of a society founded on the exclusion of contemplation should be rejected. In the modern setting, the contemplative's flight from the world requires, in my opinion, a renunciation of all hope in possible social avenues to contemplation. It leads to believing that man must become an island to himself, communing only with relics of Tradition. Of the various callings that were made possible in past civilizations, only the individual search for truth helped by the texts of Tradition is perfectly safe nowadays.

A few remarks should be added about some methods that might be picked up in the Western tradition.

The traditional prayers in their traditional form may edify us as they did the host of saints that employed them. The Scriptures and the classical practices may open on the same vistas that were disclosed to the holy and wise in ancient times, provided we read them in the same spirit as of those times. The acts and thoughts thus reproved as sinful should be avoided, since the experience of the past teaches us that they would upset the serenity of the mind.

Among the methods of contemplation that are no longer available, save for exceptionally rare cases, is the liturgy. If it is to be a workable method of contemplation, a liturgy must answer certain basic requirements.

1) Its conscious and sole aim should be glorification; the celebrant and the onlooker should acquire, thanks to it, a contemplative state.

Preaching should be a meditation on transcendent realities. When the preacher does not conform to this rule, he destroys the contemplative effect and the power of the ceremony is impaired.

2) With the aim of the liturgy being to detach us from the world, its music, its language, and its general setting should be distinct from what the ear and the eye and the nose are used to in the world.

Sacred music is different in the various traditions. In the West its canons were fixed by St. Gregory the Great.

Renaissance polyphony and the Lutheran chorale are sublime, but cannot replace the purity, simplicity, and anonymity of Gregorian chant. The latter has nothing to do with the soul; it expresses exclusively the life of the spirit. While the other great Church music of the West may be described as solemn, majestic, tragic, and so forth, all adjectives apart from "simple" and "pure" are slightly misplaced when applied to Gregorian melodies.

3) The same applies to the language. In all traditions the liturgy uses a different idiom, which can be a secret, mystical "spirit-language" or an archaic or foreign tongue. The Babylonians used Accadic, the Romans an archaic Latin, the Aramic-speaking Jews Hebrew.

The first Christian liturgies used the local idioms but created a sacred jargon with an archaic ring, studded with new words and Semitic turns of phrase.

In his treatise on Egyptian and Chaldean mysteries, Hyamblichus illustrated the liturgical use of words in unknown tongues.

4) The same criteria of otherwordliness that apply to music and to language determine the character of the solemn dance of the celebrant and of his vestments.

5) All liturgies hinge on three main moments: a foreclosure to the world, a sacrifice, and a sealing off of the sacred time prior to a return to everyday time.

6) All elements must be symbolical. Nothing should be allowed to appear that does not hide a spiritual meaning.

If one stepped into a Medieval Church at the beginning of a Mass, one saw the clergy enter preceded by tapers and by burning censers. They symbolized God condescending to Incarnation. But God has chosen us in Christ before the foundation of the world, says the Epistle to the Ephesians (1:4): If we hope to be of the chosen, we shall see *ourselves* represented as entering the realm of death-bound reality.

7) The sacrifice at the heart of the liturgy leads to the beginning of everything. All the faculties, all the senses are called on to take part in the action of actions: the origin must be seen as a host soaring heavenward, heard as the host being divided, tasted and swallowed, smelled as wine. The senses are overwhelmed and this excess should project us beyond them. The recollection of the sacrifice in all its horror and the rejoicing over its blessings puts man beside himself. His reason has been gorged with meanings and is past reason. The ordinary personality is silenced; only the intellectual intuition of the spirit survives.

For if such holy Song
enwrap our fancy long,

130

time will run back, and fetch the age of old,
and speckl'd vanity
will sicken soon and die,
and leprous sin will melt from earthly mould,
and Hell itself will pass away.

Milton's verses are the nearest verbal approximation to what goes on at the culmination of a liturgy.

8) If this effect is to be reached with some measure of ecstasy, the execution must be impeccable, impersonal, and traditional. The process is so delicate that the slightest defect will upset it.

Candles provide a good example. They have many symbolic meanings: their beeswax is the virgin soul, their light is the spirit, which, nourished by the purest essence of the soul, strives heavenward. Candles are lit, among other reasons, not only in order that reason feed on these emblems and concepts, but that the eye perceive them speaking through shapes and colors. When they are lit or put out, the creation of light and the coming of darkness and sin are not only thought of but seen. By seeing ideas one thinks them out more profoundly and more richly. They become more than mere signs in the computations of the brain.

A flood-lit church is unusable.

A candle burning there no longer enlightens our minds. But what is this tampering with tapers by comparison with the innumerable desecrations, the shame of microphones that falsify the voices and change the source of sounds? All they can symbolize is counterfeit. When symbols are used carelessly they only represent shoddiness. When they are not taken in dead earnest they only convey self-deceit.

The liturgical path to contemplation in the West is no longer open. But the few cases in which a liturgy may be seen without too much spiritual danger might help to imagine what it was like in its heyday. The last Benedictine bastion of liturgical contemplation was described by J.K. Huysmans in *La cathédrale* and *L'oblat*. It was the same liturgical scene that conveyed to Simone Weil the sense of contemplation.

Another collective method of the West used to be the spiritual exercises preached during retreats.

The best known are those of St. Ignatius in which a technique of breathing and a method for the training of imagination are employed.

The Jesuit school did not dispatch fancy by a prompt suppression, as was the custom with other schools, but on the contrary, it endeavored to put imagination to the best possible use. The Ignatian exercises are drills that keep imagination in a condition of obedience and fitness. The mind becomes a theatre where the grand baroque scenarios of hell and of the heavenly court are dressed up one after the other as the process of meditation unfolds. The imagination is the tool of the Jesuit stager, who in the eighteenth century often was the same person that had the theatrical churches, the grand colleges built in the cities of the world.

The Jesuit's will masters the imagination as it dominates society at large. The Jesuit creates his interior landscape, to use the words of Keat's *Ode to Psyche:*

> Where branched thoughts, new grown with pleasant pain
> Instead of pines shall murmur in the wind . . .
> And in the midst of this wide quietness
> A rosy sanctuary will I dress
> With the wreath'd trellis of a working brain. . .
> With all the gardener Fancy e'er could feign.

The result is a strengthening of the will, a capacity for accurate planning.

Very rarely, inventiveness.

The pupils of the Jesuits assimilated their worldly techniques but seldom grasped the moving principles behind them.

But even the Jesuit method of control of the imagination was rather undeveloped by comparison with the Hindu or Buddhist complexities, which have no counterpart in the West.

Some Buddhist schools pursue a control of the imagination as conscious self-hypnosis and train it to produce hallucinations of godly presences or of frightening scenes that, in Keats's phrase: "doth hiss fancy into belief." When these appear in all their effectiveness, the mind dismisses them as deliberate productions of its own will. This is a sudden awakening from a dream that was taken for reality, and it frees the mind from the hold of reality. The workings of *maya*, of universal illusion, are seen through. Besides, imagination projects in the body a network of vessels of "energy" that wind up in wheels or centers of energy. By regulating the flow of energy in this system, one causes material changes in the body. A method very vaguely similar was produced in the West only by Gichtel the Behemenite.

The West has developed only certain methods — breathing techniques and projections of the imagination are either absent or undeveloped. Its particular private techniques were the reading of the Breviary with its items of meditation attuned to the day of the year, and the Rosary that could lead with its whirling movement up to incantation, but that even when it fell short of that mark, induced a sense of quiet remoteness from the world.

[1]An illustration of this idea of tradition as distinct from religious custom is provided by a particular tradition of many faiths, the Rosary. In its Catholic version its aim is to engage simultaneously and separately the various parts of man in the act of telling the beads: imagination and feeling concentrate on the single mysteries or crucial events of a divine destiny, from the Annunciation of the descent of the seed or word into the virgin soul up to the soul's Assumption into heaven or beatitude; reason may elaborate on the meaning of these mysteries while at the same moment meditating on the various prayers; all the time that the higher faculties are thus at work, the rhythmic functions of the body are quieted down by the circling, spiralling movement of the prayer, the voice becoming more and more impersonal and wavelike. The sense of touch is engaged by the roundness of the beads and thereby the unconscious absorbs intimations of permanence, of concentration, of circular infinity.

The rosary is traditional, therefore, because its aim is contemplation. But it is traditional besides because it is implicit, present in a virtual or potential state, in all systems of contemplation. One may say that the followers of any system are bound to rediscover the rosary, given a sufficient number of generations and a long period of constant observance untroubled by adverse factors.

The rosary emerged in Christendom not through a sudden reformation or discovery, but apparently as the outcome of a natural growth. Probably what was to become the Byzantine type, of knotted wool, was divulged by St. Anthony in the third century, while the Western beads came into use in the thirteenth century. Their birthplace is unknown. The legend relates that they were revealed to St. Dominick by the Virgin.

The rosary was not a borrowing from previous traditions; the fact of its being practiced in other religions would actually have been a deterrent to its adoption in an exclusive faith like Christianity. It was an emersion rather from the structure of mystical life in itself, and therefore it is found in the Muslim world as in the Buddhist Hinayana, in the Shivaite Hindu tradition as well as among the Jainis, and among many primitive tribes. All these historically unrelated cases go to prove that this method of separating the fixed parts of man from his volatile element belongs to the methodology of contemplation in itself. But the faithful who adopt it do not need this kind of proof furnished by a comparative study of religions — for them it is enough that they have "been assured of knowing of whom they have learned it," to use St. Paul's words.

²The first sacrifice is that of one's personality, of everything that in us says "I": "Blessed are the poor in spirit." This sacrifice uproots the saturnine, icy and dry sin of pride. The corresponding gift, the fear of God, is cultivated by meditating on God's power, by repeating "Our Father which art in heaven, Hallowed be thy Name," which sweeps us off our selfhood.

The sacrificial trial of persecution will be endured patiently by the poor in spirit (bearing witness to the Name is the Hebrew expression for martyrdom).

The reward is the right to the Kingdom of heaven, which means an inner life of contemplation ruled by God and not by ourselves.

The second petition shall therefore be "Thy Kingdom come," which corresponds to the sacrifice of all emotions to meekness, through the gift of piety, which dispels the hot and dry martial sin of wrath. By accomplishing everything only in order to please God, and thereby in the spirit of meekness, one becomes the master of one's inner emotions, for the meek "shall inherit the earth," their soul, their inner earth.

The third sacrifice consists in mourning over one's sins: "Be afflicted, and mourn and weep: let your laughter be turned to mourning and your joy to heaviness. Humble yourselves in the sight of the Lord, and he shall lift you up," explains the Epistle of James (IV: 9-10). The mournful sight of one's sinfulness dispels the mercurial sin of envy, for it shows that one is entitled to nothing. It is cultivated by impressing on oneself the sense of one's weakness, by repeating the third petition of the Lord's prayer: "Thy will be done."

St. Paul explains what the will of God is: "And be not conformed to this world: but be ye transformed by the renewing of your mind, that ye may prove what is that good, and acceptable, and perfect, will of God" (Rom. 12:2), "for this is the will of God, even your sanctification, that you shall abstain from fornication . . . that no man go beyond and defraud his brother in any matter."

The fourth sacrifice, which helps to cultivate the gift of fortitude, consists in going against one's bent, by being kind to the hateful, by avoiding what excites one's curiosity, by accepting mortification. These actions are prompted by a craving for justice, which is inner order and peace and dispels the jovial, moist, and warm sin of sloth.

"Blessed are they which do hunger and thirst after righteousness: for they shall be filled"; the corresponding petition is "give us our daily bread." In Heb. 1:9 St. Paul adds: "Thou hast loved righteousness . . . therefore God . . . has anointed thee with the oil of gladness . . . ."

The fifth sacrifice consists in placing everything in relation to God, thanks to the gift of knowledge, which reveals the nothingness of created things. It destroys all attachments and all greed, which are of cold and moist grasping Venus. The resulting sentiment is mercy, for things appear pitiful in the light of knowledge. "Blessed are the merciful: for they shall obtain mercy." The corresponding bliss is a cleansing of sins, mercy attracting mercy: "And forgive us our trespasses as we forgive those who trespass against us."

The sixth sacrifice consists in avoiding all sensual gratification, all kinds of gluttony, which is a hot sun — like thirsty sin. It is overcome by means of understanding which is the art of discovering ... symbols, out of a thirst for the hidden spiritual meanings in things and circumstances. Purity of heart is the result and accompaniment. One begs of God "lead us not into temptation" because temptation overclouds the pure heart. "Blessed are the pure of heart: for they shall see God."

The seventh sacrifice subordinates everything to the burning need to spread peace around you. It corresponds to wisdom, the peak of contemplation, the full relish of contemplative bliss. Lust, which is a humid, lunar sin, is thereby dispelled: "But deliver us from the Evil one." The satanic contagion of lust undergoes a radical change into something opposite, a peaceful sweetness that radiates from the man who with a flaming, overbrimming heart seeks quietude. This passionate love of peace makes man godlike: "Blessed are the peacemakers: for they shall be called the children of God."

# The Hesychastic Tradition:
# An Orthodox-Christian
# Way of Contemplation

ANDRÉ SCRIMA

*Editor's Introduction:* Although situated at the innermost core of Eastern Christian spirituality, the Hesychastic tradition, curiously enough, has not been, until very recent years, truly recognized, studied, and proclaimed (a status, after all, to which it never aspired). Organically integrated into the life of Oriental Christianity (which is in place, time, and symbolic significance the "origin" of the Christian faith), the Hesychastic way expanded from the primitive eastern Mediterranean regions to the Eastern European countries; and down to our days it still represents a hidden source of life and creation. It would be difficult, moreover, to deny deep affinities, or at least rigorous formal analogies (by no means reducible to mere "historic influences"), with the "metaphysical" traditions of the Far East or with those of Jewish and, especially, Islamic mystics. The spiritual life remains for the Hesychast an "experience" never dissociated from the cosmic, anthropological, and symbolic patterns, but is always an endeavour to transfigure (literally: "go beyond figures") them. "A man who prays only when he prays, is a man who does not pray at all": this traditional Hesychastic dictum may characterize this vision, always called to transcend itself.

However, when the monks from Mount Athos conceded to the publication of the *Philokalia* (an anthology of coded writings of the spiritual tradition) at the end of the 18th century, Hesychasm met history, moreover modern Western history, although still on its spiritual way. While outlining here the general articulations of the Hesychastic way and doctrine, this brief survey also ventures into reflections on the extremely complex and essentially open question of contemplation and the historic destiny of modern man.

The eighteenth century of the Christian era is drawing to a close. By the year 1782 there is nothing apparent to distinguish it from the preceding centuries. The ebb and flow of events indicates now as always the passage of time and the existence of man. The world is going fairly badly or fairly well. Nothing would appear to mark this period as an epoch all its own when we scrutinize it — as we have now chosen to do from the standpoint of Athonite spirituality.

Mount Athos is an almost imperceptible tongue of land which in a way eludes geography and even history, and which since the turn of the tenth century (963) has occupied this corner of the eastern Mediterranean in the form of a silence and an enigma.

Yet for those almost everywhere who are awakening and questioning what is not yet visible, the signs are beginning to form a pattern, and the horizon is beginning to split asunder. The United States of America have just declared their independence and William Blake, in his poetic frenzy, prophesies on the subject of the new "angels of the nations" of Europe, America, and Asia, heading towards the fantastic gigantomachia of the future. The great French Revolution, so near as to appear incredible, is soon to burst into history — an event which is to be a mere precursor echoed by later revolutions, industrial, technological, and social. A revolution also of ideas: the philosophical logos inherited from the dawn of Greek civilization turns against pure reason and discovers the ecstasy of action dominating over reality. Hegel and Marx necessarily appear on the scene or, to be more exact, they rise up in the name of the necessity for action. Hölderlin, a contemporary who is lucid to the point of losing his reason, sums up the immensity of what is happening: the universe takes its *Abendländische Wandlung,* its turning towards the West. Man is turning away categorically from what he considers to be the "retreat of the divine." The difference between "up to this time" and "from now on" becomes essential. Something decisive, something that can be compared to the vast cosmic changes is stirring in the depths of being. "Aspice nutantem convexo pondere mundum."[1] (Vergil,*Eclogues* 4:50).

Does it not seem, then, rather out of place to link up the historical heights — or abysses — with what is so inapparent, so obliterated as this promontory of the Chalcidian peninsula curiously entitled the "Holy Mountain of Athos"? Yet for those who are capable not of seeing the invisible (which happens more often than people think), but of seeing how invisible is the invisibility of the visible, the book with which we are concerned — the book which

137

now appears in Venice (cultural hinterland of Athos) — represents an awareness of and a transcending response to the Western revolution. To its unexpected title of *Philokalia* some explanation is added in the subtitle: "Collection of *neptic* saints (i.e., those who have reached awakening), eminent model of the active life, guide to contemplation." Its editors, Nicodemus of Naxos (1749-1809) and Macarios of Corinth (1731-1805), thus bring the Hesychastic tradition unseasonably into the play of history — but only to a certain extent, let it be understood. While the revolution of temporal cycles is accelerating, the Hesychast considers these revolving orbs from the axial position at which, according to the philokalic expression, "the intellect, motionless as the axis of the heavens, gazes as towards a center into the depths of the heart" (Callistos and Ignatius, fourteenth century).

Hesychastic spiritually had hovered over Athos since the year 1000. This complex period situated at the threshold year 1000 corresponds, in fact, to the great cleavage of our civilization, when in the space delimited by the religions that are said to be of the "Book" and by the Semitic, Greek, Latin, and Germanic institutional and intellectual structures, "our" East and West branch off and commit themselves respectively to this divergence. Various mutations take place at this epoch in the Western Middle Ages. The social and political institutions of the *civitas christiana* become stronger; the cities shelter universities in which theology and the spirit of the times are questioning one another, while in the depths of men's minds is born the new anxiety which is to prove so fruitful for the future of Western history: will faith ever be able to catch up with the times? Can it ever be integrated into what is soon to be plainly called the evolution of mankind? (Secularization, at the other end of the West's historical curve, will try one day to give an answer.)

This is the period during which, on its side, Eastern Christianity, whose historic center is still in Byzantium (but toward which converge all the traditions of the eastern Mediterranean and of the surrounding Asian regions), begins to shrink. In order to survive a history which has now come to a standstill, the itinerary of this Oriental Christianity becomes interior and prepares to become essentially "tradition." The foundation in 963 of the first large monastery, on Mount Athos, soon to be followed by others, marks the emergence of the new center where the different currents and descendents of Orthodox spiritual life are to be found and more deeply explored. Four centuries later (halfway between the Athonite foundation and the publication of the *Philokalia*), the Hesychastic controversy between the Christian East and West was to break out. This confrontation, which certainly comes as a shock to cultures and institutions, as a semantic challenge to doctrines and theological theories, affects up to a certain point, the concrete understanding of contemplation. Western Christianity, where the passage from symbol to concept characteristic of the new scholastic theologies is taking place, cannot but misunderstand the Eastern spiritual tradition, for which God is the unknowable absolute, totally inobjectifiable and imparticipable and at the same time in his very "Being" participable and "experimentable." In reality there is implicit reference to the meaning of contemplation. Is it not, after all, just a higher form of intellectual activity ("Das Mystische ist das Spekulative," Hegel was to say later on, thus carrying the concept to its extreme limit), a "supernatural state" brought about by the Divine Cause? Or, rather, is it not an intrinsic part of the first and last end of the created being, independent, of course, of all "statistical" considerations as to the frequency of its occurrence? "By His Incarnation," asserted Gregory of Nyssa in the fourth century, "God has shown how natural is the supernatural and how supernatural is the natural," thus suggesting the overcoming of false oppositions. The Athonite spokesmen for Hesychasm are moreover aware of this fact and in a document of primary importance in the fourteen century, the Hagioritic[2] Tomos, they calmly acknowledge the exceptional meaning of the objective distinction (but without separation) between the essence (or the "beyond-essence") of God, which is here implied rather than expressed in words, over and above every name and knowledge, and His "uncreated energies" manifested in the world, whereby He enters into real union with the creature who is thus deified. "God is all the more invisible the more He shines forth in the soul" (St. Symeon the New Theologian).

The course of history is not to be reduced, then, to its mere chronological evolution. It also entails moments of *Kairos* — the secret consummation of yet unmanifested events — by which the contemplation of truth bursts into its midst.

It is rather in the *Kairos* that Hesychastic spirituality moves forward as its name already suggests. It comes from the Greek *hesychia*, whose root *kathezestai* corresponds to the Latin *sedere*, "to be seated, fixed": a stability which implies, on the one hand, *concentration* as the way and, on the other hand, access to the *center* as a place (or "no-place") of *peace* and *silence* (the other two connotations of *hesychia*). Meister Eckhart's expression "Wesen ist Schweigen"[3] reflects fairly closely a possible aspect of the Hesychastic spirituality. Moreover, the stability to which Hesychasm refers is undoubtedly verified at several homologous levels of intelligence. We would refer to the notions of *yesod* (foundation) and *metatron* from the Sephirothic doctrine of the Kabbalah in order to circumscribe (without any facile syncretism or concordism) a certain type of language. In all contemplative traditions certain words are bearers of the Spirit and correspond to one another and answer one another like so many signals along the way. When St. Bernard pronounces the phrase "Solus sedet Deus," a certain Hesychastic intuition of the Latin Middle Ages is expressed through him.

While this particular moment of the fourteenth century "reveals," as it were, the Athonite Hesychasm, its traditional itinerary goes back much further than that date. Some marks which are "historical" up to a certain point enable us to retrace it, provided we decipher the content embodied in symbols and signs (icons, allusive texts, etc.). Sometimes these clear indications proceed from "those who know" what Tradition is (". . . tacit and mysterious, a secret instruction which our Fathers observed in silence, restraining all curiosity" [St. Basil the Great, *On the Holy Spirit*, fourth century]), or, from those who went out into the desert to seek the "knowledge of contemplative prayer" (St. John Cassian, fourth-fifth centuries). However, one never follows faithfully a traditional trail unless one has understood its co-implication with the Origin (the *Principium*). Obviously this is not merely a historical or cosmic origin but the transcendent "place" (or, again, "no-place") to which the totality of manifested things is related and with which — as in the Byzantine liturgical space raised up by the Pancrator — the contemplative interiority of being comes face to face.

The *Philokalia,* which issued forth in the eighteenth century from the Hesychastic silence, proposes through its own tradition a remembrance, a reinsertion into the Origin. Its title repeats the name given in the fourth century by Basil the Great and Gregory of Nazianzen to a collection of ascetical and mystical writings. At a different level of meaning, however, the word *Philokalia* answers implicitly to a decisive beginning of our history, that of Greek and Western *Philosophia,* which was to be the great educator of active mankind in the future. The "Love of Beauty" (Philo-Kalia) understood as the illumination of Truth ("transcendental source of life and ultimate desire of desires") proposes another means of approach to the mystery of "being": "Beauty will save the world," as Dostoievsky, an assiduous and tormented reader of the *Philokalia,* was to cry out in the middle of the nineteenth century.

The *Philokalia,* in fact, at the beginning of the nineteenth century, reached a Russia still on the fringe of Western history, which it entered into only after her "revolution" was achieved. It was in a Romanian monastery that the *Philokalia* was immediately translated into the Slavonic language (and later into Romanian) by one who remains a great bearer of the Hesychastic tradition of modern times, the monk Paissios (1722-1794). From this monastic center it made its way towards Russia. The first edition appeared in 1793 in St. Petersburg (Leningrad today) and there is no need to recall to what extent the Russian spirituality and culture of the ninteenth century were influenced by it. It will suffice to mention once more the example of Dostoievsky who echoes the "unseen warfare" in which contemporary Russia and indeed universal history are involved at the time. It is a matter of the "choice" between new ideologies and Western techniques on the one hand, and the contemplative knowledge of man's destiny on the other hand. The "choice" — or its impossibility — no longer belongs to history, rather it makes our history.

THE "NO-MAN'S-LAND" OF CONTEMPLATION.

*The path beyond knowledge.* For the Christian East the way as well as the experience of contemplation is inscribed in a living Tradition. This term, or rather this reality, remains essential, for it expresses inseparably the creative, prophetic way of actual experience (*experientia magistra*: experience is the only master) and the light of doctrine that is both rigorous and liberating for the intellect. Tradition alone prevents them from separating and wrongly opposing each other in an individual "mysticism" on the one hand, and an abstract "doctrine" on the other. In reality the Greek word for tradition, *paradosis*, completely excludes this risk of rupture (a risk inherent in our temporal condition) since it signifies both the act or manner of transmission and its actual content. "There is no other way to speak of God than to live in him; he alone knows God who allows himself to be transmuted into him" (Gregory of Nyssa). It is not surprising that the Hesychastic tradition insists on the "methodical" character of the spiritual life. This idea of "method," successfully taken up, as we know, since the sixteenth-seventeenth centuries by the rational knowledge and technical sciences of the West, was already recognized by the Christian East in its primordial sense: *methodos* means 'going along with', 'itinerancy', a normative way. The two disciples of Emmaus (Luke 24) had to go along with the Unknown before recognizing the Risen Christ in the Eucharistic sign. And Moses, who before the Burning Bush replied "Here I am" but did not dare to raise his eyes, ventured to know on the Rock of Horeb, but glory was refused to the audacity, and Transcendence — a pure passing — manifested only when it passed by. It is a trace to be followed up.

*Apophasis, way of the Living God.* It is always rash to try and sum up in a single word the intimate dominant, the "figure" of a spiritual universe. It is legitimate, however, to attempt a first approach. In the spiritual tradition of the East, apophatism, rather than a current or school of thought, indicates a style, an essential intention to which is linked a whole coherent series of symbols (icons, hymnography, liturgical rhythm). Here again we must be careful and know how to interpret. In this domain what is said is "nothing": the fundamental intuition signified conceptually is realized (and "de"-realized also) in an experience which leads to something beyond itself.

The Greek noun *apophasis* immediately defines negation, but when we probe more deeply, this is a particular negation which goes beyond categories, beyond words. Thus it faces up to the *kataphasis*, the affirmation which is the very structure of all language (even of language which formally denies a thing or an idea, since this invariably presupposes adherence to what I affirm by my denial).

The first form of apophatism is that which the Eastern as well as the Western spiritual traditions know under the name of *via negativa*. A mysterious writer of the fifth-sixth centuries, who goes by the name of Dionysius the Areopagite, made this form famous. The intellect in its ascent to God passes through a noetic catharsis, a gradual purification in the course of which it perceives that God is nothing of that which is (hence the negative terms composed with the alpha privative are more suitable: *atheatos, akatonomastos, aperiliptos*), that to name Him we must go beyond all possible names (this is why He must be called by names surpassing all others, connoted by the prefix *hyper: hyperarrhetos, hypertheos, hyperagathos*), that, in sum, God lives in the superessential darkness where ecstasy alone can transport the intellect *(noûs)* beyond itself, in perfect union with the only One it desires. Contrary to what may be believed, the Hesychastic tradition has been rather reticent with regard to the Areopagitic schema of the *via negationis*. Its principal merit undoubtedly consists in preserving on the one hand the divine transcendence from all confusion with the cosmological order, no matter how exalted it may be, and, on the other hand, making the soul aware of its total inadequacy to penetrate by itself the mystery of the Living God. But apophatism here is far from its real meaning. "We know that the intellect invariably understands what negative theology denies," said the great Hesychastic witness of the fourteenth century, Gregory Palamas. "With the latter we go downwards instead of ascending to the ultimate mystery."

This is why we must proceed by what is called the "living apophatical experience." The intellect (*noûs*), the cognitive-contemplative faculty, the apex or "ground" of the soul, is considered more fully here, from its "existential" aspect as an expression of total human existence. It tends essentially to connaturality in silence and peace (*hesychia*), having left behind it every vestige of the perceptible, of the imaginary, of intellection. To describe this new apophatic passage, the words "nudity," "formlessness" (which might partially capture the known meaning of *śunyavada*) are employed. In the living experience, however, the emphasis is on "purification of the heart" (the center and root of being) and on "liberation from the passions" (*apatheia*). It is difficult to translate this last notion: its etymological root, *pathe*, combines in a single word two aspects which are different but inseparable: "active passion," which is expressed by ontological pulsion (desire, self-assertion, domination), and a passive aspect, "the invasion of being by nothingness." Those who enter this state already have a foretaste of the Resurrection of which Christ is the beginning and the end. "The death of what is created, on the seventh day — the mystical Sabbath on which death dies — introduces to the Resurrection on the eighth day" (St. Maximus the Confessor). (The "eighth day," the "Sunday of eternity," announces the passing beyond the created horizon symbolized by the biblical account of the seven days of creation.) The heart thus restored to its true state, and having become like unto God, sees creation in its entirety as though in a cosmic liturgy illuminated internally by the divine sense (the *logoi*) which it always possesses, and "becomes inflamed itself with infinite compassion for all beings, for men, for the birds, the beasts, the demons. . . . It prays unceasingly for the enemies of truth, for those who commit evil, so that they may be saved and purified" (Isaac the Syrian). To such a heart, "He who never ceases to show himself can, in the end, appear" (Gregory of Nyssa).

It is at this point that the apophatic approach discloses its "last" teaching, and, for the Hesychastic tradition, which was the chosen instrument of its communication, its full meaning. It is true that human language itself experiences its death and the presentiment of possible resurrection. "The essential relationship between death and speech is dazzling, but it is as yet unimagined."[4]

In point of fact the Logos of origin here transfigures the human word in order to enable it to grasp the "compenetration" of the Uncreated and the created. Formulae become antinomic and paradoxical when attempting to describe the Living God "beyond all affirmation and negation, even beyond the *coincidentia oppositorum*, and entirely present in His uncreated energies fully communicated to the creature. This doctrine reveals the distinction-identity in God of the uncommunicable and unshareable essence and of its uncreated energies in which this essence manifests itself *without going forth from its nonmanifestation*. The Hesychastic tradition contemplates in these fomulations the doctrinal expression of deification, just as it calls by a name which has no parallel the total appropriation of man by God and God by man. "Even if it is metaphorically called knowledge, it [this deification] is beyond all knowledge. It no longer belongs to the domain of the intelligible. . . . It is also beyond unknowing. And no matter what we choose to call it — vision, knowledge, feeling, illumination — it is none of all these" (Gregory Palamas).

*The deified being (theosis).* The way of Hesychastic contemplation is, in the end, a way of deification. Once the "liturgical pilgrimage towards the heart" is achieved by the intellect impelled by the remembrance and invocation of the Name of Mercy and Power ("Lord Jesus Christ, Son of God, have mercy upon me") and confirmed by the "grace of breathing," man becomes the seat of divine uncreated action. Beforehand (during the phase of intellectual seeking and ascetical purification) God sustains the effort of the created being, and whereas formerly He was hidden to man, now it is man who is hidden in God.

The Hesychastic tradition refers insistently to the episode of Christ's Transfiguration in order to awaken the intelligence to a knowledge of deification. Before the eyes of his disciples on Mount Thabor Christ appeared radiant with "uncreated light," a reverberation of inaccessible divinity. (Maximus the Confessor says in enigmatic fashion: "On Thabor God became his own symbol.") Deification assumes a realistic significance: "Man, while remaining entirely man, in body and soul, by nature, has become entirely God, in body and soul, by grace" (Maximus the Confessor). "And he who ascends never stops, going from beginnings to beginnings, by beginnings which have no end" (Gregory of Nyssa).

ANDRÉ SCRIMA

CONTEMPLATION AND ACTION

"Behold . . . before thee an open door, and no man can shut it . . . (Rev. 3:8).

The polarity "contemplation-action" would at first sight appear to be a form of language. In order to place these two terms together, we must name them singly, or in other words, place them in opposition to each other, even if only in a relative opposition. But already at the ungratifying level of language their complementarity would show up as the reflection of a dynamic unity which cannot express itself save in the dual refraction or the tensions which issue literally from "misunderstanding." It is hardly necessary to stress how this polarity corresponds for the contemplative to an axial reality: "acting as a contemplative and contemplating as an active person" (Maximus the Confessor). God creates for that matter from His virtuality in our act as from our virtuality in His act. The two concepts — contemplation and action — converge towards a state of reintegration in which they disclose and conceal at the same time the fulfilled presence of the human being. However, in actual fact a certain dissymmetry subsists which enables us to recognize and "define" them. In other words, contemplation envelops and carries action, while action "signifies" and possibly "conveys" contemplation. For the latter is preeminently the consummated act as an act, with all its metaphysical, cosmic resonance, and, it must be said, especially with its human resonance, because it is up to man to bring together (or to separate temporarily) one dominion from the other, "heaven" from "earth."

This will enable us, in passing, to touch on another aspect involved in the unity of — and distinction between — contemplation and action, the aspect which concerns the typology (altogether relative) of the various religions in their current pursuit of meeting and dialogue. It is obvious — and this is very likely a sign of the times that we have still to decipher — that in a certain sense the age of exclusions, anathemas, attempts at domination, and facile apologetics is virtually past for religious conscience (even though in actual behavior it still continues). It is not merely a question of tolerance and courtesy: there is, apparently, a *dialogical* dimension (in the strong sense of the word — that which allows the

146

logos to pass; for, just as there is a *dia-logos*, there is also the great obstacle of the *dia-bolos*) which invites not so much an intercourse by words as an exchange, so difficult and demanding, of real experience. But even this might merely belong to some substructures of contemporary history or to general cultural events. It is all the more useful, then, to call to mind at this point a traditional truth according to which all apparent progress in the visible order is followed by an as yet invisible ordeal to come.

Now, it seems difficult to overlook the fact that both contemplation and action are being confronted today with a totalizing form of space and time which is called "history." Both contemplation and action find themselves, as it were, *intimately* obliged to take their place in this "history," to take it into account and even up to a point to justify themselves before it. Undoubtedly, the contemplatives will speak (or be silent) on history as based on their transcendent knowledge. But it may be that history awaits from them, consciously or not, as a fulfillment or a judgment, the signs capable of opening the "door" (cf. Rev. 3:8), leading to its *eschaton*. Certainly the "active" members of all religions are more or less at ease in the apparent progression of our history unless, according to Hegel's idea about the cunning of history, history itself maneuvers them surreptitiously by enclosing itself into a temporal finitude — an absolute enclosure simulating the Absolute.

It has often been observed that we lend to the horizontal transcendence what we take from the vertical, and that we conceive infinite and progressive history as an "external Power" of which we would be only the instruments without interior substance. This type of history secularizes a rudimentary conception of God. "Moreover, no philosophy of history has ever carried over to the future the whole substance of the present, nor destroyed itself to give place to another. No philosophy has ever consisted in choosing between transcendencies — for example, between that of God and that of the future of mankind; all philosophies have been busy mediating them."[5]

Now, here are the facts. This spatial setting — vertical, horizontal — which, far from denoting a simple abstract metaphor of existence, expresses the dimensions and the topography of the unfolding of being, is confirmed, one might say, by the other two cardinal reference points, East and West. There would obviously be a strong temptation to assimilate the East to "vertical" contemplation and the West to "horizontal" action. In any event, the fact remains that today as yesterday it is difficult to name a form of contemplative research which does not go back sooner or later to its Eastern horizon. (To put it bluntly, the origin of contemplation is the contemplation of the Origin.) Equally, it would be contrary to the evidence to deny that history in its totalizing and active sense represents the very act of the West, its original project, its impossible innocence. ("Atheism as the will to establish a new origin in time, and the presentiment of second innocence, are inseparable,"[6] said Nietzsche.)

Actually, the temptation would be too strong and, in fact, simplistic. Indubitably "the contemporary situation, which takes on the aspect of a new beginning and which is in reality the destruction of the original advent of the unveiling of the world, lies like a snare in the path. The interrogation regarding God in such an extremely misguided period must be kept up."[7] And quite probably the deadliest snare in the path of a "history" understood as "action" in times and on the times is the fall in "concepts" and "things."

This is not, of course, the proper place to dwell scrutinizingly on the multiple strata of semantic and philosophical implications of *thing* — the word-concept, and the concrete fact of what it designates. Be it sufficient to note that its essential meaning, underlying the current use of our modern languages, traces back to an ambivalent function: it may as well "close" as "reopen" time and reality. The Greek *pragma* relates itself to *prasso, praxo*, the achieved effect of a temporal action (akin to the Sanskrit *Karman*), whereas the Anglo-Saxon *thing*, subsuming the Northern and Germanic linguistic layers, apparently refers to an old and obscure Gothic root, *theihs*, "accomplished time." On the other side, the Neo-Latin *chose, cosa*, etc., eluding the old Latin *res* (nearer, in its etymology, to the Greek *pragma*), derives itself from *causa*, again in obvious relation to the time, but equally suggesting "that which puts us in question." And, strangely enough, with a rather unexpected intuition, when the Andalusian algebraists established the sign for a mathematically operational unknown, they expressed it as "x," from the Arabic name for "thing," *sh(ay)*.

Both things and concepts are implied, moreover, in the essential structure of "technology" (in the broad sense): this could mean either the triumph or the entropy of action. For "to act" requires something immediately visible (material or intellectual) and totally controllable: the invisible and the gratuitous then become mere subproducts of the imagination. For the living man, a mere relay point between "thing" and "action," will there be any room left any longer?

That, between concepts and things, "she errs, the divinity of the gods" (Sophocles, *Oedipus Rex*) has been the lament of Oedipus's chorus since the Hellenistic dawn of the West.

Nevertheless, the contemplative gaze could illumine with a strange light the day (or the evening — "and the evening and the morning were the first day" [Gen. 1:5]) of our Western history. For the West, over and above the action which it is to pursue to the very end, is itself placed beneath a destinal sign. It is a question of being able to recognize this sign written on the countenance of the true man of the West. According to its more enigmatic poets and artists (Hölderlin, Nietzsche, Van Gogh, Segalen . . .), the true people of the West are the *Hesperians*, the "adventurers" (*ad-venire*: to reach the end) seeking in their passage through time the previous future, the return of the matutinal origin (of which the immutable memory is entrusted to the East) as *eschaton*, the dawn which is to come at the setting (*Occidens*) of the sun. The final consummation can only be brought about by the one who seeks, inquires, and acts. The historical "body" of the West has in actual fact become the "final" horizon of our planetary cycle, a body made up of "things" and imbued with the resulting quantophrenia (*ad perpetuam rei memoriam*: the daring phrase inherited from the Roman ancestors of the West, seems now to have become a universal countersign). Nevertheless, it must not deceive us by its outward semblances. It may perhaps be merely the *vehicle* of a much deeper *vocation*, of which the value and meaning come not from the past, very little from the present, almost entirely from the future. And there again, the realm of contemplation by no means appears either contradicted or

149

contradictory. It dwells and peregrinates both "here" and "elsewhere." *Ad perpetuam Dei memoriam — donec veniat* (for the everlasting remembrance of God — until He comes).

[1]"Behold the universe shaking with its vaulted mass."

[2]Hagioritic: of the Holy Mountain.

[3]"Being is silence"

[4]Martin Heidegger, *Unterwegs zur Sprache* (Pfullingen: Neske, 1959), p. 215.

[5]M. Merleau-Ponty, *Signes* (Paris, 1960), pp. 88-89.

[6]*Die Frohliche Wissenschaft* (Leipzig: C. G. Naumann, 1895-97). Frederich Nietzche's Werke, Vol. 5.

[7]M. Heidegger, *Nietzsche*, vol. I, (Pfullingen, 1961), p. 24.

# Contemplation and Action
# in Judaism and Islam

## LEO SCHAYA

*Editor's Introduction:* Contemplation as well as all spiritual and human activity that flows from it has basically to do with a universal reality in which all beings endowed with intelligence participate on different levels. This reality is the pure and universal Being Itself, the divine Principle of all being, intelligence, and action. Whosoever removes himself from divine Being, from its presence and its will, is degraded into his particular being, lapses into nondivine existence, ignorance, and delusion.

Contemplation of the One is in itself the unitive act of the One, its beatific act of knowledge. The One contemplates itself according to various human spiritual needs and sacred modes of communication that correspond to them. At the level of pure Contemplation of the One, the spiritual reality of a Jew is no different from that of a Muslim. Israel and Islam, like all other revealed forms, are, at this level, completely transformed into the only Truth and Reality, the One God, whatever the name by which He is called or the form in which He is worshipped.

## DEFINITION OF CONTEMPLATION AND OF ACTION

Before considering contemplation and action in their specifically Judaic and Islamic modes, it may be useful to define them generally in the light of what Judaism and Islam have deeply in common and of what they share, each in its own fashion, with universal spirituality. We shall take the Latin etymology of the words "contemplation" and "action" as the point of departure since we shall use these terms throughout our exposition, and the etymological analysis will serve at the same time as a bridge between the Western terminology and that of the two Semitic traditions we are going to consider. So let us first recall that the word *contemplatio* is composed of *cum* and of *templum* and that *templum* denotes in

151

general a consecrated place, but signified in particular the square imaginarily traced in the sky by the rod of the augur, the Roman priest whose function it was to interpret the omens read in the flight of birds, amongst other things, within this celestial field of observation.

But contemplation of the sky has not been restricted to the soothsayer looking for signs: men of all peoples and all times have raised their eyes towards the celestial vault, their gaze transfixed and ravished by the myriads of marvels there revealed to them. And men everywhere have been transported from this natural *contemplatio caeli* to spiritual *contemplatio Dei,* as in the case of the prophet Isaiah, who cried out: "Lift up your eyes on high and behold who has created these (things)" (Isa. 40:26). In this verse from the Scriptures, apparently so simple, the word "who" (Heb.: *mî*) signifies, according to the esoteric exegesis of the Kabbalah, the supreme and superintelligible Essence; "to create" *(bara)* is a synonym of "cause to emanate"; and "these" *(eleh)* are all the intelligible aspects of the divine Being, the eternal archetypes of all things.

But *contemplatio Dei* does not follow naturally from contemplation of the heavenly phenomena alone. Thus Cicero, in Rep. 6,15, expanded the idea of *templum,* hence of *contemplatio,* to the magnitude of omnipresent Divinity, of "God, who has for his domain *(templum)* all that you behold" *(Deus, cujus hoc templum est omne quod conspicis).* And the Object of contemplation, at once supreme and universal, revealed itself in the Qur'an: "To whatever side you turn, there is the Face of Allah" (II, 109). Then the Prophet passed on to his companions, and through them to all the faithful, in the definition of spiritual "virtue" *(al-iḥsân),* the almost unconditional principle of contemplation. This contemplation does not start solely from apparent things but also from those that we do not see; it is dormant within our mind itself, before the mind reveals to us the light of its divine Object: "Virtue *(iḥsân)* consists in your worshipping (or serving) Allah as though you were seeing Him, and if you do not see Him, He sees you." This, finally, is the contemplation of Him whom man would not be able to see by himself, but who sees man and sees Himself through man by making the superhuman spirit of man participate in His own Vision; the Omnipresent One contemplates Itself in man through the "eye of the heart," until the earthly contemplator is able to say, with Al-Ḥusayn ibn Manṣûr al-Ḥallâj: "I saw my Lord with the eye of my heart and said to Him: 'Who art Thou?' He said: 'Thou!'" Spiritual contemplation has as its object divine Reality, which is likewise the pure Essence of man: it leads to knowledge of the only Truth, the only Reality, which is also the true knowledge of self, of our divine Self. Mohammed said: "Who knows himself knows his Lord."

Contemplation can be the outer action of a sensory look attentively fixed on a given physical object. It can also be an inner fixation of the mind on an object which is imagined or remembered, seen in a dream or in a prophetic vision; and it may be the essentially supramental or nondiscursive concentration on an idea or abstract truth, on the Infinite, the Absolute, God, or on the reality itself of such an idea, on its direct or purely spiritual revelation. Furthermore, contemplation may be outwardly sustained by a physical symbol and, at the same time, inwardly supported by a meditation such as deepens the truth or reality of the symbolic object by reflection; and finally, contemplation may pass from these two concomitant and peripheric activities to the very heart of its own action, namely to a direct and purely spiritual vision of the essence of the object or symbol. But passage from outer to innermost contemplation by way of meditation of an eminently discursive nature may also be bypassed by the simultaneity, the complete coincidence of the sensory perception and the suprasensory, spiritual knowledge of an object. The object perceived will be the revelation, at once formal and supraformal, of its own divine essence: its form will be "transparent" to the point of unveiling immediately its spiritual content, and so the "eyes" of the body and of the soul will participate directly in the contemplation of the "eye of the heart," which is the "eye of God" in man. The contemplative will thus see his object with the "eye that sees all": he will see God, the Omnipresent, in the object and he will see Him in the sensory mode and in the spiritual mode at the same time; as the prophet Mohammed promised believers: "You will see the Lord with your eyes." This promise was already fulfilled on Mount Sinai where the elect of Israel "saw God, and did eat and drink" (Exod. 24:11) and will be fulfilled again at the end of time, when "they will see with their eyes the return of YHVH[1] to Zion" (Isa. 52:8).

In the sense in which we are taking it, contemplation is distinct on the physical plane from all sensory looking without a noble motive or object related to a spiritual source, as well as distinct on the psychic plane from all reflection having nothing to do with Truth or divine Reality. Spiritual meditation, though it may serve as an entry to pure contemplation, is distinct from that contemplation insofar as its function remains discursive, i.e., welded to the indirect and dual knowledge of the mind. When meditation reaches its aim, it arrives — to quote the Kabbalah — at the "end of thought," at the entrance to pure contemplation, which is a supramental or nondiscursive concentration of the spirit on the supraformal and universal essence of the cognitive object, seen until then under the veil of its form, whether bodily or intellectual. Stripped of this form, the spirit of the object meditated upon is directly open to the spirit that contemplates it, and they become totally united. And in this union, the contemplator knows that his spirit and the spirit of all things are not two, but eternally and infinitely one: the "Spirit of Spirits," the One without a second.

But let us return again to meditation, which occupies an important place in the *via contemplativa* for, in the broadest sense, it already begins with the study of the revealed doctrine, which immediately incites the thought to God-centered reflection. Indeed, the revealed doctrine, with the sacred exegesis, teaches a man all he needs in order to realize the All. It enables him to know what the world is and what the human being is and — in some measure — what God is; how visible things reflect the invisible Reality, at once transcendent and immanent, how they connect in thought and interact with their divine Source which is our own Essence. Starting from there, a man can, in principle and on the microcosmic scale, integrate the multitude in the One. Thought, itself multiple and symbolically coextensive with All-Reality, instead of being dispersed and lost in a multitude of phenomena that it would have been unable to interpret correctly without the aid of sacred doctrine, discriminates between the illusory aspects and their profound reality; it brings all things back to their real and divine causes, even to the "Cause of Causes." This is the domain to which meditation belongs, the mental integration of the multiple in the One, as encountered in most traditional methods, whatever their particular modes of regarding and approaching the Absolute.

Every transcendental Cause, every eternal Archetype of a thing being an Aspect, a Quality, a Name of God, offers also a direct access to the One. Having conformed his actions and his qualities to those of the One and having mentally brought all things back to Him, it is then sufficient for a person to meditate on one truth, one Aspect, one Quality, and one Name of God for his thought to fulfill the whole of the work assigned to him: to bring the thinking being back, step by step, with all its content, to the end of all thought, which coincides with the birth of the being to the Spirit, which contemplates, in the depths of the heart, the supreme Principle of all things. This gradual raising of thought towards absorption in the Spirit is symbolized, amongst other things, by the pyramid, whose volume diminishes and is "concentrated" progressively with the approach to the apex, where it finally vanishes in the "highest Point," without extension, infinite.

In other words, the broadly extended base of the pyramid of reflection or theocentric meditation represents the study of the revealed doctrine, whose richness reflects the incommensurable plenitude of the aspects of the divine All-Reality. On that basis begins the mental and spiritual integration of the multiple in the One; this integration becomes pure contemplation inasmuch as the thought unceasingly relates all things to their divine archetypes and, by way of consequence, to the "Archetype of Archetypes," to the Unique Essence of all that is. Arriving at the "highest Point," the thought can no longer reflect, meditate, expand as such, and is of necessity effaced in its pure inner light, which is the superhuman Spirit, the divine ontological cognitive Essence of man. This is the Essence of all things revealing Itself in the highest contemplation, in uninterrupted intuition; this is the direct seeing of Him who alone sees and whom alone is seen. Thanks to meditation — beginning from the study of the teaching and leading to pure contemplation as its end — a man thus realizes, on the mental plane, the microcosmic reflection of the divine and universal integration of all things in the

One. In that way he participates really in God's unitive work; he fulfills his function of mediator between creation and Creator. This cosmic or objective aspect of meditation is, by definition, inseparable from its subjective aspect relating to the individual himself, who, by meditating, integrates himself with all things in the One: it is only through his own union with God that the one who meditates is able to unite all with Him. If he is dominated by things, if his mind is attached to their ephemeral nature, lost in their multiplicity, he is unable to make their real synthesis, to realize their union in the One, for he is unable to make the union in himself: he remains distracted, dispersed, lost in the multiple.

After having studied the sacred doctrine, after having reflected on it, meditated on the connections and the essential unity of man, the world and God, the one who meditates — normally under the direction of a spiritual master — then reduces the host of objects of meditation to a few fundamental themes that summarize them, or even to one universal theme, one sacred formula, one divine Name, that embraces all the aspects of Reality. He concentrates all his thought upon this theme, this truth, this access to the One, and his concentration has to be such that meditation "flows in an uninterrupted fashion, like oil into a jar." Every distraction, everything that is opposed in the man to the truth he is meditating, must be eliminated with the help of this truth itself, and, if need be, of a supplementary "means of union" used at the same time as meditation, such as the invocation of a divine Name or the repetition of a revealed formula, identified in either case with the Truth or Reality meditated. This combination of meditation and invocation or repetition of a divine Name or revealed formula has its sufficient reason in the Real Presence of God, who dwells both in the heart or spirit of the man who meditates and in the Word issued from the divine Mouth so that it might be voiced by man here below. But neither meditation nor invocation should be considered as acting automatically, like the formulas in the practice of magic. We have seen that these spiritual exercises demand not only a knowledge of the sacred doctrine, but unflagging discrimination as well, between the True and the false, the Real and the unreal, and, *ipso facto,* attachment to the One. This attachment is itself not only correlative to detachment from the illusory multitude but also to realization of the One in the multiple, of His Perfections in the soul, of the virtues and right, godlike attitudes of man. Thus not only must a man try to assimilate the truths upon which he meditates, he must also apply them in daily life. The *via contemplativa* and the *via activa* have to be inseparably united; contemplation itself is nothing other than the first and innermost of all activities and all activities have to be determined by it. If a man acts against the truths he is meditating or contemplating, this contradiction will reappear in his meditation or contemplation in the form of an obstacle to the actualization of the real Presence, to spiritual union with the One. If, on the contrary, his way of acting and behaving in outer life is in harmony with the content of his meditation or contemplation, it will prove to be a strong support for his inner activity, a "throne of union": thought crystallizes into virtue and right attitude; truth through thought becomes flesh; the spiritualized flesh is not opposed to thought but sustains it and becomes one with it in contemplation of the only Truth and the only Reality; the being in which body and soul are united contemplates Him until it becomes one with the One Being.

In this contemplative union, the individual and formal unity of body and soul must disappear and be transmuted into the infinite, universal, supraformal Unity of God or of the divine Self in man. All that has form, whether body or soul, all feelings, thoughts, reflections, meditation — all that must cease. Meditation has played its part positively in the return to mind of the Truth which man, in essence, is, which he saw, therefore, before his birth here below and which is deep inside him. This role of meditation implies the negation of every negation of the Truth, the elimination of all that is opposed to the inner Light, to pure Reality, to our own Self. Having played this part, meditation ends by denying itself insofar as it is in turn a screen which veils the Reality. By meditation, thought is transmuted into "being," and now the individual, formal, human being remains to be transformed, by pure nondiscursive, supramental contemplation, into divine, universal, suprahuman Being. After the final negation of all that is not the "One without a second," effected during meditation, there is the eternal, direct, and total affirmation of the One ... the contemplation proper to It, wherein the one contemplating and the one contemplated are at last but one. Any state of pure contemplation is a participation in this supreme state of *contemplatio Dei*; and the participation that comes about every time the individual being is effectively absorbed in its own universal center, in its heart where God dwells, can become total, complete identification, full union, the final and highest spiritual state, pure Being. A state of contemplation — a state of grace, light, and union — can therefore be at first a passing result of spiritual efforts, and this passing result can be repeated and intensified before being definitively acquired. Actually, if one considers contemplation in its broadest sense, i.e., as the *via contemplativa,* it represents the entire way of effort or spiritual exercise in the direction of the spiritual state properly so-called; the entire path from natural perception to divine inner vision, from meditation to suspension of thought in pure concentration of the mind; the entire process of passing from the cognitive act to real union with the essence of the object contemplated, from all action to pure Being, and, by that very fact, the transition from all movement, all form, to the immovable, supraformal Reality of the Infinite: the bridge between the multiple and the One — deep continuity in the midst of discontinuity, the very One in all multiplicity, the One contemplating Himself in the multiple.

In fact, contemplation of the One is the unitive Act of the One Himself: His beatific Act of Being, Knowledge, and Union. In contemplating the One, man actualizes in himself His Being, His Knowledge, His Unity: he is Being through Being, he knows all that is knowable through Him who alone knows; he is unified in himself and united to the One through the One. Perfect contemplation is the act wholly in conformity and essentially identical with Being; it is the act by which man realizes his being, and in his being, pure and supreme Being. It consists in "eating from the Tree of Life and living eternally" after bodily death. And this applies to every act that, as in contemplation, is truly in conformity with the divine Being, His Reality, and His Will. But of all these acts — whether of prayer, meditation, invocation of a divine Name, repetition of a revealed formula, visualization of a sacred symbol, or love of one's neighbor, any of which can easily be a direct support of contemplation — it is always contemplation itself (or, from another angle, the contemplative "effort," i.e., pure, nondiscursive concentration of the mind) that effects in the most immediate way the transition from act to Being.

Spiritual contemplation, although a human act, is not done by man alone; in the image of its divine Object, it assumes both an outer and an inner aspect. It is in itself its own object: the Reality, Being, Knowledge, and Beatitude of the One. Just as the divine Being is outwardly revealed by its creative and redemptive Act, so is our contemplation extrinsically an act, but an act through which we participate directly in God's Act, whereas the essence of our contemplation is one with His Essence. Seen from the outside or from below, contemplation is passing from act to Being, from spiritual activity to spiritual Essence; seen from within, or from above, it is Being, Essence itself, or again: the passing from Being to Act or that of the supreme Light to Its own receptivity, which, in the heart of the Cosmos, becomes Its contemplative receptacle, the creature, man.

In defining contemplation in this way, from the earthly point of view as the passing from act to Being, and from the ontological point of view as the passage from Being to act, we have not used the philosophical vocabulary inherited from Aristotle, where the term *actus* itself designates what really is, so that pure Act is thus pure Being without any restriction due to some or another virtuality of being. *Actus* then is equivalent to God himself, for all one can conceive of true being is possessed by God and He has no need to acquire it by passing from potency to act. God, pure Being, is pure Act and, as such, the Prime Mover, the motionless Mover. In other words, God moves all things by His very Being, which is pure Act, the first Act, the supreme Act. And according to the Stagirite, this supreme Act is not only divine Being but also divine Thought; since it is divine Being, pure Act, the Thought in this sense could only have a divine object, namely Itself. It is therefore not comparable with human thought, as the great Master of Kabbalah, Moses Cordovero (1522-1570), so clearly pointed out in *Pardes Rimmonim:* "The Creator's Knowledge is not like that of creatures, for in the latter, knowledge is distinct from the subject of knowledge and has to do with objects that are likewise distinguished from the subject. This is what is referred to by the three terms: thought, what thinks, and what is thought. On the contrary, the Creator is Himself at once Knowledge, Knower, and Known. Indeed, His manner of knowing does not consist of applying His Thought to things as it were outside of Him; but it is by knowing Himself and of Himself that He knows and sees all that is. Nothing exists but is united with Him and found by Him in His own Essence." Divine "Thought," *Mahshabah*, according to the Kabbalah, is none other than the infinite "Wisdom" of the One, *Hokhmah*, His first ontological Emanation, His intelligent Being which is also His intelligent Act, His Knowledge or Contemplation of Himself which determines and produces all things; such is also the teaching of Hermes Trismegistus, inscribed on the Emerald Tablet: "All things come from the One and from the Contemplation of the One."

And so the Aristotelian terminology, from which our own differed somewhat at first sight, finally corroborates what we have said about the true nature of contemplation, namely that it is the Act, the very Being of the One, or His Act of Being, of Knowing and — seen from below — of Supreme Union. It follows, besides, from this that if we speak of contemplation and action, we have to keep well in mind that these are not opposite terms, since contemplation is the first and pure act from which all other acts flow and by which they are therefore determined. "Act" or "Action" derives from the Latin *agere*, "to act," which is opposed neither to *contemplari* nor to *cogitare*, but to *pati*, "to undergo"; *actio* or *actus* is the opposite of *passio*, "what one undergoes," whence the opposition "activity," "passivity." On the ontological level, the agent, the act, and what is acted upon are but one: Being "is" Being, Knowledge knows itself, Light contemplates itself, and its rays create and illuminate what is created until it is finally reabsorbed in its divine Essence. This is the definition of contemplation and action in itself. This is the supreme identity of contemplation and pure Act or pure Being. To contemplate is to actualize the pure Act, is to be Being, Knowledge, Beatitude.

From the *contemplatio Dei*, which is His Act, His very Being, proceeds every being, every act, all contemplation, by way of His "adaptation" matched to all levels and receptivities of existence, as Hermes Trismegistus likewise taught: "All things are brought forth from the One by the way of adaptation" of Himself to things. This is why normally everything should be in conformity with His Being, every act with His Act, all knowledge or contemplation with His Knowledge, His Contemplation. But it is not so: everything issued from pure Being, pure Act, does not remain united to His Presence as it descends to this lower world. Now, everything which digresses from divine Being, from his Presence, is degraded in its particular being, in its nondivine existence, in its knowledge become ignorance, in its action no longer in conformity with the divine Act or Will. Only pure contemplation and any act that is contemplative or willed by God unites with His Presence, even if in a more or less direct manner; and the being who contemplates or acts in that way is by the very fact united with the One. This is how Plotinus defines contemplation *(theoria)*. as a state of the soul directly united with God by its higher part; contemplation and whatever in the soul contemplates God escapes from the degradation of doing *(prattein)* and making *(poiein)*. The act of contemplation and what con-templates — to return to our own terminology — are essentially one with the pure Act, pure Being. On the contrary, what does not contemplate God and does not do His Will is — by definition — not united with Him and, having gone away from Him, is degraded and denies its own reason for being: the only Being, the one and universal Act.

Every action here below, whether perfect or deformed by man, is a manifestation of that Act, of that Being. The essence of act is Being and its immediate reason for being is the actualization, the realization of Being. Action that is not in conformity with Being, instead of actualizing Being, of realizing it, tends to stifle it, to kill it. And since such action cannot annihilate the eternal Being, it inevitably turns against the one who has acted against Him and who thereby denies and kills his own ephemeral being. Action that kills being is the sin of mankind, sin carried to extremes by our own contemporaries. They cultivate action for the sake of action without regard to being, His Being: hence, agitation without any true aim, collective suicide, loss of soul. Modern man preaches "progress," progress towards the abyss, and commits himself body and soul to an activity that does violence to being; he cultivates a "Tree of Science," which proves to be a "Tree of Death." He rejects contemplation as being something ineffective: men who devote their life to contemplation are considered useless, idle people, enemies of society. Countries which have remained more or less traditional are regarded as "unproductive" to the very extent that they retain signs of contemplation. Modern man has no notion that contemplation is the purest and highest form of action, and the most powerful; that it actualizes the supreme Being, the universal Act; that in contemplation the real presence of the Lord of the worlds reveals Himself, manifests here below. Our contemporaries do not know that contemplation is in itself not the act of man, but of God, in face of which all actions initiated by man vanish like the mirage. God contemplates the world in Himself and the world is. God contemplates the end of the world in Himself and the world is finished. And a man of God contemplates with God, acts with Him, is conscious of God in himself and in all things. He contemplates the One "withersoever he turns" — "on high" where absolute Truth is enthroned, in the "heart" where His real Presence dwells, and in the "neighbor" filled with the same Presence. His contemplation embraces all — it is the infinite knowledge and universal love that unites all to the One.

## THE OBJECT OF CONTEMPLATION IN JUDAISM AND IN ISLAM

When one has become aware of what contemplation is — as of all the spiritual and human activity that flows from it — one knows that basically it has to do with a universal reality in which all beings endowed with intelligence participate on different levels. This reality is the pure Act, the pure and supreme Being, the Principle of all being, all intelligence, and all action. To contemplate means actualizing the pure Act, being pure Being, resting in pure knowledge amid the variety of modes of contemplation, and of the ways or traditions to which they belong. Contemplation — and any essentially spiritual activity — in Judaism or Islam is an adaptation of these universal principles in regard to one mode of spiritual receptivity or another, crystallized in religious form. And for the universality of contemplation — as well as for the relationship between Judaism and Islam — we will find analogies among their contemplative modes, which, the nearer they come to their object, gradually become also at one with it. In pure contemplation, all revealed ways, all true contemplators come together and are united, all being receptacles open to the One and filled with the One.

The One contemplates Himself in Himself and in His receptacles, and communicates with them according to the depth of their receptivity; this variable predisposition or receptivity is translated in this world as much by the diverse spiritual needs of humanity as by the diverse sacred modes that correspond to them and in which men worship and contemplate the only Reality and manifest His Truth and His Will in their outer action. The world of contemplation and of godlike action is His Kingdom, is the world of the One but also the world of the One in the many, to which Israel and Islam, among others, belong. In this world of pure contemplation and godlikeness, Israel strictly signifies Judaism as such, the Mosaic religion or the Hebrew people insofar as they follow that religion, the "holy nation," the theocracy of the Bible. In the same way, Islam is the Mohammedan religion concretizing the Qur'anic revelation and the *Sunna*, the sacred "custom," received from the Prophet and supported by his *aḥadîth*, or "sayings" that have crystallized the Moslem tradition. In these two sister religions, the revealed letter is clarified by the exoteric exegesis and by the spiritual doctrine or esoterism, both going back, on the one hand, to Moses, and on the other, to Mohammed. As for the two esoterisms, Kabbalah and Sufism, they represent the innermost or highest interpretations and the actual spiritual realization of the divine revelations in question: the heart of Israel, the heart of Islam. From a certain historical point of view, these are two worlds of contemplation arising from the heart of Abraham and united in his faith in the One: in the innermost depths of these two hearts there is nothing but the One (*ehad* in Hebrew, *aḥad* in Arabic), the "One without a second" (*hu ehad we-en sheni* in Hebrew, *waḥdahu lâ sharîka lahu* in Arabic). Can there be two "Ones," two "Ones without a second?" One is one without any

163

division; One without a second is One without any associate. Such is the God of Israel: "Hear, O Israel, YHVH, our God, YHVH, is One" (*Sh'ma Israel* YHVH *Elohenu* YHVH *ehad*) (Deut. 6:4); and such is "The Divinity" (Allâh) of the Qur'an, who enjoins every Moslem: "Say: He, Allâh, is one" (*Qul huwa-Allâhu ahad*) and who excludes every false divinity, any pseudo-absolute, by the credo: "There is no divinity if it be not The Divinity" (*Lâ ilâha illâ Allâh*). There is only the one Divinity, unique and universal; this is why the prophet Malachi asked the great question: "Have we not all one Father: Hath not one God created us?" (Mal. 2:10).

Judaism and Islam exoterically declare the "One without a second" to be the "only God"; and this God is worshipped by man, who coexists with Him as a "second." Jewish and Moslem esotericism (the Kabbalah, Sufism) pursue this monotheistic profession of faith to its ultimate conclusion by affirming the "One without a second" as the absolute One, the only Reality, who integrates all in Himself — this without falling into the traps of pantheism, which, on the contrary, integrates the Divinity in the world and leads mentally to confusion of the Real with the unreal, of the Infinite with the finite, the imperishable with the transitory. According to both of these esoteric doctrines, what is transitory appears and disappears in the Infinite without affecting it; All-Reality, of which the eternal and the transitory are aspects, remains forever what It is. It is at once absolute Super-Being, causal Being, and universal Existence; it is simultaneously superintelligible Reality, which rests in Itself, intelligible Being, which contemplates Itself, and Existence, which goes out from Being (*ex-sistere, ex-stare*) without going out from It in reality. Existence is irradiated from God's revelatory and creative contemplation; it remains linked with Him by the ray of His ontocosmological contemplation and returns to Him in His self-contemplation. Divine All-Reality cannot be reduced to Existence, as pantheism would have it; on the contrary, Existence finds itself forever integrated in the divine All, either in His Transcendence or in His Immanence. The one Reality of Existence is its divine Essence that is at the same time transcendent and immanent, whereas its relative unreality is the pure expression of the creative, revealing, and unifying will of the only One: from His self-contemplation emanates the illusory appearance of an other-than-Him, so that this other may know and contemplate the fact that in reality, in essence, he is not other than Him — that in truth there is none other than Him, the One without a second. This is what the Prophet says: "Allâh was and nothing was with Him and He is now just as He was." When a mirage appears or disappears in a desert, is the desert changed thereby? "The thirsty man runs towards it and there waiting for him is Allâh." So long as the illusory existence of the "other" lasts, this other will find nothing real, nothing positive, nothing good outside of the only real Being; and whatever this existence itself may be, perfect or imperfect, it subsists as such thanks solely to the Being, the only Reality, the "One and Only Essence" (*Dhât al-wâḥidah*) of all that is. Thanks to this essential Unity or "Unity of Being" (*Waḥdat al-Wujûd*), every being comes in the end to contemplate the One Being, to be that Being, to be one through the One, with the One, in the One.

While pasturing Jethro's ewes in the desert of Midian and on arriving at the foot of Mount Horeb, Moses saw and contemplated in the burning bush the real Presence of this one Essence of all that is: the Presence revealed itself to him as *Ehyeh*, the one and universal "Being," as the "Being that is Being" (*Ehyeh asher Ehyeh*), beyond and within all existence. But It also revealed to him that It is not only the Essence and Principle of existence, but simultaneously rests in Itself, in Its Super-Being or Non-Being — called in Kabbalah, *Ain*, the divine "Nothingness." In fact, *Ehyeh* means not only "I am," but also "I will be." *Ehyeh asher Ehyeh* means not only "I am that I am," but also "I will be that I will be," on this side of My Non-Being or Super-Being, of My superontological and superintelligible Reality; and in My Being "I will be with you" (*Ehyeh imokh*), with all existence, with all that is born from My Being, with all My "children," the "children of Israel" and all the "children of God."

Because the only Father and God is with all His children — because the "Being-and-Super-Being" is the spiritual Essence in all existence — the spirit of man, all his spiritual being, is in principle capable of immersing itself not only in pure and intelligible Being, but even in the bottomless abyss of the divine "Nothingness," in the more-than-luminous Darkness of the supreme and superintelligible Principle. This is what happened to Moses at the foot of Mount Horeb, in Sinai, face to face with the burning bush. He realized in secret all that he was later to reveal to the children of Israel from the summit of the same sacred mountain, when he went up step by step until he entered into the darkness of God's cloud. Then, according to Denis the Areopagite, "He penetrated into the truly mystical Darkness of unknowing; there he closed his eyes to all positive knowledge, escaped completely from all grasping and all vision, for he belonged wholly to Him who is beyond all, no longer belonged to himself, or to anything alien, but was united through the best of himself with Him who is ungraspable by any knowledge, having renounced all positive knowledge, and knowing, thanks to that very unknowing, beyond all intelligence. May we also [here the Areopagite addresses Timothy and through him all Christian contemplatives] penetrate into this Darkness more luminous than light and, renouncing all vision and all knowledge, may we thus see and know Him who is beyond all vision and all knowledge! For that is true vision, that is true knowledge, and from the very fact that one gives up all that exists one celebrates the Superessential in a superessential mode."[2] This is what in Kabbalah is called *bittul ha-yesh*, the "annihilation of existence" in *Ain*, the divine "Nothingness," implying the annihilation of human reason in "contemplation of the Nothingness." On this subject, the Hassidic[3] master Rabbi Levy Yitshak of Berdichev (d. 1809) said: "There are men who worship the Creator with their reason, and there are other men who contemplate the Nothingness [*mistakel el ha-Ain*], if one may express it like that; and for human reason it is not possible, but only with God's help. . . . When a man succeeds in contemplating Nothingness, his human reason is annihilated; later, when he returns towards reason, he is filled with [divine] superabundance." To "come down again" from "Nothingness" to "Being," from superintelligible contemplation to ontological and universal Knowledge not only brings with it the instantaneous reconstitution of existence, of human being, but its full illumination. The highest Contemplation itself is not — as we have just said — positive knowledge or vision; it is "being united by the best of oneself [by the pure and highest 'Self'] with Him who cannot be grasped by knowledge." So it is not a question of the union of a subject with an object of positive knowledge, but of absolute identity of the subject and the object in the "contemplation of Nothingness"; or, more precisely, there is in this case no subject contemplating, no object contemplated, there is only a divine "Nothingness" and a contemplation that is not contemplation, that is itself "Nothingness"; and this "Nothingness" is the Absolute, the more than luminous, unknowable, infinite, and unconditioned Essence of all contemplation or knowledge. Here all affirmation and all negation are surpassed, all existence and nonexistence are effaced: this is the Sufis' "extinction of extinction" *(fanâ' al-fanâ')*.

Here man is no longer a human being nor any intelligible being whatsoever: he is transformed into his own superhuman and superintelligible Essence, the divine Super-Being which reposes in itself without any exteriorization, emanation, revelation, or manifestation; since, from eternity to eternity, He "made Darkness His hiding place" (Ps. 18:11). This is the Obscurity of the divine Cloud, into which Moses penetrated, the "dark Cloud" *(al-ʿamâ)* where, according to the Prophet, Allah dwells "before creating the world," that is to say beyond everything that relates in any way whatsoever to the creation. In Sufism this more than luminous Obscurity is identified with *al-ʿadam* or *al-ʿudum,* Non-Being, absolute non-Manifestation, the highest degree of divine All-Reality, where Allah dwells like a "hidden and unknown Treasure." He says to His Prophet: "I was a hidden Treasure; I wished to be known and I created the world. . . ." Wishing to be known, He descends, so to say, from His superintelligible "Non-Being" to His state of self-Knowledge — the state of His intelligible "Being" *(Wujûd).* Here He contemplates Himself as *Aḥad,* the "One" in Itself, and as *Wâḥid,* the "unique" Principle and Cause of all existence; in this latter contemplation He creates the world and from there His "ways" are revealed in their variety, as they surge out in all the "directions of the universe" and shine forth resplendent in all the possible shades of the divine "Colors" or Qualities.

From here, Islam comes down as a spiritual sword flaming with affirmation of the One, as a luminous axis linking heaven and earth, as the "straight path" *(Şirât al-mustaqîm)* going from God to man and leading man to God. This descent of the One, this vertical hyphen, is particularly symbolized by the *Alif,* the first letter of the Arabic alphabet, whose numerical value is one. This symbol of the One and of His descent is also the initial letter of the names Allah, "The Divinity," and *Aḥad,* the "One," as also of the word Islam (the first letter of which is an *Alif* pronounced as "i"). This quite simple design therefore reflects the eternal archetype of Islam, the direct revelation of the One, which is the summary of all His revelations: the *Alif* contains, reveals, and reabsorbs all the other letters that come after it, just as the primordial Sound, creative, revelatory, and redemptive, which manifests all things and in which they return to the eternal silence, to the absolute nonmanifestation of Allah. Islam represents, from the historical point of view, the restoration of the monotheism of Abraham, which — still in the aspect of its temporal filiation — goes back to the primordial revelation of God, to the religion of Adam, the unanimous tradition of humanity in the dawn of time. The spiritual reality of the Prophet is even prior to the first man; Mohammed said: "I was a prophet when Adam was still between the water and the clay." And he also said that at his advent "time turned back in a circular movement to the aspect it had on the day when Allah created the heavens and the earth." If the *Alif,* the vertical axis, signifies the revelation of Islam or the direct descent of the One, the said circular movement is none other than the movement of the same *Alif,* whose end comes to join again with the beginning by integrating all things in the One; this is the inner, spiritual movement of Islam, which actualizes the universal circle of the *religio perennis.* It is the primordial spirituality of man, which was due to rise again before the end of time in the form of the last religion, the one preceding the unanimous tradition of the Messiah, destined to be that of the world to come. In other words, Islam is the "last point" of the present circle or cycle of revelations — sealed by the "Seal of the Prophets," Mohammed — the final point which rejoins the primordial Point, the One revealing Himself to the whole of Humanity. This is why the Mohammedan religion confirms all earlier true beliefs, which it represents as at once the everlasting quintessence and the final synthesis. From vertical axis or straight ray of the One, Islam thus becomes the hidden circle, connecting all the revelations of the present cycle of humanity going from Adam to the Messiah of the *parousia*. We find this symbolism in the letter "m" of the name *Muḥammad*, the *Mîm*, being circular in form. And we find this same symbol of the circle in the deep meaning and graphical development of the letters or consonants of the name *Allâh* or *Allâhu*.

اللّه     =ALLâHu

One of the traditional representations of the divine name clearly shows, by means of a certain stylization, the passage from the "vertical axis" to the "universal circle," namely:[4]

الله

The axis of the *Alif* | curves at its lower extremity and becomes the first *Lâm* ل , and continues to curve in the same way in the second *Lâm* ل , until the curve is complete and closed on itself in the *Hâ* ه , reappearing in the stylization of the final vowel *u* (the *dammah*- ذ above the *Hâ*) as purely and simply a circle O . In one of the variants of this representation, the name of the Prophet appears in the middle of the final circle. Now all this symbolizes the mysteries hidden in the "Supreme Name" *(al-Ism al-aᶜẓam)*, each letter of which reveals a fundamental aspect of the divine All-Reality, or of the wholly real "Divinity," Allah. Among the many Sufic ways of considering these mysteries, we choose the following due to the teaching of Ibn al-ᶜArabî: The *Alif* — which at the beginning of a word always remains alone, not joined to the letters that follow it — represents the only Reality, the One without a second, *Allâh*, outside of Whom there is no divinity." The first *Lâm* —in which the *Alif* bends towards itself—is the One who contemplates Himself, His pure Unity. The second *Lâm* is the One who contemplates Himself through His "All-Possession," which comprehends the illusory appearances of an "other-than-He." This same second *Lâm*, in passing to the second *Alif* — which is not necessarily written, but always pronounced, and with which the *Lâm* forms the word *lâ*, "no," — is the eternal negation of the illusory "otherness," the reabsorption of all things in the one and only real Unity of *Allâh*. Lastly the *Hâ* is *Huwa*, "He," "He who alone remains": He rests eternally in Himself, absolutely hidden in Himself; and all things rest hidden in Him, are not other than Him, this being symbolized — in the form of the circle poised over the "h" — by the final "u" of *Allâhu* — because everything is in It and because It is the Essence of all things, the Name of the Essence is also the Name of all that is. This is why the Shaikh al-Akbar adds, in his "Book of the Name of Majesty: Allâh," that the Name Allâh, although it designates solely the supreme Essence *(al-Dhât)*, appears also on the different degrees of the All-Reality: it is often named when a particular Name of God is intended to refer to one of His "Qualities" *(Ṣîfât)* or "Activities" *(afᶜâl)* characterizing His relationships with the universal existence comprised in His Essence. Thus, besides the "essential" Mysteries that are being identified in the symbolism of the letters of the name *Allâhu*, all the other Mysteries of Essence and Existence are hidden in it: "All the divine Names are contained in this Name. From it they come forth and toward it they reascend"; it is the "supreme Name," the Name and the real Presence of the highest Object of all contemplation, all invocation, all action of the *muslim*.

While Allah is the Name proper to the Essence, and to all its aspects, *al-Raḥmân*, the "Merciful," is the Name proper to the preeminent divine Quality and to all the other Qualities and Activities of God that proceed from it. According to ᶜAbd al-Karîm al-Jîlî the meaning of the divine Name *al-Raḥmân* is "the Quality which includes all the divine "Qualities"; he places it — so to speak — between the "Essence *(Dhât)* of God and His "Qualities" *(Ṣîfât)*. According to another traditional point of view — put forward notably by Ibn al-ᶜArabî — *al-Raḥmân* belongs directly to the order of *adh-Dhât*. Al-Raḥmân is in that case the equivalent of the Vedantic *Ananda*, the "Beatitude," which designates an intrinsic aspect of *Atma*, the divine "Self." It is for this reason that it is said in the Qur'an: "Invoke Allah or invoke *al-Raḥmân;* by whatever Name you call upon Him, His are the most beautiful Names" (XX, 7). Allah, the Name of the *Dhât* or Essence of God, becomes, in *al-Rahmân*, the Name of the personal Divinity or of the "divine Person" *(al-Nafs al-ilâhiyah)*; for it is through His *Rahmâniyah* that Allah relates Himself to His creatures. Whether the created are conscious of it or not, whether they are grateful for it or not, the "merciful Lord" *(al-Rabb al-rahîm)* gives His "Life" to all that exists. His creatures exist thanks to His Being in them, know thanks to His Knowledge in them, have will thanks to His Will in them; and they hear, see, and express themselves thanks to His "Hearing," His "Seeing," and His "Speech" in them. The true contemplative is not only conscious of this and grateful, but he never ceases, apart from the carrying out of the Law, to seek, contemplate, and actualize in his own person the Being, Qualities, and Activities of the divine Person; and when his being is filled, absorbed, and "replaced" by the divine Being and His Qualities and Attributes, his spirit as well as his spiritualized body live what the Sufis have been able to describe—as for instance ᶜAbd al-Karîm al-Jîlî in his book *Al-Insân al-Kâmil,* "Universal Man." Then the words of Allah addressed to His Prophet are verified in him: "Nothing of what is pleasant to Me brings My servant closer to Me than the performance of the duties I have imposed upon him. My servant will not cease [as well] to come closer to Me by practices beyond the call of obligation, until I love him; and, when I come to love him, I shall be the ear through which he hears, the look by which he sees, the hand with which he grasps, the foot with which he walks ...." Allah will reveal himself to His servant in every one of his contemplations and actions and will unite him with Himself so intimately that the true name of His friend will be Allah. All this He made known to Al-Jîlî: "My friend, savor Me in perfumes, eat Me in what is eaten, imagine Me in the imaginable, know Me in thoughts, contemplate Me in the objects of the senses, clothe yourself in Me! My friend, you are My aim, through you My name is mentioned and you it is who are called when I am named!" Such is the revelation of the One in Islam, His descent into the man who contemplates Him in truth and acts according to His Will: the total union of the *muslim* with Allah.

In Judaism also, the supreme Object of all contemplation and action in the end takes the place of the human subject, who contemplates Him and becomes at last His representative on earth. The "rightful" *(Tsaddiq)* is so permeated by God that his whole being is finally but one with the divine Being: his activity actualizes God's Act, his thought reveals the divine Thought, and when he wishes something it is God who wishes it and makes it come true. In spite of that, the *via unitiva* of Judaism differs in form from that of Islam. The Revelation, the descent of the One into the midst of "His people" is peculiar to Israel, and is by definition the particular reason for being of Judaism. Whereas, in Islam, the One appears as a single direct ray whose flaming path traverses all levels of existence and becomes a circle integrating all things in God, in Judaism the ray of the One breaks, at the point of departure, as soon as the golden calf is worshipped in Sinai. In fact, the first Sinaitic revelation of God to His people, which united all the children of Israel with Him and was crystallized in the first Tables of the Torah, was broken, as they were, in face of this sin, this renewal of the original sin by a group of humans which the Lord had mercifully led back to the state of innocence. According to the Kabbalah, God wished graciously to bestow His Messianic Revelation on Israel, but His people were not ready for the final deliverance; the "Messiah flew away" from Sinai and the Lord had to replace the "first Tables whose transparent stones were made of Unity without duality" or of the "Tree of Life," by other Tables "emanating from the Tree of Good and Evil." From then on, Israel was subject to the dual Law, which veils the One; if obeyed it leads to eternal Life, but if not respected it may lead to hell. This was the institution of the Mosaic exoterism, which like a shell, enclosed the esoterism of the first revelation; purely contemplative life in the One became thenceforth a spiritual kernel hidden in the multiple forms of a religion, of an existence filled with ritual practices intended to purify man and keep him constantly attached to God. The traces of the first Revelation on Sinai, concentrated in the esoteric tradition, the Kabbalah, were reserved for a rigorously chosen few consecrated by initiation to the Mysteries of the Torah; but the Kabbalists also had to serve God by observing the Law, which, for them, signified a whole of ways for actualizing the Mysteries. This, furthermore, is why every Israelite who is faithful to God by being faithful to the Law, and whose sincere aspiration and other qualities fit him for initiation to the Mysteries, is in principle given the opportunity to become a Kabbalist.

It is true that one finds the same polarization of esoterism and exoterism in Islam, but in this case it was instituted at the very beginning and not as the consequence of a collective sin, a "break" in the ray of the One in the soul of a whole people. In Islam, as we have seen, the divine ray pierces directly through all degrees of existence, like an axis or central pivot, which links them harmoniously and bestows upon each degree what is suited to it; and we have also seen how the straight ray curves on its return and becomes a circle that brings everything back to its Point of departure: the One. Thus, passage from one degree to another and even the direct return from any point of existence to the highest, divine Degree, are mercifully made easy in Islam, the same being true, consequently, as regards the transition from exoterism to esoterism. Indeed, initiatic adherence to Sufism, although subject to certain strict conditions, is far less difficult than entering Kabbalah, the access to which is guarded, like the lost paradise, by a fiery sword of hidden forces. That is not merely a negative effect of the "break" long ago between the Divinity really present in Sinai and the idolatrous people, but also the positive sign of the permanence of "fiery" spiritual effects going back to Sinai and actualized in the esoteric rites of Kabbalah. The dazzling Revelation of the real and intemporal Presence of the One, His direct descent onto the sacred mountain, is repeated and its effects are so powerful that only initiates who have been well prepared and tested can bear it and assimilate it. This exceptional grace of sudden illumination, ascent, and spiritual union offered to the "chosen people" is confirmed in the Qur'an, where it is revealed that God "raised Israel above the worlds" (II, 47). Indeed, as the Kabbalah on its side attests, all the souls of the Israelites were raised immediately in Sinai up to the Throne of God, so that Israel might be a "holy people" and reveal the One to all humanity. But, also in Sinai, there was the break between Israel and the One, and this break, in spite of the continuity of the "Covenant," reappeared again and again in the history of this "people" whose sole reason for being is nonetheless the One and union with Him. Israel wrestles with Him — as its very name recalls — until the day when this sacred vessel, broken by its own faults, will be finally repaired: "On that day YHVH will be One and His Name will be One" (Zech. 14:9). The ray of the One, descending into the midst of His people, will no longer be broken; the Light of the first Tables of the Torah will reappear in its original, redemptive, Messianic Unity; the very real Presence of the One will rise up in place of the two destroyed Temples and will fill the world with His unitive Grace; the remaining righteous of Israel will worship the One in adoration shared with the other remaining "flocks of the Lord" — affirmation, contemplation of the only Reality will be unanimous, as it already is for the contemplatives of all authentic ways. *Al-tawḥîd wâḥid,* "affirmation of the One is itself one," say the Sufis.

There have always been groups of Jews who have sought to prefigure this ideal state in the midst of their own community; their endeavor has been to carry out the divine Will as perfectly as possible, to sanctify themselves in the image of the Most-Holy One and thereby contribute to the advent of the Messiah. This elect was not confined to the restricted circles of the Kabbalists, but radiated outward to create a living passage between the domain, so difficult to enter, of the Kabbalah and the domain of public or exoteric study and application of the Torah. The Truth of the One, His divine Wisdom, the Wisdom of the Kabbalah, had to be given back to the body of the people of Israel, who always had a tendency to backslide, if not toward loss of faith or a superficial observance of the law, at any rate toward a sterile and congealed formalism barring the path to real union with God. This was already the chief aim and mission of the prophets of Israel: they came to break up from within, by their revelations and their example of a godlike life ruling the whole of man's existence, the dark incrustations formed again and again around a Torah neglected or taken literally, so as to leave no opening for the heart and spirit of the divine Speech and Presence. A last echo of this repeated effort to renew Israel spiritually sounded in Polish Hassidism, which arose towards the middle of the eighteenth century, and in whose midst one can find more than one analogy with certain aspects of Sufism: the insistence on total attachment to God and to the spiritual master, on fear and love of the Lord as inescapable conditions of knowing Him, on all the spiritual and human virtues. But the characteristic element in Polish Hassidism — whose followers are still to be found today, in Europe as in America, and notably in Israel — is love of God, of His people, and of all creatures; love filled with fear and knowledge of God; the love that integrates all existence in spiritual life; the joy of meeting the Omnipresent in everything; the happiness of freeing His sparks that have fallen into the darkness of this world and of raising them toward Him, thanks to the power to rise which is natural and proper to the soul when, praying with unbounded fervor, it springs up towards Him, unites with Him. Hassidism is an emotional and collective mysticism everlastingly fed by the memory of the Only One, the Well-Beloved; it explodes in sacred songs and dances and is demonstrated in the extraordinary intensity of common prayer; it is seen in the radiant faces at holy meals eaten together, in the extreme recollection of all those gathered around the master teaching,[5] and in their study together of the sacred Doctrine. It does not exclude silent contemplation, or prayers, or meditation in solitude; but apart from the purely esoteric exercises performed in secret and reserved for the elect, the initiates, the Kabbalists, who form the nucleus of Hassidism — a nucleus of actual or potential masters — the way in Judaism revolves here around the pivot of spiritual integration of all the elements of life, soul and body, of compassionate conversion of all earthly darkness, of all evil, which is merely a degradation or inversion of good, hence of the affirmative and unitive absorption of the whole of this lower world in the Highest. And this way is open to every Jew, however humble and ignorant, to the simpleminded who, not knowing how to articulate a prayer, cry out to God — with cries that tear asunder the veils of the world, open the doors of Heaven, causing the Father's heart to incline towards His unfortunate creature. In these aspects of pure universal love, Polish Hassidism is distinct from earlier movements which, like it, formed a bridge between esoterism and exoterism, but were founded rather, like German Hassidism in the thirteenth century, on ascetic practice. However, in the latter also we find an extreme manifestation of the love of the neighbor, just as one finds the communal life, with all goods shared, in the midst of that other group of Jews who, more than a thousand years earlier, attempted to embody the wisdom and holiness of Israel at the cost of an ascetic discipline of the highest degree, namely the Essenians. What characterizes these and other similar eso-exoteric movements which have marked the course of Jewish history, can be summed up in the affirmation of a contemporary descendant of a Polish Hassidic family, who is not interested to know "that two and two make four, but that God is one — that man and God make one — the secret is in the *Alef.* in the One." [6]

We have seen that the Sufis contemplate the only Reality, the All-Reality, in the *Alif.* amongst other things, and the Kabbalists do the same in regard to the *Alef,* the first letter of the Hebrew alphabet. Like the *Alif,* the latter has the numerical value one and symbolizes the One Himself, but here the One insofar as He reveals Himself to Israel. In other words, the *Alef* represents all of the following: the One Himself; the One who descends into the midst of His children; His single Light, His pure straight Ray, which is broken in Sinai before the golden calf; His first Tables, made of His Unity and broken by this sin — an initial break, repeated throughout the history of Israel, in betrayals leading to the destruction of the two Temples, the dispersion of the people all over the world, where they are persecuted and almost exterminated. All this, as well as the return of Israel and of all peoples to the One, is written eternally in the *Alef* א which is not, like the *Alif,* a simple straight line, a lightning bolt from the One falling straight from the heavens and symbolizing what we have said of it above, and more. The *Alef* is a broken shaft, a wavering light, a flame flickering in all directions to reveal the eternal Archetype and the earthly destiny of Israel, and above all (1) the "Point (or Center) above" ׳ , the supreme Principle, the transcendent Divinity, the "Holy One, blessed be He"; (2) the "line of Union" between divine Transcendence and divine Immanence: ׀ the slanting line stylizing the letter *Vav* ⌐ , itself symbolizing the "Son," the "Messiah descending" as from the mountain top — onto Sinai, where he is received by Moses as the Light and Word of the Torah, and (3) the "Point (or Center) below" ◢ , the immanent Principle, divine Omnipresence revealed as real Presence, the *Shekhinah* which is the *corpus mysticum* of Israel and cares in the same time for all people "as a mother does for her children." The "lower Point" ◢ is like an inversion of the "Point above" ◤ ; it looks above on its own transcendent Essence, which is united with it; this is the "union of the Holy One, blessed be He, with His *Shekhinah*" and this very union, implying the union of all creatures with the Creator, is symbolized by the "line of union" ◥ ; thus we see the "Union of all" in the א , the One.

But that is only one way of contemplating the *Alef*, which in truth encloses all the Mysteries of the One and of His descent into the midst of the children of Israel. There is, for instance, another way of contemplating the *Alef*, a variation on the same theme of the Transcendence, Descent, and Immanence of God, which is the contemplation of the ten fundamental Aspects of the One that are also the ten supreme Archetypes of all things, the ten *Sefiroth* or synthetic "Enumerations" of the Infinitude of the divine Realities. While in Islam and particularly in Sufism, every reality whatsoever is tirelessly and directly brought back to the One, in Judaism, and above all in Kabbalah, all things are constantly related to their ten supreme Archetypes, the ten *Sefiroth* or fundamental Aspects of the One, His tenfold Unity, which is reflected in the whole Mosaic Revelation, in the Ten Commandments, first of all, as well as in the "sacred Community of Israel," which is valid ritually only in the presence of ten Jewish men. Here the absolute Unity of God is contemplated at the apex of contemplation of His tenfold Unity, the indivisible Unity of the ten Sefiroth; for the absolute One is the very first *Sefirah*, the highest, the "Supreme Crown" (*Kether elyon*), the pure Essence of the nine others that emanate from it in the ontological plane, the first emanation being *Hokhmah*, His eternal "Wisdom," His own Knowledge, the Knowledge of His infinite Unity. The second Emanation is *Binah*, His ontocosmological "Intelligence." *Kether*, *Hokhmah*, and *Binah* are the supreme Tri-Unity, which is revealed in the *Alef* in the form of the "upper Point" ◆ , identified with the letter *Yod* י . The fine upper point of the *Yod* itself signifies *Kether*, its thick stroke *Hokhmah*, and its fine lower point *Binah*. From this "supreme Point" with three aspects descend the seven "Sefiroth of cosmic construction," the seven fundamental aspects of God the creator, revealer, redeemer, and of His universal Immanence. The oblique stroke of the *Alef* — identified with the *Vav* ו , which has the numerical value six — symbolizes the six active *Sefiroth*, namely *Hesed, Din, Tifereth, Netsah, Hod,* and *Yesod* (Grace, Judgment, Beauty, Victory, Majesty, and Foundation), to which is added the "lower Point" , the *Yod* directed upwards, symbolizing the last *Sefirah, Malkhuth* (Kingdom) or *Shekhinah* (divine Immanence). The latter therefore receives the real Presence of all the other *Sefiroth,* constituting with them the divine Decad, symbolized by the numerical value ten, proper to the *Yod.* The last *Sefirah* is the whole of Divinity present "below" in the "lower *Yod,*" called *Adonai,* "My Lord": the personal God who is immediately accessible to each creature, the God who dwells in all hearts.

In the *Alef,* the One descends from His highest degree to the terrestrial degree, amid His people, to be Himself the *corpus mysticum* of the latter — to be contemplated, known, and realized by Israel. This sacrosanct body is at once that of God, His *"Sefirothic* Body," and that of Israel, the Spirit of Israel, which carries out the Ten Commandments — the ten Acts of the *Sefiroth* or of the tenfold One — on earth. The child of Israel who obeys His Will, causes the "divine Body" to act in his human body and is united with Him; whereas if he sins, "he sins against the very Body of the divine King." Thus the history of Israel is thereby the very history of their

God here below; it is eternally written in the *Alef,* inscribed in the One, whose descent calls forth from Israel — which is YHVH's own "portion" — either reception of Him and union with Him, or negation of Him and fall, destruction of the receptacle.

The spiritual way of the Jew traverses the body and the history of Israel, its body at once ethnic and spiritual. By this permanent identification with its own history, as by every observance of the Law of Moses, as well as by contemplation of the *Sefiroth* and the invocation of their divine Names, the Jew becomes really "YHVH's portion" (Deut. 32:9): he is united with the *corpus mysticum,* with the *Shekhinah,* which is the "final H" of YHVH, His Immanence. YHVH transcendent is represented by the *Yod* — or by YH-*Yâh* — and YHVH immanent by the final *He,* whereas the *Vav* — situated between the two *He*'s — signifies the descent of the Transcendent into the realm of the Immanent. Now Israel, although fallen from its first and highest degree, the *Yod,* has remained inseparable, at its lowest, from the *"He* below," from the *Shekhinah.* The latter has accompanied the children of Israel in their dispersion throughout the entire world and is what will bring them back to "Zion," to the One. But, for the Kabbalists, the "final *He,"* the *Shekhinah,* means not only the *corpus mysticum* of Israel with all its sacred institutions, laws, teachings, and rites, the whole Torah in short; they unite with the "final *He,"* through every door opened by the many means of grace deriving from the Torah, in order to rise, starting from this last "letter," or directly accessible reality of YHVH, toward the higher "letters" or degrees and finally to the "highest Point," to the *Yod,* to YHVH transcendent. At the summit of all his observance of the Law, of all his study of the Torah, or all the steps of his exegesis of the scriptures, the Kabbalist rises, by the initiatic means belonging to Jewish esoterism, to the *Vav,* the immediate descent of the Transcendent. He receives the direct inflow of the *Yod* — or of YH-*Yâh* — and thanks to this inflow it is given to him to actualize the last spiritual ascent to the "highest *Yod,"* to the "supreme Crown" *(Kether elyon),* which is none other than the "God Most High" *(El elyon).* Thus the finished Kabbalist is not only "YHVH's portion," thanks to union with the "final *He,"* but comes to be but one with all the "letters" or realities of YHVH. He is man united

179

with the highest Archetype of the whole of humanity and of the universe, with the Archetype of Archetypes.


## JUDAIC AND ISLAMIC MODES OF CONTEMPLATION AND ACTION

In Judaism and Islam, God is worshipped, contemplated, invoked, and served, not through some image drawn from one or another of the four terrestrial kingdoms, and not through a human or angelic mediator, but through His Name or His Names, which designate respectively His Essence, His Qualities, and His Activities. It is true, however, that in these two noniconic ways the image of man reappears, if not as a figurative symbol, at least in the indirect anthropomorphism characterizing the Names of the ontocosmological Attributes and Activities of God and even of certain intelligible Aspects of His pure Essence as revealed in the Torah and the Koran. The evident reason for this anthropomorphism is that the Infinite, in order to establish relations with man, to make Himself understood and known by man, must necessarily enter the latter's field of vision: He must, so to say, espouse the form of man and of his universe and speak in human language. In other words, the Infinite reveals Himself to man through the eternal human archetype reposing in Himself as a mode of His own receptivity, as a receptacle, in which He gives Himself to Himself and receives Himself, taking on — according to an expression of the Sufi al-Junaid — the "color of His recipient." But it is not His Essence as such which assumes the "colors" of the receptacles: the Essence is eternally "beyond what they attribute to Him" (*ᶜan-mâ yaṣifûn*). It is the infinite Perfection of "Quality" belonging to the Essence, which, being revealed, is translated first into the essentially single multiplicity of its ontological Qualities, then , in the midst of the Cosmos, into the effective multitude of Its manifested Qualities and Activities. Thus it is that the Infinite takes on in the eternal human receptivity the "color," the principial form of man; in other words, the eternal archetype of man is the Infinite which makes Itself anthropomorphic, so that the form of man is theomorphic and by becoming conscious and fully realizing his godlikeness the human recipient may, even in this lower world, find again his divine Content, both in Its Perfection and in Its Essence.

Man realizes his likeness unto God by conforming his acts to the Will of God — which itself is manifested through the activity and the whole of human existence — and by imitating with all his faculties the divine Perfections, of which the human qualities and virtues are the terrestrial reflections and vehicles. When this likeness comes to maturity, it produces, according to Sufism, the *fanâ' al-afᶜâl*, the "extinction of (human) activities" in the divine Act, and the *fanâ' al-ṣifât*, the "extinction of the (human) qualities" in the divine Qualities. Thereby the human being reaches *fanâ' al-dhât*, "extinction of the (individual) essence" in the universal and divine Essence, which corresponds, in the Kabbalistic way, to the *bittul ha-yesh*, the "annihilation" of individual existence and its transformation into "Being-and-Super-Being." The supports for this spiritual realization in Judaism and Islam are by definition all the traditional modes of human existence, the many sacred forms of the outer and inner activity of man and, in particular, those of contemplation. Now here we shall not go into the traditional or ritual practices belonging to the exoterism of these two religions, which are sufficiently well known. We propose to look briefly, beyond the religious prescriptions, at the esoteric domain, which in no way implies that the contemplatives in the two ways would neglect the observance of these prescriptions; for them, all outer activity, every application of virtue, every manifestation of faith, faith and virtues themselves, prepare, sustain, and rejoin the innermost activity, pure contemplation, the *unio mystica* itself. While exoterists remain attached to their domain simply as a point of departure for gaining a salvation correlative to a posthumous paradisial coexistence with God, the esoterists start every day from that same domain in order to rise to their own sphere of spiritual activity, that of pure Truth, of the One without a second. Every exoteric activity becomes for them a mode of contemplation, beginning with the purifying ablutions, the canonic prayers, the prescribed fasts and almsgiving, met with in both of the religions in question, and to which can be added, for the Moslems, above all the pilgrimage to Mecca and, for the Jews, the prescriptions and prohibitions of which there are as many as 613 in all.

The elite in both of these ways thus respond affirmatively to the truth expressed in the divine saying quoted above, where God declares: "Nothing that is pleasant to Me brings Me so close to My servant as the performance of the duties I have set for him"; furthermore, they actualize the following: "My servant shall not cease to come closer to Me by practices beyond the call of duty, until I love him . . . ." Now, these practices can be summarized as all modes of study or exegesis of the sacred Scriptures and the spiritual realization of their content, starting from initiation to the "Wisdom of the Kabbalah" (*Hokhmat ha-Qabbalah*), which is in essence — to make use of a Sufic term — the "divine Wisdom" (*al-Ḥikmah al-ilâhiyah*), the Knowledge proper to God Himself and in all things. This divine and universal knowledge is in principle the end result of "study of the Torah" (*Talmud Thorah*) or of the Koran, and initiation to "Mysteries of the Torah" (*Sithre Thorah*) or to the divine "Truths" (*Ḥaqâ'iq*); this means initiation to the Mysteries or Truths of the "Name" of God (*ha-Shem* or *al-Ism*), which comprises all reality and all revelation. Indeed, the divine Name takes on the highest importance in the contemplative life of Judaism and of Islam; and it is not only a mnemonic or ideographic support for contemplation but also—and above all—the support for invocation of God, of His real Presence. While concentrating on His Presence, while meditating on His qualities, contemplating the Light — or the more than luminous Darkness — of His Essence, the Kabbalist, like the Sufi, calls upon His Name, whether pronouncing it with the mouth, or formulating it mentally, or actualizing its informal reality in the heart.

In Judaic esoterism, the simultaneity of meditation and invocation as supports for contemplation appears, amongst other things, in the combination of the "way of the *Sefiroth*" (*derekh ha-Sefiroth*) and of the "way of Names" (*derekh ha-Shemoth*). In other words, those of the divine Names are invoked which correspond to the *Sefiroth* that are contemplated, which incidentally represents only one of the many combinations of the "contemplative Kabbalah" (*Qabbalah iyunit*) with the "operative Kabbalah" (*Qabbalah maasit*).

The characteristic modes of Jewish esoterism, the combination of "contemplative Kabbalah" and "operative Kabbalah," is also met with in the various methods of the Science of letters — which is also the Science of numbers — since the letters of the sacred alphabet express, as do the proper names or the divine names of the *Sefiroth*, the fundamental archetypes of all things. More precisely, the twenty-two letters of the "celestial alphabet" represent the eternal relationships between the *Sefiroth*, that is to say, between the unchangeable Aspects and Qualities of the divine Essence; and these relationships are at the origin of all the acts, or revelatory, creative, and transforming movements, of God: they are the eternal agents of the *Sefirothic Decad*, the immediate principle of the divine Activity. Each of these "eternal letters" is by itself alone a Name—a particular determination—of God, and their innumerable combinations are in turn so many divine Names or Words, actualizing their eternal content in the midst of the Cosmos. The revealed Scriptures—the Torah, the Prophets, and the Hagiographs—are none other than the scriptuary actualizations of the transcendent letters of the eternal relationships between the *Sefiroth*. These letters, combined differently in Names, Words, or Truths of God, all operate in the midst of the world and of man: they carry out the whole of the divine work. The man who goes deeply into the letters and their combinations through the four degrees of sacred exegesis, and who meditates on them, contemplates them, recites them, chants or invokes through them, the man who prays by uniting the letters in formulas of worship or of supplication, he who arranges them in different ways according to the "Science of (their) combinations" (*Hokhmat ha-Tseruf*), cooperates with God. With the Lord, man actualizes in himself the "Letters" that He "writes" in eternity, and man unites them till they become His "one and only Name"; for "YHVH is One and His Name is One." Thus the servant finally unites all things in himself and unites himself with the One by actualizing His real Presence, which dwells in his heart and in the holy Name.

Now, this unitive work begins with the study and application of the revealed letters as such, which is the first step, at once exoteric and esoteric, of traditional exegesis and activity. The "simple" or literal interpretation *(Peshat)* of the sacred Scriptures leads, in the first place, to the perfect carrying out of religious practice — of the "Law" — in all the prescribed modes. Then a man can rise to the second step or degree of exegesis, which is still common to the exoteric oral Doctrine, the *Talmud*, the public "study" of the Torah, and to the esoteric oral Doctrine, the Kabbalah. Having reached this degree, called *Remez*, "allusion" to the many meanings hidden in each phrase, word, letter, sign, and point of Scripture, a man passes from the domain of chiefly external activity to that of inner activity, mental and spiritual, to reflection, meditation, contemplation. Here, the Talmudist, like the Kabbalist, no longer proceeds simply by means of elementary reasoning, but examines carefully the truths enclosed in the literal expressions in the Scriptures, beginning from the overall symbolism of a whole section relating to a particular event in sacred history, and then proceeding to a closer reading, on the scale of a sentence, a phrase, a letter, all of which are symbolic, as is each revealed vowel, sign, and point. In this study in depth of the Scriptures is used, among other things, the Science of the combination of letters or numbers, whose best known methods are the *Gematria*, involving the numerical value of letters, *Notarikon*, involving the initial, middle, and final letters of words, and the *Temurah*, based on the permutation of letters. Mastery of the two fundamental degrees of exegesis, *Peshat* and *Remez*, as well as of all the Talmudic modes of interpreting the Torah, allows the Talmudist to pass to the third degree, called *Derash*, the homiletic "exposition" of the doctrinal truths, by way of anagoge, which rises from the literal or exoteric interpretation of the Scriptures to their spiritual exegesis. The Talmudists come up to this third degree, but without approaching its "fine upper point," the esoterism which alone constitutes the fourth degree of exegesis, called Sod, the "Mystery," to which only the Kabbalists accede: this is the domain of initiation to the pure *Hokhmah*, the divine "Wisdom" hidden in the Scriptures and called, in respect to the teaching, *Hokhmat ha-Qabbalah*, the "Wisdom of the esoteric Tradition."

This fourth method, its object being the "Mysteries of the Torah" *(Sithre Thorah)*, consists essentially of the exegesis and spiritual realization of the first chapter of Genesis *(Maasseh Bereshith*, the

"Work of the Beginning"), and of the first chapter of Ezekiel's Prophecy, namely the vision of Man of the divine Throne and of the Throne itself, which is like a "Chariot" (Merkabah); hence this chapter is called the "Work of the Chariot" (Maasseh Merkabah) and the name given to initiates who carry out this work is Yorde Merkabah, "those who come down into the Chariot" hidden in their heart, the descent being in reality their ascent through all the heavens up to the divine Throne. But apart from these revelations from the Scriptures relating to the emanation of the divine Principle and reintegration in It, the whole of the Torah, the Prophets, and Hagiographs serve as a point of departure for the exegetic and operative methods of the Sod. The ten Sefiroth play the part of fundamental supports of contemplation, while the divine Names here represent the essential operative means; along with all the other means of union given, they lead the Kabbalist through the four degrees of PaRDeS (the word in which we find the initial letters of the names of these degrees themselves, namely, Peshat, Remez, Derash, Sod, and which signifies "Paradise"): they lead him beyond even this Paradise of Knowledge to the superintelligible realm, to the "Nothingness" which is the Absolute.

The other means or methods of spiritual realization in Judaism represent for the most part variants or combinations of those previously cited. In all these ways, a great Kawwanah is required, that is to say, a theocentric "intention" which, in conformity with its sacrosanct object, calls for the greatest "attention" from the contemplatives, total "concentration" of his mind on the Principle contemplated, and the "recollection" of his whole being in the only Truth and only Reality — these being some of the many possible translations of the term Kawwanah, to which one can add that formulated by Rabbi Moshe of Kobryn (d. 1858): "To direct the heart toward God." This essential and universal way of all contemplation, this necessary condition of all spiritual realization, is founded in Scripture on the commandment: "And thou shalt love YHVH, thy God, with all thy heart, with all thy soul, with all thy strength" — this fundamental commandment being itself insepara- ble from another that has particularly to be carried out in external activity: "Thou shalt love thy neighbor as thyself." For God is all in all and it is necessary to contemplate Him and inwardly unite oneself with Him in order to see Him and approach Him in all things; as the Kabbalah testifies: "In all things there is a 'drawing near' [to God] for him who understands how to accomplish the union [with Him] and to worship [or contemplate] the Lord ..." (Zohar, Tetsaveh 181 b).

The ultimate aim of all modes of contemplation and of action in Judaism is *En Sof,* the Infinite, the Unity of Being *(Ehyeh)* and Super-Being or Non-Being *(Ain).* Now, all the fundamental Judaic modes of "union" *(Yihud),* the various *Kawwanot* or ways of concentrating on the One, the permanent "attachment" *(debekut)* to Him, all modes of "prayer" *(tefillah),* of "invocation" *(qeriyah),* of "meditation" *(hirhur* or *hitbonenut),* of "contemplation" *(histaklut),* all "fervor" *(hitlahabut)* or intense love for the Only One and all "fear" *(yirah)* of nonconformity with Him, in a word, all "service" *(abodah)* of God and of one's neighbor, the performance of the *mitsvot* or "commandments" — all that is to be found again in other forms, revealed by Allah, in Islam, and in particular in its esoteric or contemplative domain, Sufism.

The immediate aim of Sufism, to which we come back once more, is *ḥaqîqah,* pure, supreme, universal "Truth," whereas the immediate object of the majority of Moslems is the carrying out of the *Sharî°a* or Qur'anic "Law" and sacred customs going back to the Prophet. The practice of the *Sharî°a* is to Islam what the practice of the *mitsvot* prescribed by the Torah and its Talmudic interpretation is to Judaism. What is in question are outer actions, but actions which normally are motivated by the faith of those who perform them — many degrees of faith, from the seeking for a posthumous paradise to the pure love of God, the pure knowledge of Him, by which the works of the *Sharî°a* are transformed into as many modes of contemplation.

Spiritual elevation of being, starting from outer activity and rising to the inner contemplative act, takes place by three fundamental steps which are (1) *al-Islâm,* "submission to the divine Will," effective observance of the Law: (2) *al-îmân,* "faith" defined as true belief in Allah, His angels, His books, His messengers, and the Day of Judgment; (3) *al-iḥsân,* preeminent "virtue," which implies the purely spiritual element in all religious practice and in faith itself: the "vision of God," contemplation of Him, whether luminous or obscure. *"Iḥsân* consists in worshipping God as though you saw Him, and if you do not see Him, He sees you." If our contemplation is not filled with His Light, it must be filled with our faith in Him — the "believing without seeing" — and with our works willed by Him. These three degrees of the Islamic Way are found in its esoterism in the analogous triad: *makhâfah,* "fear," *maḥabbah,* "love," and *maʿarifah,* "knowledge" of God. Here, "fear" consists above all of *al-furqân,* theoretical and practical "discernment" between the true and the false, between the only reality, Allah, and unreality — the "I" and the "world"; "love" is the direct and permanent aspiration to the only Truth and the only Reality, to the one and only well-Beloved; and "knowledge" is none other than contemplative union with the "One without a second." These are the three fundamental degrees of the *tawḥîd,* of the Sufic affirmation of the One, and these degrees are repeated again in other analogous triads, such as that which starts from the idea that man is above all an *ʿabd,* a "servant" of God. Regarded in this way, the spiritual way becomes the threefold service of the Absolute, beginning from *al-ʿibâdah,* the rigorous or ascetic "service" of all the faculties of the being who submits to the spiritual exercises; then *al-ʿubûdiyyah,* "servitude," which is the central idea of the present triad and gives it its global significance — all the patience, all the endurance required by the search, often of long duration, for the spiritual Goal; lastly, *al-ʿubûdiyyah,* total "enslavement" of the servant to his Lord, his complete "extinction" *(fanâ')* in Him, the "loss of the awareness of his servitude in contemplation of Him who is served." But on coming back to himself, "the servant remains the servant," submitted *(muslim)* to the Will of the Lord with the submission *(islâm)* with which he set out on his quest of the Absolute and which played its part in the spiritual exercises of his *ʿibâdah.*

In Moslem exoterism as in Moslem esoterism, man is *ʿabd,* the servant of Allah, but in esoterism he becomes a true "poor man before his Lord" *(faqîr ilâ Rabbihi). Al-faqr,* "poverty" or spiritual receptivity in face of the only Truth and the only Reality, is his fundamental way of existence from the day when he ceases to lead

187

the illusory existence of a "second" beside the "One without a second"; from that day on he follows a spiritual "path," *ṭarîqah,* thanks to the initiatic "blessing" *(barakah)* received from a "Master" *(murshid* or *shaykh,* lit. "old man"). Thenceforth he is *murîd,* "aspirant" to Truth, linked by the "pact" *(al-bayᶜah)* of an initiation to an esoteric "chain" *(silsilah),* which goes back to the Prophet. From then on, the *Sharîᶜa* or exoteric "law" represents for him a whole of modes of spiritualization, beginning from the first of the "five pillars," or fundamental obligations of *islâm,* the *shahâdah,* the creed or "attestation" of the One God and of His messenger Mohammed. By affirming that "there is no divinity if not The Divinity" *(La ilâha illâ Allâh),* the *murîd* renounces himself as being a false "divinity" *(ilâh),* and by adding that "Mohammed is the messenger of the Divinity" *(Muḥammad rasûl Allâh),* he affirms his exoteric and esoteric imitation of the Prophet, who is the model of all believers, keepers of the *Sharîᶜa* and *fuqarâ'* alike. As for the second "obligation," prayer, for him it is not limited to the prayer that has to be made at least five times a day: it is continued in other forms, such as the recitation of the Qur'an or of the Rosary, and above all in the form of the *dhikr,* the permanent "remembrance" of Allah in its various and often simultaneous aspects of the "invocation" of a divine Name, of the "meditation" *(tafakkur)* of a truth or of an aspect of He who is invoked, or of the "contemplation" *(mushahadah)* of His Presence *(ḥuḍûr);* the sacred song and dance also play their part — insofar as they are true "means of union" — in the *dhikr.* The third "obligation" — the fast in the month of Ramadhân, in which the descent of the Qur'an took place — is often carried on beyond that period by the *faqîr,* particularly when he is in *Khalwah,* the spiritual "retreat" devoted to the *dhikr;* but in a deeper sense still, the "poor in spirit" abstains to the greatest extent possible from all psychic food, even thought itself, in the permanent and non-discursive concentration of his spirit on the supreme and universal Principle — and this in fact is the essential meaning of fasting: the *vacare Deo* into which He sends down His Presence, His Light, His Word, the Qur'an. The same applies to the fourth "obligation," almsgiving, which, in the eyes of the *faqîr,* is the gift of oneself to God in the neighbor; his almsgiving or tithe is not limited to the legal percentage to be withheld from one's revenue: he gives himself to those who have need of him. Lastly, the "fifth pillar" of *Islâm*, the pilgrimage to Mecca, which retraces here below the journey of the soul to the Throne of Allah, for him takes place everyday and everywhere: each day he makes his pilgrimage to Mecca in his heart, to the universal Center hidden in himself, where Allah dwells in all His Majesty and Beauty.

This daily inner pilgrimage of spiritual man, his search for the Absolute, is his "gradual 'approach' *(taqarrub)* to God which implies partial (inner) liberations (from the 'I'): these are the 'stations' *(maqâmât)* of his growing poverty on the way to his complete extinction in God. ... This gift of oneself to All-Reality calls for virtues and cognitive efforts which together constitute all aspects of spiritual 'poverty' *(al-faqr)*, a synonym of the 'unitive way' *(al-tawḥîd)*. Among these virtues figures above all the 'struggle against the soul,' *(mukhâlafat al-nafs)* insofar as the soul, through its ignorance and its passions, masks the pure and divine 'Self' of man; this negation of the 'I' implies not only every kind of 'renunciation' *(al-zuhd)* or 'abstinence' *(al-waraᶜ)*, but also every virtue which affirms the Reality through a positive symbolism, such as 'love' of God *(al-maḥabbah)* and 'confidence' in Him *(al-tawakkul)*, 'gratitude' *(al-shukr)* and 'contentment' *(al-riḍâ)* in regard to what He grants us, 'patience' *(al-sabr)* or 'hope' *(al-rajâ)* concerning what He has not yet given us, 'truthfulness' *(al-ṣidq)* and 'purity' *(al-ikhlâṣ)*, which manifest the Truth present in us. The 'warfare' *(al-mujâhadah)* of man against his ego is not waged solely because of the divine 'Self' immanent in him but in view of the Presence of the 'Self' in all things: man also meets his divine 'Self' in the 'non-I' around him and it is likewise by affirming the latter through 'altruism' *(al-ithâr)*, 'generosity' *(al-sakhâ')*, 'chivalrous spirit' *(al-futûwwa)*, 'politeness' *(al-adab)* that he fights and overcomes the ego. Apart from these virtues which relate to the divine Omnipresence, there are others which derive above all from the unfathomable distance between the 'I' and the Transcendent or from the (relative) absence of God — such as 'fear' *(al-khawf* or *al-taqwa)*, 'sadness' *(al-ḥuzn)*, and 'humility' *(al-khushûᶜ)*. Finally all the virtues are summarized in 'servitude' *(al-ᶜubûdiyyah)* towards God, 'submission' *(al-Islâm)* to His Will, 'faith *(al-imân)* in Him and worship of Him 'as though you saw Him, and if you do not see Him, He sees you' *(al-ihsân)*. As for the initiatic way of the 'poor man,' it presupposes his spiritual 'conversion' *(al-tawbah)* and consists of the initiatic 'pact' *(al-bay<sup>c</sup>ah)* with the (spiritual) Master, inner 'attachment' *(al-ṣuḥbah)* to him, 'retreat' *(al-khalwah)*, 'invocation' *(adh-dhikr)*, 'meditation' *(al-tafakkur)*, 'observation of the Omnipresent' *(al-murâqabah)*, etc. All these virtues and all these spiritual efforts to which one could add many others, are crystallized in the *tawḥîd,* permanent concentration on the One, which implies the 'effort of actualization' of His Presence *(al-istiḥḍâr)* intended to lead to 'realization of the Essence' *(taḥqîq al-Dhât).*" [7]

We have just seen that besides the attitudes, stations, or spiritual degrees characterized by the virtues, there are some which refer more directly to knowledge. The cognitive ladder of *islâm* ending in the pure *tawḥîd* begins with the literal assimilation of the Qur'an and goes on to the exoteric and esoteric exegesis of the Qur'an, the latter being concretized in the spiritual actualization of the revealed Truth, the "realization of the (divine) Essence (itself)." Now, from the point of view of Sufism the whole of the Revelation of the Essence, of the Truth, of the divine Qualities and Activities, the Revelation of the All-Reality in the Universe and in the Qur'an, is nothing other than the descent of the Supreme Name of Allah and of all the divine Names comprised therein. This is why in Islam — as in Judaism, where the whole of the Torah is nothing but the multiform revelation of the Name of the One — the sanctification of the divine Name by invocation, meditation, or contemplation is of capital importance, and this is why here, as in the sister religion, we find a veritable science of the divine Names starting from the "Names of the Essence" *(asmâ<sup>c</sup> dhâtiyah),* the highest of which is Allah and amongst which are to be found *Huwa,* "He," *Al-Aḥad,* "the One," *al-Ṣamad,* "the Independent," *al-Quddûs,* "the Most Holy," descending towards the "qualitative Names" *(asmâ<sup></sup> ṣifatiyah)* such as *al-Raḥmân,* "the Merciful," *al-Salâm,* "Peace," *al-Karîm,* "the Generous," and towards the Names of the divine "activities" *(al-af<sup>c</sup>âl),* such as *al-Muhyî,* "He who gives life," or *al-Mumît,* "He who gives death." The various categories of these Names — which also include the *shahâdah* — are actualized above all by the *dhikr,* contemplative invocation, with its various methods or techniques, which often differ from one *ţâriqah* or Sufi brotherhood to another and of which we cannot here draw up a complete list.

All these initiatic techniques of contemplative invocation, like every esoteric science of the divine Names and of the Letters of the sacred alphabet, enter into the general category of knowledge that the Sufis call *ᶜilm al-yaqîn,* the "Science of certainty." This is a degree of *furqân,* of "discernment," acquired thanks to the teachings of the spiritual master, to assimilate which demands from the disciple *muḥâḍarah,* the "presence of the heart" or of the "intellect" *(al-ᶜaql)* that dwells in it; the latter grasps the teachings through their intrinsic "proof" *(burhân),* a logical — and deeply ontological — proof which reveals the truth in the discursive or rational mode. In fact, *al-ᶜaql,* the intellect, is first of all regarded here in its peculiarly human or mental aspect: reason, which assimilates Truth by "reflection" or "meditation" *(tafakkur)* of the discursive order. But, while there is a discontinuity between this rational order and the purely spiritual and nondiscursive realm of "contemplation" *(mushâhadah),* it is not absolute: the discontinuity hides a continuity which is none other than the universal Logos relating human logic to ontological, divine Reality. This is *al-ᶜilm* in the universal sense, divine "science" or "omniscience" which, in the midst of discursive meditation, discovers the Truth or Reality that is its object; reasonable reflection is suddenly absorbed by intuition or inspiration, by the direct vision of the cognitive Object which has no need of rational proof. When the "eye of the heart" *(ᶜayn al-qalb)* opens, looks, and sees, the disciple is raised to the degree of knowledge called *ᶜayn al-yaqîn,* the "Source" or "Eye of Certainty." This is the degree where sacred thought, methodical meditation, becomes a key to *mukashâfa,* the direct "unveiling" of the Object of meditation; *al-bayân,* the "evidence" of the cognitive Object, is found instead of logical proof, and *al-ᶜilm,* the divine "omniscience" dwelling in the pure spirit of man, acts in place of his "reason," *al-ᶜaql.* Now, the true object of all spiritual search, hence of all doctrinal reflection and methodical meditation, is none other than the "One without a second," in which the "second," the one who searches, reflects, and meditates has to be effaced and integrated. And indeed the "evidence" of the sole Reality finally becomes so strong that all human thought, even all human being is extinguished as the shades of night vanish at sunrise: there is no longer anything but the divine Sun, the luminous Eye of Allah infinitely open in the midst of the heart, there is no longer anything but Him looking at Himself and contemplating Himself in His servant, while the latter is truly in Him like a spark indistinctly comprised in His boundless Clarity. This is the entrance to the highest cognitive degree, called the "Truth of Certainty," *Ḥaqq al-yaqîn;* this is the degree of *mushâhadat-al-Rububîyah,* "the Lord's own Contemplation" in the servant who, on coming back to himself, is an *ᶜârif bi-Allâh,* a "knower through Allah."

When the soul of the servant is reduced by its extinction to what it was in the beginning, a divine spark, it becomes again what it is in truth and in eternity: the Infinite. And when the servant comes down again from eternity into time, he finds his terrestrial body in its primordial beauty. His earthly body is filled with Light from above, with the Presence of "God, the Light of the heavens and of the earth." In the middle of his invocation the servant became silent because the sound of the divine Name, its whole articulation, was transformed into pure Light. The Essence of the servant is light, his spirit, his soul, and his body are light, even though, from the outside, one sees a man, a body. His head no longer thinks, for it is open to the Infinite and filled with light; his heart desires nothing, for he has become a source of light which radiates in all the directions of the universe toward the Infinite. His being is but one with the pure Being, his act one with the pure Act, the Act of Being and of Knowledge. To be Being is to be infinitely happy, is to be conscious of the Plenitude of Being, is to know oneself as infinite Light. To be the Light is to be the Clarity of all knowledge, is to have no further need of thinking or of acting unless the Light wishes it. Then the Light which is pure Being manifests as pure Act, as divine Will, and with this Will, Life comes down from on high like a beatific stream. It fills the terrestrial body which before that was full of suffering and the body becomes a paradise of light.

Existence is suffering. Being is bliss. To exist is to go out from

Being, is to leave happiness behind. To act is to actualize either Being or Existence, either Light or the *chiaroscuro* of transient life on earth. Contemplation is the pure act by which one passes from all action and from existence itself to Being, to eternal Life, to infinite Light. If all men were immersed in contemplation of the only Truth and only Reality, where would be the problems of humanity? And if all those who have become incapable of such contemplation were to pray, if they were to serve the contemplatives and follow their advice, where would be their difficulties? Heaven would send them its blessing and the earth would give them its fruits in abundance; it would no longer be an "accursed soil" but a paradise, and mankind would rediscover the happiness of Adam before his fall. For the true destiny of man is contemplation: to contemplate the One, pray to, call upon, and serve the One and thereby be united with the One. Outside of the One, no salvation, no peace, no grace, no light, and no happiness; apart from the One, only dualism, struggle, suffering, and death.

"See, I have set before thee this day life and good, and death and evil; in that I command thee this day to love the Eternal, thy God, to walk in His ways and to keep His commandments and His statutes and His ordinances, that thou mayest live . . . . But if thine heart turn away, so that thou wilt not hear, but shalt be drawn away, and worship other gods [the false gods fabricated by man, the *idola mentis*] and serve them, I denounce unto you this day, that ye shall surely perish . . . . Choose life, that thou mayest live . . . . " (Deut. 30: 15-18, 19).

---

[1] Following the Jewish custom, we write this divine Name without vowels. It has been forbidden to pronounce it for more than two thousand years.

[2] *Oeuvres complètes du Pseudo-Denys l'Areopagite*, trans. by M. de Gandillac (Paris: Aubier, 1943) pp. 179-80.

[3] The mystical movement of the *Hassidim*, the "Devotees," was founded by Rabbi Israel ben Eliezer, known as the *Baal-Shem* (the "Master of the [divine]

Name"), towards the middle of the eighteenth century in Poland. It first spread through Eastern Europe and finally all over the world.

[4] Let us remember that Arabic, like Hebrew, is written from right to left.

[5] For genuine Hassidic teaching translated into English, see *Liqqutei Amarim* (Collected Essays) by Rabbi Schneur Zalman of Liadi, trans. Dr. Nissan Mindel (Brooklyn, N.Y.: "Kohet" Publication Society, 1962).

[6] Elie Wiesel, *Célébration hassidique* (Paris: Ed. Seuil, 1972).

[7] Leo Schaya, *La Doctrine Soufique de l'Unité,* p. 88-89. (Ed. Adrien-Maisonneuve: Paris, 1962) [author's translation].

# The Complementarity of Contemplative and Active Lives in Islam

SEYYED HOSSEIN NASR

An hour of meditation is better than sixty
years of acts of worship.

Prophetic tradition—ḥadîth

Knowledge without action is like a tree
without fruit.

Arabic proverb

The quotations cited above, in the light of the discussion at hand, express the just relationship between contemplation and action in Islam, a religion which because of its unitary perspective has never allowed contemplative and active lives to become divorced from each other. For the modern world, which is so completely immersed in a way of acting and doing bound to purely terrestrial ends as to have lost sight of the meaning of contemplation—let alone its primacy over action—it is hardly conceivable that in a civilization such as the Islamic, action and contemplation should exist harmoniously. Today it is difficult to imagine a universe of thought, action, and being in which contemplation leads to action, and action on the spiritual plane becomes the way of access to the inner garden of contemplation.

Contemplation in Islamic spirituality, as in other integral traditions, is essentially a knowledge that relates the knower to higher modes of being. It is identified with *shuhûd* (vision) or *taᶜammul* (literally "to regard attentively") and is related to *tafakkur* (meditation) in traditional Islamic sources. It is referred to constantly in the Qur'an, which commands man to contemplate the beauties of the Universe and their divine prototypes. The essentially gnostic character of Islamic spirituality in fact lends a contemplative air to all the authentic manifestations of Islam, including, of course, its sacred art, and causes the soul of the Muslim to tend towards contemplation as that of a Christian tends toward sacrifice. There lies deep within the texture of the soul molded by the message of the Qur'an a tendency to pull its roots from the world of multiplicity and to establish itself in the center of that "void" which reflects Divine Unity and which is reflected in virgin nature and Muslim sacred art. There is the tendency to contemplate a single flower, a blade of wheat, a solitary bush or tree, which, being all epiphanies of the Divine, provide even more than the contemplative eye needs to behold, and all serve as the gateway to the Infinite. For as the Persian poem by Hâtif of Ispahan states,

If you dissect the heart of an atom
you shall behold a sun within it.

Moreover, in the Islamic context, this contemplation has been forever wed to action understood in its traditional sense. The contemplative form of Islamic spirituality has never been contradictory to correct action, and has in fact often been combined with an irresistible inner urge to action. It is this inner unity that made Islamic civilization at the height of its power one of the most virile and active in human history while harboring within itself a most intense contemplative life.

Here again the message of the Qur'an expresses the rapport which was divinely ordained for the Islamic community concerning the question of the relation between contemplation, or knowledge, and action, between al-ʿilm and al-ʿamal. Throughout the Qur'an the injunction to contemplate God's wisdom in creation as well as in its metacosmic reality, is followed by injunctions to act correctly and according to principles derived from that wisdom. The call to prayer in its Shiʿite form, based on formulas drawn from the Qur'an, summarizes the hierarchic relationship between God's wisdom, man's knowledge of it, and the action which issues from this knowledge. The second part of the call to prayer (adhân) consists of three phrases: *ḥayy ʿalâ al-ṣalât,* hurry to prayer; *ḥayy ʿalâ al-falâḥ,* hurry to salvation; *ḥayy ʿalâ khayr al-ʿamal,* hurry to the best act, good works, or correct action. Prayer, which in its highest form is contemplative and unitive, leads to salvation or deliverance of the soul from all bondage and imperfection and this in turn leads to correct action. Without prayer or contemplation one cannot *be* in a state of grace or goodness, and without *being* good one cannot *do* good. Correct action depends on the correct mode of being, which in turn issues from the correct relation with the source of all existence through prayer, which in its most exalted mode is contemplation.

Therefore, while contemplation and action are complementary, they are not on an equal footing. Contemplation and meditation— they are closely related—stand above action, as the *ḥadîth* "An hour of meditation is better than sixty years of acts of worship" reveals. At the same time correct action follows from contemplation and is related to the realized aspect of knowledge which contemplation in fact makes possible. Theoretical knowledge is incomplete if not brought into realization—which in turn leads to a transformation, in fact man's "death and resurrection," and thus the correct mode of action issuing effortlessly from the newly acquired mode of being. Contemplation alone can turn this theoretical knowledge into realization, leading in turn to correct action which may be inward or outward depending on the conditions chosen for man by the hands of destiny. It can turn the theoretical metaphysical doctrine which is like a purifying snow in the mind to a fire in the center of the heart, a fire which not only melts the heart but also enlivens the limbs and provides them with a new vitality.

The relationship between contemplation and action in human life thus described is an echo in the matrices of time and space of the principal domain and an image, although in reverse, of the cosmogonic act itself. In the Qur'an the act of creation, the *fiat lux,* is expressed in this majestic verse: "But His command, when He intendeth a thing, is only that he saith unto it: 'Be' and it is" (XXXVI, 81, Pickthall trans.). Creation is related to an act which at the same time bestows existence and knows all things in principle. The act of God is at once the Word of Logos (*al-Kalimah*) and the Intellect (*al-ʿaql*). Therefore not only does God utter the word *kun!*

(Be!), but also the spiritual root *(malakût)* of all things resides in His presence.

Furthermore, in Sufi metaphysics and cosmology, which are based directly on the Qur'anic revelation, the creation of the world is conceived as a "breathing" by God upon the immutable archetypes *(al-aᶜyân al-thâbitah)*, which are God's knowledge of all things as well as the spiritual essence of all things. The "breath of the Compassionate" *(nafas al-Raḥmân)* externalizes the divine possibilities in the form of external objects. The divine act creates the world through contemplation, a world which itself *is* the result of God's contemplation of Himself. For it was in order to contemplate His own Beauty that God created the Universe.

Likewise, according to the Islamic philosophers such as Ibn Sina, the very substance of the Universe is the result of God's contemplation of Himself. By contemplating Himself the necessary Being *(wâjib al-wujûd)* brings into existence the First Intellect, and the First Intellect, the Second Intellect, down to the world of generation and corruption in which man resides. Contemplation and being are interrelated, and on the highest plane God's act and self-knowledge are ultimately the same.

In the process of spiritual realization, which is in a way the reversal of the cosmogonic act, a journey by means of the arc of ascent *(al-qaws al-suᶜûdî)* through all the degrees that have been traversed in the descending arc *(al-qaws al-nuzûlî)* of cosmic manifestation, contemplation and action are also interrelated. Contemplation leads to correct action, and action, conceived as inner spiritual travail as well as external acts which put the soul in the right state to undergo the inner alchemy, leads to the doors of contemplation. But because man must know in order to act, contemplation, as primary, always precedes action. Thus the contemplative man is held in higher esteem in traditional Islamic society than the man of action, as testifies the famous *ḥadîth* stating that the ink of the man of knowledge is more worthy than the blood of the martyr.

But precisely because there is no monasticism in Islam, because Islam is a society "of married monks," because the Divine Law of Islam (the *Sharîᶜah*) is at once a code of action and a way of preparing the soul for the flights of contemplation of the spiritual world, and because of many other factors, the ink and the blood have never been totally divorced and the Islamic order has preserved a remarkable balance between the contemplative and active lives, a balance which cannot be fully understood by a mere theoretical discussion of the subject from the outside. As long as man does not participate in tradition in an operative manner and does not benefit from the grace or *barakah* issuing from its rites and other sacred forms, the complementarity of the contemplative and active lives is most difficult to conceive.

The many men who rely only on reading traditional sources, and simply speak about tradition without practicing it, are never able to perform correct action in the spiritual sense, not to speak of reaching states of contemplation, which by definition belong to the traditional Universe alone. The man who does not practice a spiritual way cannot experience that inner certitude, that inner attachment of one's being to the Divinity, which makes of action an application of immutable principles and the gateway to the world of contemplation, and which brings about a state of unity whereby contemplation and action are wed in an indissoluble union. In fact, what is invocation *(dhikr)* but such a wedding between action and contemplation at its highest level? There is an immeasurable difference between the man who does not practice a tradition and does not live "existentially" attached to a traditional world and one who participates actively in such a world and feels motivated at every moment by the "hands" of God, according to the Qur'anic verse "The Hands of Allah are above their hands" (XLVIII, 10). As the Alexandrian Sufi Ibn ᶜAtāʾ Allāh al-Iskandarānī states,

> He who is negligent awakens by
> considering what he should do,
> And he who is wise by considering
> what God will do with him.[1]

There is an immense difference between the two, even in the context of the traditional world. How much greater is the difference in a world in which many men live in a state of total amnesia or at best a simply theoretical and cerebral understanding of tradition. In either case there is obscured the possibilities of practicing the traditional life in an active way, and of opening inner doors to the world of contemplation amidst external circumstances and situations which, seen only from the outside, appear as opposed to such possibilities and incongruent with the spiritual life.

As previously mentioned, Islam bans monasticism, but this institutional ban does not imply by any means that the door to the life of contemplation is closed. On the contrary, Islamic spirituality activates a tendency toward contemplation which is combined with combativeness (*jihâd*), understood in its esoteric sense of removing all the obstacles which veil the Truth and make It inaccessible. Sufism, the main manifestation of Islamic esoterism, contains within itself the possibility of the most intense contemplative life, not because it is a *monachisme érrant*, as some orientalists have called it, but because such a perspective lies by nature within the Islamic revelation and constitutes its essence.

The unitary principle of Islam, however, could not permit this contemplative way from becoming crystallized as a separate social organization outside the matrix molded by the injunctions of the Divine Law or *Sharî'ah*. It had to remain as an inner dimension of that Law and institutionally as an organization integrated into the Islamic social pattern and inseparable from it. As a result, contemplatives of the highest order often have combined their life of contemplation with the most intense form of activity, and throughout Islamic history outstanding Sufis have been known to be scholars, artists, teachers, and even administrators and rulers.

One often finds it difficult to understand the possibility of the contemplative life for a woman in Islam. Putting aside the case of certain female ascetics like Râbi'ah, most contemplative Muslim women have, like men, found the possibility of the contemplative life within the matrix of the Muslim social order itself. To accept one's destiny as the wife and mother who is of necessity concerned with small daily problems and to submit oneself to one's social position and duties with the awareness that this is in reality submitting oneself to Divine Will, has led many a Muslim woman to an intense contemplative inner life amidst the active life of being a wife and mother. Her acceptance of her role and duty as specified by Islamic teachings echoes the state of *fanâ'* or "annihilation" in

God and can lead, when combined with true piety and devotion to spiritual practices, to that state. For both men and women in Islam the contemplative life lies, not outside, but within the active norms of life specified by the *Sharî'ah*.

The most essential rapport between contemplation and action in Islam is to be found in prayer, especially quintessential prayer, which is the invocation *(dhikr)* practiced by the Sufis. Perfect action which is the *dhikr* leads to contemplation *(shuhûd* or *mushâhadah)*, while contemplation is itself the *dhikr* inasmuch as the *dhikr* is unified with "Him who is involved" *(madhkûr)*. In perfect invocation, he who invokes or performs the act of invocation *(dhikr)* becomes united with the *dhikr* and the *madhkûr* in a supreme union which transcends the dichotomy between action and contemplation, knowledge and existence, the knower and the known; in this supreme union all polarities are embraced within the essential and at the same time primordial unity.

The incantatory methods of Sufism, if practiced under the direction of a master and within the protective matrix of traditional orthodoxy, are all forms of contemplative action at the highest level, leading ultimately to union with God. Inasmuch as the process of realization is in a sense the reversal of the cosmogonic act, the traversing of the ascending arc *(al-qaws al-su'ûdî)* to return to the Source and Origin results in going from a state in which knowledge and existence are separated to a state of union. As a result, in a mysterious fashion the agent who performs the contemplative act is able to transcend his own limited existence as agent through his very action. The secret of this paradox lies in the fact that in the *dhikr* man performs an act, but an act preceded by contemplation, an act which is also a state of being, an act which is ultimately not the act of man but the act of God. Hence in the same way that, through the Word, God created the world, again through His Word—the *dhikr*, which is mysteriously the act of man participating in the eternal and immutable act of God—creation returns to its source. Quintessential prayer is the act which leads to pure contemplation and finally union.

As for active contemplation, it too is the *dhikr* from another point of view. Sufism is not a passive form of mysticism. It is a journey (sulûk) after Divine Knowledge, the attainment of which leads to union and the overcoming of the separation between man in his fallen state and man as the Universal and Perfect Man (al-insân al-kâmil), who is in union with God because he is the perfect mirror in whom the Divine Names and Qualities are reflected. There is then in the very method of Sufism or the dhikr, as it is combined with various forms of meditation (fikr), an active contemplation of the spiritual realities. For those who actually tread the path, the sâlikûn, in contrast to the stationary members of Sufi orders who remain satisfied with being simply blessed with the grace of initiation (the mutabarrikûn), the whole of the spiritual work is continuously combined with the element of active contemplation in which progress upon the spiritual path is achieved through an active participation of the whole being of the adept.

That is why in Islam one of the symbols of the Universal Man, who embodies the full realization of the truth and in whom the dhikr has become fully operative, is the seal of Solomon, of whose triangles the one with the base toward heaven symbolizes contemplation and the other, in the reverse position, action. It is this perfect wedding between the two that makes the act of the contemplative at once the sword that discriminates between truth and error and establishes harmony and justice, and the brush that paints upon the canvas of time and space the beauties of the spiritual world and thereby opens the gate of return to that world.

The relationship between action and contemplation thus described on its most essential level in quintessential orison is reflected also on the plane of the study of nature and of the creation of art. Islamic science certainly enabled man to gain knowledge of nature and also to act upon nature, as we see in agriculture, medicine and the like. But the final goal of this science was to enable man to contemplate nature and to aid him to act upon himself and to remake himself with the help of the contemplative knowledge thus gained. Islamic science was concerned with a process which also implied the possibility for nature considered as the Divine theophany (tajallî) to act upon the soul of man, as well as the possibility for man to "act" upon nature through the contemplation of its epiphanies. Islamic science thus began with an objectivization of nature which made it an "object" of study to end with a unitive knowledge which finally integrated man with his own prototype as well as the prototype of nature, so that at the end nature became a "thou," an intimate witness to the Divine Presence. Moreover, action upon nature has always been regulated and limited because the traditional Muslim knows fully that ultimate happiness comes not from endless action turned outwardly toward the plundering and devastating of nature but from acting inwardly upon oneself to tame and "Islamize the satan of one's own being," as the Sufis would say.

In direct contrast to this perspective, modern science has sought since the seventeenth century to drive a wedge between man and nature by extending further and further the edge of objectivity, with the end result that this objectivity has finally led to total alienation of man from his natural environment, an alienation which, combined with a theory of action conceived of as an aggressive externalization of human energy, an indiscriminate reaping and plundering, has led the world to the present environmental crisis. The relation between contemplation and action in the Islamic sciences of nature derived from the central relationship described contains a message of the utmost importance for modern man seeking to save himself from his own folly.

Likewise in Islamic art there is an intimate relation between action and contemplation which recaptures in the world of forms the complementarity existing between these two in the principal order. Whether it be the courtyard of a mosque, an arabesque design, a verse of Sufi poetry, or a traditional musical composition, various forms of Islamic art serve the function of strengthening the wings of the soul for its contemplative flight into the empyrean. Their beauties are in fact so many reminiscences of the beauties of paradise, which man can taste even here on earth on the wings of contemplation and spiritual vision. In Islamic art, as in the Islamic sciences of nature, contemplation and action are intertwined and complementary, while the hierarchic relation of contemplation over action is always preserved.

The complementarity between contemplation and action in Islam has naturally found its most perfect terrestrial embodiment in the life of the Prophet. He remains the perfect model *(uswah)* to follow, and in him the union of action and contemplation manifests itself in that blinding *coincidentia oppositorum* which transcends all duality and opposition.

The end of human life according to Islam is to act according to the Divine Will and finally to reach through purity such a state of knowledge and vision or contemplation as to see God everywhere. The Prophet was that perfect being who acted according to the Divine Will at every moment of his life while having his gaze fixed at every moment on the Divine realities, contemplating God everywhere in every speck of His creation. Thus one finds in the Prophet the perfect manifestation of the complementarity of contemplation and action culminating in union which lies at the heart of the Islamic way of life and which characterizes at the highest level of meaning the central method of realization in Islamic spirituality.

[1]P. Nwiva, *Ibn ᶜAtâ Allah et la naissance de la Confrérie Shadilite* (Beirut, 1972), p. 133, no. 106.

# Ibn al- ᶜArabî's
# Theory of Journeying

YUSUF IBISH

Lo! We are Allah's and Lo! unto Him we are returning.

Qur'an II: 156

Lo! We it is Who quicken and give death,
and unto Us is the journeying.

Qur'an L: 43

The path of Allah, unto Whom belongeth whatsoever
is in the heavens and whatsoever is in the earth.
Do not all things reach Allah at last?

Qur'an XLII:53

Allah's is the Sovereignty of the heavens and the earth, and
all that is between them, and unto Him is the journeying.

Qur'an V: 18

The Qur'anic verses cited above, among others, define the general
Muslim conception of the cosmos and its relation to the Divine
Origin as well as the Divine End. It follows that the study of the
universe and its component parts is not only a valid but a necessary
step toward the knowledge of Divine Realities. The world is nothing
but the work of Allah and the study of it becomes incumbent on the
believers as part of their religious duty. "The universe at all levels of
its existence emanates from Pure Being and ultimately returns to
it."[1] Therefore nature is not to be studied as an object of curiosity,
or just because it is around us, or for its own sake. The study of
nature cannot be an end in itself but only a means to an end: to

acquire knowledge of Him who created it; to catch a glimpse of His Tremendous Majesty; to have an insight into His Wisdom, which is "reflected" in "the order of things" (i.e., the cosmos); and, inevitably, by relating particulars to Universals, to attain knowledge of the Creator Himself, as "He is what He is."

Ibn al-ᶜArabî wrote as follows of the Creator:

> He is, and there is with him no after nor before, nor above nor below, nor far nor near, nor union nor division, nor how nor where nor when, nor time nor moment nor age, nor being nor place. And He is now as He was. He is the One without oneness and the Single without singleness. He is not composed of name and named, for His name is He and His named is He. . . .
>
> Understand therefore . . . He is not in a thing nor a thing in Him, whether entering in or proceeding forth. It is necessary that thou know Him after this fashion, not by knowledge, nor by intellect, nor by understanding, nor by imagination, nor by sense, nor by perception. There does not see Him, save Himself; nor perceive Him, save Himself. By Himself He sees Himself, and by Himself He knows Himself. None sees Him other than He, and none perceives Him other than He. His veil is [only a "consequence" and effect of] His oneness; nothing veils other than He. His veil is [only] the concealment of His existence in His oneness, without any quality. None sees Him other than He — no sent prophet, nor saint made perfect, nor angel brought nigh know Him. His Prophet is He, and His sending is He, and His Word is He. He sent Himself with Himself to Himself. [2]

This knowledge helps man attain an understanding of himself: who he is, where he is, why he is here, what is expected of him, where he is going, and what is the true meaning of what is happening to him and around him. Man can attain such knowledge through the "Revelations" of God and because he is "endowed with an intelligence capable of conceiving of the Absolute and with a will capable of choosing what leads to the Absolute."[3]

Ibn al-ᶜArabî's theosophy leads to the doctrine that knowledge of the cosmos is reached by means of journeying through it. Symbolically all natural phenomena become encompassed within a "Huge Circle," which in turn is internalized within the being of al-ᶜArif (the gnostic), who is thus able to journey from any point of the circumference inwardly along one of the radii, "paths," or "Ways" (*Ṭuruq*, plural of *Ṭarîqah*) to reach the Center, which is the

Divine Presence *(al-Ḥaqq)*. The journey is both inward toward the Center, the Self, the Absolute, and outward, away from the human self, the finite form. To Ibn al-ʿArabî the process resembles breathing, inhaling and exhaling, contracting and expanding, inwardly and outwardly, in a cyclical manner. The universe pulsates in the same manner through the "Breath of the Compassionate" *(nafas al-Raḥmân)*, for everything in existence emanated from an articulated "Breath of Him" *Kun fa-kâna* (be! and it was), and "unto Him is the journeying."

In order to understand the traditional view of man in general and Ibn al-ʿArabî's in particular it is necessary to understand that the "healthy" man is one who is "detached" from the world of illusions and "attached" to and living in "Reality." The "sick" man, in need of help and cure, is the one who is "detached" from Reality and "attached" to illusions and living in his delusions. The first is a *muwaḥḥid* (monotheist), the latter is a *mushrik* (polytheist) who suffers from the most heinous sin. It is not sufficient to testify verbally to one God; one must also live and act by the *Shahâdah, La ilâha illâ Allâh* (there is no divinity outside the Only Divinity).

To live up to God's expectations, man must realize that his true role is to be His *Khalîfah (vicegerent)* on earth, observing His *Sharîʿa* (revealed law) and reflecting the Divine Names and Qualities. One of the implications of the *Shahâdah* (Testimony) is self-purification from all polytheistic tendencies of earthly life and worship of the only Divinity. As it was said by the Prophet (upon whom be Peace): *Iḥsân* is to adore Allâh as though thou didst see Him, and if thou dost not see Him He nonetheless seeth thee." Another implication is remembrance of *al-Mîthâq* (the solemn Covenant of God) and paying heed to it. A further implication is following the example of the Prophet, *al-Insân al-Kâmil* (the Perfect Man) in whom all the potentials of man have been actualized and realized. God confirmed this when He said to the Prophet: "And Lo! thou art of a tremendous nature" (Qur'an LXVIII: 4).

Perfect Man implies cosmic man, thoroughly one and forming an integrated whole inwardly and outwardly and in all his desires. Ibn al-ʿArabî in *Fuṣûṣ al-Ḥikam* quotes the *Ḥadîth:* "Of this world, three [elements] are worthy of my love: women, perfumes, and *Ṣalât* [ritual prayer]." These three elements are external symbols of the love of the Inward Reality. Woman symbolizes for man the other part of the whole, and she draws unto herself him who wants to become a whole; as such she is an expression of Divine Concern on the Path to requital. This is what makes her so lovable. As for "perfumes," they synthesize the fragrance of the Garden and provoke in man memories of his original State before he fell into the terrestrial condition of separation from his divine prototype. Here we find memories provoking remembrance of an Inward Reality for which man yearns and which impel him on the road to self-realization and eternal felicity. "Verily with hardship cometh ease" (Qur'an XCIV:5).

As for *Ṣalât,* mentioned in the Tradition, its basic aim is to help man enter into communion with God through an inward movement *(Qurrat al-ʿAyn).* God participates with us in our prayer, helping us to remember who we are in relationship to Him, step by step, from the beginning to the end, from the *Basmalah* to the *Ḥamdalah,* for when we recite: "In the Name of Allah," He concurs: "My worshiper has Named Me"; and when we continue: "Most Merciful and Compassionate," He concurs: "My worshiper has described Me" and so on to the end, when we say the *Ḥamdalah* and He says: "My worshiper is duly grateful."

The reader who was at the beginning shocked by the apparent worldliness of the *Ḥadîth* quoted above might realize now that the outward form of the symbol can be integrated, by contemplation, in the love of God. This integration takes place by virtue of *Istiʿdâd* (an inward quality of the heart). The mystery that enshrouds the symbol is unveiled by *Tajallî* (resplendency) in the same way that the morning sun illuminates the obscurities of the night. When there is reciprocation of *Tajallî* and *Istiʿdâd,* a *hâl* (spiritual state) is attained by the traveler on the path of the Divine Presence, the goal being always to reach and live in Him and not to remain fixed in a particular *maqâm* (spiritual station). Living in God implies annihilation and requital by Him. ʿAlî ibn Abî Ṭâlib related the following *Ḥadîth Qudsî:*

Who seeketh Me findeth Me

Who findeth Me knoweth Me.
Who knoweth Me loveth Me.
Who loveth Me, him I love.
Whom I love, him I slay.
Whom I slay, him must I requite.
Whom I must requite, Myself am his Requital.

Ibn al-ᶜArabî sums up his position on the end of contemplation in a masterly way: "Thus God is the mirror in which you see yourself, as you are His mirror in which He contemplates His Names; now His Names are not other than Himself, so that the analogy of relations is an inversion."[4]

To Ibn al-ᶜArabî action, all action, implies motion and motion is journeying from, to, and in a destination. Thus for him there are only three types of journeys and there is no fourth: away from Him, towards Him, and in Him.[5] The first, away from Him, is a journey with a purpose, leading to a reward or a punishment, and shrouded with dangers unless the traveler is "carried" by Divine Ordinance to his destination. Ibn al-ᶜArabî says this first form of journeying is of three types. The first is a journey in banishment from Him such as the journey of the fallen angel Iblis who disobeyed God's command. The second is a self-inflicted journey away from Him, not in banishment, but in shame. Those who journey this way cannot endure remaining in His presence and they draw away from Him because they have disobeyed Him. The third type is the journey of those who are envoys from Him to mankind; they carry a particular message and are the Prophets and Apostles of God.

The second journey is towards God, and this again with a purpose, implying reward or punishment, and full of dangers except for those who are summoned by Him and are "carried" by the Divine Ordinance towards Him. This journey is also of three types. The first type includes those travelers who, as polytheists, worship Him among other gods, yet are excluded from His Mercy and therefore will never obtain a vision of Him, for they are separated from Him by a veil; among them are those who disobeyed Him and did not repent. The second type of journey is of those who, though free of disobedience, have yet ascribed associates to Him in creation, and they reach a threshold but never enter His presence. The third type is that of the impeccable ones who journey to Him by His Divine Ordinance and with His protection, and between Him and them there are no veils.

The third journey is in Him and has no rewards; the traveler gains only himself, but it involves danger. This journey may be of two types. The first type comprizes those who travel only by their rational faculties — philosophers and the like — and inevitably lose the way because they have no other guide. The second type contains His prophets, Messengers, Apostles, and the chosen and beloved *awliyâ'* (His friends).

Then Ibn al-ᶜArabî recounts for us in *Kitâb al-Asfâr* a number of journeys he has found in the Qur'an. First there is the journey of the Merciful from Sublimity to the Throne of Establishment, under which it can be said that God has established Himself firmly on the Throne. Second is the journey of Creativity and Originality, when God said, "Be," and the universe was. The third journey is that of the Qur'an, which descended on that Blessed Night of Power. The fourth journey, the ascent of the Prophet to Heaven, is known as the journey of Vision. The fifth is the journey of Calamity, when God ordered Adam and Eve to descend from the garden to the earth for having disobeyed Him. The sixth is the journey of Grandeur and Splendor, that of Idris. The seventh is the journey of Safety, such as Noah's. The eighth is the journey of Guidance, such as Ibrahim's. The ninth is the journey of Pursuit with no looking backwards, that of Lot to Ibrahim and their meeting in Certainty. Tenth is the journey of Cunning and Calamity, that of Yacub and Yusuf. The eleventh is the journey by Divine Appointment, as when Musa (Moses) went to meet God. The twelfth is the journey of Content, that of Musa towards God so that He would be pleased with him. Thirteenth is the journey of Anger and Return, Musa's return to his people in sorrow and anger. Fourteenth is the journey towards Unity with the Family. Fifteenth is the journey of Fear, as fear is in the station of faith. Sixteenth is the journey of Heed.

Implicit in Ibn al-ᶜArabî's theory of journeying is the unity of religions. To him revelation is universal and every prophet has transmitted an aspect of God's Will to mankind. Therefore, if we examine the inner contents of all religions by journeying inwardly from the external forms toward the inner one we will find a transcendent unity: they all emanate from the same Supreme Center. It should be clearly understood that Ibn al-ᶜArabî does not reject the outer forms for they remain part of Divine Wisdom. The rites and practices of any religion are points of departure toward the inner content and must be protected if that religion is to fulfill its message. What he tries to convey to us is the principle of the unity of the "Essence" within the diversity of external forms. The "Essence" here is nothing more or less than the love of God which is shared by all religions. This is why he could say without falling into error, "Love is my religion and faith."

In our modern world, when so many have lost their sense of direction and wander around looking for something which they do not know, we find that Ibn al-ᶜArabî has a message for them. Those who are taking "trips" through the use of drugs, those who are traveling out of their habitats as tourists, even those who recently journeyed into space, indicate clearly that wandering and journeying is natural to man in his terrestrial estrangement. What is abnormal and grotesque is that a sense of direction is completely lacking and these meanderings are all physical rather than spiritual. This is not surprising in our modern material world, for if the spirit is disregarded then nothing remains to be explored but the physical world around us. Modern Western man is in danger of becoming really one-dimensional. Certainly Ibn al-ᶜArabî has a profound message to mankind in his theory of journeying. He points to the Way and is an excellent guide.

[1]S.H. Nasr, *An Introduction to Islamic Cosmological Doctrines* (Cambridge, Mass: Harvard University Press, 1964), p. 276.

[2]T.H. Weir, *Translation of an Arabic Manuscript* (London, 1963), pp. 809-810.

[3]F. Schuon, *Understanding Islam* (London, 1963), p. 13.

[4]T. Burckhardt, *An Introduction to Sufi Doctrine* (Lahore, 1959), p. 142.

[5]Ibn al-ᶜArabî, *Kitâb al-Isfâr ᶜan Nata 'ij al-Asfar* (Hyderabad, 1948).

# Contemplation and Action:
# the Sufi Way

### AL-SAYYEDAH FATIMAH YASHRUTIYYAH

All Sufi masters (may Allah be pleased with them) are agreed that Sufism is the *Ḥikmah* (Wisdom) which leads to happiness in this world and the next through divine knowledge. Allah (Almighty and Exalted) said in the Qur'an: "Whoso is given the Wisdom has been given much good." He also said (may His Name be glorified): "Our Lord! And raise up in their midst a messenger from among them who shall recite unto them Thy revelation and shall instruct them in the Scripture and in the Wisdom and shall make them grow." It is imperative for anyone wishing to obtain any degree of Divine Wisdom to educate himself in the esoteric doctrines. Such Wisdom helps man distinguish between truth and error, sound and unsound, praiseworthy and blameworthy, pure and impure. Moreover, it helps man clear his heart of the accumulated errors, cures it of its maladies, and purifies it of animal tendencies. If the soul is thus purified then the mirror of the heart becomes burnished and capable of reflecting the light of Divine Sublimity out of which the springs of Divine Wisdom gush. Our master Ibn ᶜAtâ' Allâh al-Iskandarânî has said the following about this process: "Perhaps rays have made their appearance and found the heart burdened with errors, so they make off to whence they came; empty your heart of petty things, and He will fill it with secrets and illuminations."

The salvation of the soul and the attainment of the knowledge of Allah is the legacy of purification. We maintain, therefore, that Sufism is the most noble and excellent of all the sciences because its subject is the knowledge of Allah (may He be praised and exalted), His Names, His Qualities, and His Deeds. While the virtues of acquiring knowledge in all fields are the duty of the Muslim, every branch of knowledge derives its own honor from the honor of that which it seeks to know and the fruits thereof. The study of the physical world as the handiwork of Allah (and He is Omnipotent) is a natural and noble activity of man. It is obvious that man's finite intellect, if it is on the right path, is drawn and moves towards the Infinite. Thus the knowledge of Allah is more noble and complete than the knowledge of everything knowable, and the fruits of it lead to felicity in this world and the next. Moreover, the seeker of knowledge is usually impressed by that which he seeks and gradually his life and his soul are molded by the qualities and attributes of the "known." Thus the knowledge of every attribute of Allah leads the seeker to a "spiritual state." As our Sufi masters have demonstrated, the possessor of such knowledge is raised and molded by the Qualities of His knowledge. From seeking the Mercy of Allah men become merciful; from seeking the Compassion of Allah men become compassionate; and so with the rest of His Names. The experience of these states is a possibility for those who are willing to devote themselves fully to *taṣawwuf*. It is through them that the Names and Eternal Mysteries are diffused in the Cosmos. This is the true meaning of spiritual realization through intellectual and existential intuition *(bi al- dhawq wa al-wujdân)*. God affirmed this in His Holy Book when He said: "He it is Who sent down peace of reassurance into the hearts of the believers that they might add faith unto their faith."

Esotericism revolves on three elements:

1. The knowledge of the nature of God, His revelations, His Names, His Qualities and Deeds.

2. The knowledge of the nature of man: for the key to the knowledge of God is self-knowledge. How can one know God if one does not know oneself? He who knows himself knows his Lord. The Almighty said: "We shall show them Our portents on the horizons and within themselves until it will be manifest unto them that it is the truth. Doth not thy Lord suffice, since He is Witness over all things?" And He also said: ". . . and within themselves, will they not them see?"

3. Knowledge of terrestial life and the reality of the next, the

control of the soul, and the preference of the love of God to everything else. He who has sincerity in the "One" is on the path to God.

To the Sufis actions are divided into three categories: actions under *Sharîᶜa*, actions under *al-Ţarîqah,* and actions in accordance with *al-Ḥaqîqah;* or, one could say, *al-Islâm, al-Îmân* and *al-Iḥsân;* or *al-ᶜIbâdah, al-ᶜUbûdiyyah,* and *al-ᶜUbûdah.* Or, one could say further, the beginning, the middle and the end. The *Sharîᶜa* is that one worship Him, the *Ţarîqah* is that one seek Him, *al-Ḥaqîqah* that one witness Him. God Almighty says: "They say: Peace be unto you! Enter the Garden because of what ye used to do."

The true Sufi does not worship God to derive rewards nor in fear of punishment, but in order to draw near to God and to fulfill His Will.

It has been related that the pious al- Sayyida Râbiᶜa al-Adawîya (may Allah be pleased with her) used to pray one hundred *rakᶜas* each night and she would then address the Almighty saying: "O God! If I worship Thee in fear of Hell, burn me in Hell, and if I worship Thee in hope of Paradise, exclude me from Paradise, but if I worship Thee for Thine own Sake, withhold not Thine Everlasting Beauty."

Thus it is that if the Sufi speaks it is of God, if he hears it is from God, if he moves it is by order of God, and if he rests it is with God, for he lives by God, through God, and with God.

*Al-Ţarîq,* the Way of the Sufis, is the "path" taken to God. It has *Ẓâhir* (exoteric) and *Baţin* (esoteric) dimensions. Exoterically it involves the harmonization of life according to the Will of Allah, that is living in full obedience to the *Sharîᶜa* (the revealed Law). Esoterically it calls for the development of inner spiritual virtues. The adherents of this Way have a special method of attaching themselves to *al-Ḥaqq* (the Truth) in all their actions, even in their very breathing, until the Truth completely reigns over their hearts and the world and its concerns and calamities dwindle and fade away.

A group of Sufi masters have maintained that Sufism is not

reading books on the subject but striving to mend the heart and to cleanse it from noxious diseases. It also calls for putting the soul at peace, i.e., reintegrated in the Spirit and set at rest in its original certainty. As the Almighty has said: "But ah! thou soul at peace! Return unto thy Lord, content in His good pleasure."

However many and different the "paths" may be, they all return to the same focal point and involve contemplation and action. The multiple guises of spiritual beauty demand many ways of recognizing it; hence the multiplicity of the Sufi paths. To each group of men there is a path: to the common man there is a path, to the jurist there is a path, to the narrator of *Ḥadîth* there is a path, to the theologian there is a path, to the logician there is a path and to the sage there is a path. Each man in the final analysis can start from where he is.

The all-important secret in taking a "path" is the will to take it! God Almighty said: "Who hear advice and follow the best thereof, such are those whom Allah guideth, and such are men of understanding."

Although there are many different "paths," they can be divided into two schools and their followers into two groups:

1. The first school is the *Ishrâqî* (illuminationist), and their method is spiritual exercises and purification of the soul. They compare the soul in its original state to a clean and burnished mirror upon which Divine Reality is reflected. The soul is, however, impeded in this process by two things: the image of the contingent world makes it rusty or it turns away from its intended goal, directing itself to other activities. This rust can only be removed and the right direction regained by rigorous spiritual exercises and purification. Otherwise, how can the heart reflect Divine Reality if the images of the world are impressed upon it? Or, how can one travel on the path to God if he is chained by his animal appetites? Or still, how could one penetrate to the innermost secrets if he has not repented his errors? Just as the soul is likened to a mirror, so is it also likened to a spring, the knowledge of Divine Reality being the water it contains. The Ishraqi maintain that the pressures of being preoccupied by the illusions of this world lower the water level and

the spring dries up. The water cannot be tapped unless one digs for it with the spade of *jihâd*. By abandoning the illusions of this world and by *jihâd* the spring will gush forth with water just as before, if not more powerful. This school also holds that the origin of every bodily ill is the corruption of the humor so that its actions and reactions are not in accordance with the natural course of things, and that the origin of every illness of the heart is merely the corruption of the sincerity of intention, so that its action and reaction are not in harmony with *Sharî'a* and Reality. The way in which the soul can be treated is by refraining from failings and errors and by purifying it from what already burdens it. This can be achieved in the first place by awe and self-discipline, and in the second place by repentance and conversion.

2. The second school follows the maxim that *'Ilm* (knowledge) is the key to action. The Prophet (may the Blessings and Peace of Allah be upon him) has said: "Knowledge precedes action, and action follows; he who seeks the good will attain it, and he who avoids the evil shall be spared its consequences; and he who acts upon knowledge Allah will bequeath upon him the knowledge of that which he does not know." The followers of this school seek and stress the importance of acquiring *'Ilm* to guide their actions along the straight and ordained path. They also try to redress the soul through knowledge and action. Knowledge, they maintain, is the light that dispels the darkness in which we live, and if it is added to the inner light that the soul possesses, then darkness will be dispelled from inside and outside and our way will be illuminated both ways.

The *'Ilm* needed in this respect has four branches: (a) the knowledge and affirmation of the Divine Unity (*'Ilm al-Tawḥîd*); (b) the knowledge of Muslim jurisprudence (*'Ilm al-Fiqh*); (c) the knowledge of Qur'anic commentaries and Traditions of the Prophet (*'Ilm al-Tasfîr wa al-Ḥadîth*); and (d) the knowledge of the states of soul of those who are practising Sufism and are striving on the Way (*'Ilm al-Ḥâlât wa al Munâzalât*).

The first three branches of *'Ilm* are well known and hence need no elaboration. The fourth *'Ilm* calls for some explanation. The Sufi must possess knowledge of his *ḥâl* (the state of his soul) if he is to keep up the *munâzalah* (the striving) to attain advance *maqâm* (station) and move on in journeying toward the Absolute. The best way to attain this branch of knowledge is through acting as though seeing Allah all the time. This is the Shadhili Way, while others, within the same above-mentioned school, such as al-Ghazzali, stress that action should be based on the following principle: if you do not see Him, He sees you. Both groups base themselves on the following sound *Ḥadîth*: "Adore Allah as though thou didst see Him, and if thou dost not see Him, He nonetheless seeth thee."

The *Shâdhiliyyah* is one of the leading Sufi Ways, for it combines knowledge and action, spiritual will and Divine Attraction (*jadhb*), intoxication without violating the limits of *Sharîᶜa*, and sobriety (*saḥw*) without veiling the Divine Presence. It calls for a balanced spiritual life through *dhikr* (remembrance and invocation of the Divine Name), which ultimately leads to *al-Faraḥ bil-Allâh* (rejoicing in God). Since it does not call for superhuman efforts its followers lead the Muslim life with ease and joy, admitting at the same time their weakness and shortcomings. It is also the Way of Love, that which nourished the hearts of the Prophets and of the *Awliyâ'* of Allah (the Saints).

I have endeavored to encourage all to meditate on the prayer of al-Sayyidah Râbiᶜa al-Adawîyah. Now let us all act upon the following words of al-Shaykh al-Akbar Muḥyi al-Dîn, ibn al-ᶜArabî:

> My heart is open to every form: it is a pasture for gazelles, and a cloister for Christian monks, a temple for idols, the tables of the Torah, and the book of the Qur'an. I practice the religion of love; in whatsoever direction His caravans advance, the religion of Love shall be my religion and my faith.

# Yoruba Traditional Religion

## WANDE ABIMBOLA

*Editor's Introduction:* Against some materialistic views of action held in the West, the Yoruba religion of Africa presents us with an *active vision* which is simultaneously a cosmogony, a theology, and a theory of social order and moral behavior based on contemplative communication between the human and the divine. Consequently, mere description of Yoruba myths and legends in terms of Western metaphysics would hardly suffice. One needs to know the history and the structure of Yoruba tradition, its poetic dimension, its concepts of Good and Evil, Sacrifice and Possession.

According to the author — himself a high priest of the Yoruba religion and a scholar trained in the Western academic style — the foremost tasks are: to fix this immense richness of oral tradition in written documents, and thus to make accessible to Blacks everywhere the tenets, rituals, and profound contents of this African religion; and to persuade the African governments concerned to amplify teaching about the Yoruba traditional religion in primary education, not with the purpose of proselytizing, but with a view toward restoring dignity to the people by giving them full possession of their spiritual heritage and system of values.[1]

The Yoruba are an important West African ethnic group, numbering about ten million, in the southwestern corner of Nigeria and a small area in eastern Dahomey. They are largely concentrated in the Ibadan, Ondo, Oyo, Abeokuta, Ikeja, and Ijebu provinces of the Western Region and in the Ilorin and Kabba Provinces of the Northern Region of Nigeria.[2] There are also strong influences of Yoruba culture among the Creole populations of Sierra Leone. Outside Africa, one can find traces of Yoruba culture in Latin America, where the Yoruba language has been preserved as a ritual language in combination with everyday languages — specifically in the chants and hymns of the black people of Brazil and Cuba.

The Yoruba-speaking peoples of Nigeria have had a long history of urbanization, and today several of Nigeria's most populous cities are found in Yoruba territory. The Yoruba have also come under Islamic influence since the fourteenth and fifteenth centuries. Systematic Christian influence came in the 1850s, when the first missionaries arrived. This long history of external influence resulted in the decline of the Yoruba traditional religion and value system which can be witnessed today.

However, despite their long history of urban development and contact with Christian and Islamic cultures, a large and important core of the Yoruba population still clings tenaciously to the faith of their fathers. Therefore, while the traditional religious system is not shared today by all the Yoruba, they nevertheless recognize it as their own legacy, and it continues to exert strong influence even among the powerful Christian and Muslim communities.

The main obstacle to the preservation and transmission of this original tradition is its existence in exclusively oral form. As such, it has to compete with the powerful Muslim and Christian written traditions, whose holy scriptures constitute a permanent reinforcement and system of reference for the believers. With the death of its few remaining initiated priests, the Yoruba tradition would be in danger of disappearing; this situation entails an impending religious task: the recording on tapes, transcribing, and the translation as well, of the esoteric teachings of the Yoruba peoples.

While coexistence with other systems of beliefs ought to be maintained, it is the duty of governmental educational and cultural agencies to help preserve and disseminate — not only for African peoples, but for the world at large — the treasures contained in the Yoruba traditional system of beliefs.

SOCIAL AND POLITICAL ORGANIZATION

The Yoruba cosmological vision is wholly hierarchical: at the apex is God Almighty, followed by the mythical divinities, the ancestors, the personal divinities, and, finally, man. Man himself is represented as a double figure: the internal, which is his own "inner" head (ori), and the external, which is hierarchically lower; between these two aspects there is no real separation, but actual continuity.

As well as possessing an ancestor, every man has an *ori*, a spiritual counterpart which is simultaneously his individual protector-divinity.

Sacrifice, rituals, dance, chanting, and possession are in effect the external manifestation of inwardness. Thus rituals refer inwardly to contemplation. Possession is *the total religious act,* and, as far as traditional African religion is concerned, without possession there is no religion.

Corresponding to the hierarchy of supernatural powers, Yoruba society is organized in a social and political hierarchy: the king is at its top, followed by the chiefs, the city and village heads, the family heads, and, finally, the individual heads of the households. Between the two hierarchies, there is a strict interdependence.

Traditional Yoruba society is based on a hierarchy of authority shared by powerful divine rulers and the elders. The basic political unit is the household, governed by the *baálé* (household head) who always is the oldest man. The *baálé* settles petty disputes within his household unit and sees to other matters affecting the welfare of his people, such as clearing bush paths overgrown with weeds, digging wells, and deepening rivers to produce water in the dry season. He is assisted in his function by the oldest female in the household, who is known as the *iyáálé-ilé*. She is head of the womenfolk, the midwife of the community, the deputy of the *baálé*; her authority on matters affecting the female occupants of the household is final.

The immediate superior of the *baálé* is the village head, who judges cases referred to him by all the *baálé* in his territory, and attends to other matters affecting the general welfare of the village. He is assisted in his duties by a host of counselors varying in number from place to place. Chosen by the king from a list of elders, he is responsible to the king for his actions. The village head may or may not be a descendant of the divinities.

At the apex of this hierarchical order is the *oba* (king) who holds supreme authority over everyone in his kingdom. The king usually has a council of advisers who help him in the day-to-day administration of his domain. From his subjects the king collects tolls and levies from which he draws the financial appropriations of his government. Difficult cases which cannot be handled by the village heads are referred to the king whose judgment is final. In many Yoruba kingdoms, for example, only the king can impose the death penalty.

Many Yoruba kings claim that they are descended from Oduduwa, a major divinity who is regarded as the father of the whole nation, and that therefore they rule by the divine right of kings. They are regarded by their subjects as "the supreme authority, deputy of the divinities."

## THE BELIEF SYSTEM: COSMOGONY AND MAJOR DIVINITIES

The Yoruba conceive their universe as consisting of two territories: *aye* (earth) and *orun* (heaven). *Aye* is the abode of the human beings while *orun* is the abode of the divinities and the ancestors. Normally those who reach adulthood in life go to *orun* after death and become ancestors as well. Infants and children who die do not become ancestors.[3] The Yoruba view death as a means of transferring people from a lower state of authority to a higher one. Hence the usually elaborate funeral ceremonies which the Yoruba perform. The authority of the ancestors as well as the divinities is higher than that of the kings.

Yoruba mythology states that at one time *aye* and *orun* were part of the same territory, so that it was possible for the living to travel freely between *aye* and *orun*. According to Yoruba mythology, *orun* was moved into the sky due to human failings, and thenceforth became inaccessible to human beings except by death.

According to one myth, the divinities came to *aye* before the separation of the human from the divine planes of existence. They were led by Ogun, the war and hunting divinity, who made a path for them with his cutlass until they reached Ife. But another myth states that the divinities came to Ife after *orun* had been moved, so that they descended from the sky and landed upon a hill which they named Ife.

It is believed that the creation divinity, Obatala, was the one whom Olodumare charged with the function of creating dry land at Ife with the aid of a hen and a parcel of sand. But because Obatala drank too much palm wine and slept away, Oduduwa performed the function in his place. Hence, Oduduwa, otherwise known as Olofin, became the great ancestor of the Yoruba race.

Ife is therefore the primordial earth, analogous to the Garden of Eden of the Judeo-Christian tradition. This holy city of the Yoruba, now the site of the University of Ife, was also the traditional academic center of Yorubaland, and, indeed, of a good part of West Africa. From very ancient times, Ife developed a traditional African civilization which produced the famous rock, terra-cotta, and bronze sculptures for which that ancient city is well known.

The Yoruba believe that Olodumare, the Yoruba Almighty God who sent the divinities to earth, resides in *orun*. Hence his other name Olorun, which means "owner or lord of *orun*." He is also known as *elédàá* (the creator); *olojo-oni* (owner of today); *aláàánu* (kindhearted one); and *alase* (the supreme authority). Olodumare is omnipresent, everlasting, and ageless. He is essentially good, and his supreme duty is to protect his creatures from unnecessary harm; he is known as *baba* (father). Olodumare also uses his highly potent power, known as *ase*, to govern the universe and maintain its physical laws.

Olodumare is the greatest of all powers both in *orun* and *aye*, and his authority pervades all time and space. Through the divinities who are his able deputies, Olodumare enforces compliance with the ethical values of the universe. He punishes transgressors and rewards the virtuous. Believed to be omnipresent, no images are made of Olodumare, and there is no priesthood, no temple built for his worship, and no special cult devoted to him.

Just as the king is at the apex of the hierarchy of political authority on earth, Olodumare is at the apex of everything in *orun*. Without him, there is nothing. One Ifa poem states that once there was a quarrel between Olodumare and Ile (the Earth), the one claiming superiority over the other. The quarrel started after a bush-burning exercise on earth when only one bush rat was killed. Both Ile and Orun (i.e., Olodumare) claimed seniority and therefore the right to take away the only bush rat killed in the burnt bush. When the quarrel became too intense, Olodumare left the bush rat for Ile and retired into his abode in the skies. The result was total chaos and confusion on earth:

> There was no rain.
> Neither were there any showers.
> Yams produced small but undeveloped tubers.
> Maize grew undeveloped ears.
> The bean crop developed useless buds.
> The pregnant women could not deliver their babies.
> The barren women remained barren.
> The sick remained infirm.
> Small rivers were covered up with falling leaves.
> The semen of the men dried up inside their testicles.
> The women did not see their menstrual periods.
> The famine was so severe
> That it killed the ruler of Omu.
> Tiny drops of rain fell down,
> And the chicken attempted to eat them.
> Well-sharpened razors were laid down,
> And the goats attempted to consume them.[4]

When all men, animals, birds, and other creatures on earth were faced with total extermination, Ile decided to send the bush rat which caused the trouble back to Olodumare with apologies. After several other birds had tried and failed, the vulture succeeded in taking the bush rat to Olorun. The result was that rain fell once again and life returned to the earth. But from that time, Olodumare was never again challenged by any divinity. His authority over the whole of the universe was complete.

The many divinities known as *orisa* are the representatives of Olodumare on earth. Each of them performs a function for Olodumare: Òòsàálá, otherwise known as Obatala, is charged with the creation; Ogun, the war and hunting divinity, with all matters requiring the use of iron and physical force; Ifa, with using his great wisdom for the divine ordering of the young earth. Esu, also known as Elegbara, is the universal policeman and keeper of the *ase* (power) which the divinities have to borrow to perform supernatural deeds.

Ogun, the iron divinity, assumed prominence among the major divinities as one upon whom the survival of the community depended. He is believed to be in charge of all acts of heroism and warfare, and supervises and regulates the occupation of hunting (he and his wife Ọsóọsì were the originators of the cult of hunters). Ogun also sanctions all wars before the warriors take to the field of battle. Furthermore, Ogun initiated the smelting of iron upon which the Yoruba Iron Age civilization was based. Because he controls the secrets of the iron industry, all people who make use of iron in their day-to-day life must propitiate him, including blacksmiths, farmers, bricklayers, motor drivers, mechanics, and even housewives. Hence these lines on the multiple roles of Ogun:

> There are seven Ire.
> There are seven Ogun.
> The Ogun of the city dwellers
> Does not refuse meat.
> The Ogun of the farmland eats rats.
> The Ogun of the villagers does not see blood.
> That of the hunters eats plenty of blood.
> That of the circumcisers drinks blood.
> There is another Ogun who belongs to the king of
> Ire in the city of Sambebe.
> There is another one who built a workshop for
> the production of iron tools.
> But there is another one who did not.
> Another one built a house of palm fronds.
> The torrent made the house of another one
> its own abode.
> Travellers on the road to Àwoyè,
> My own Ogun is placed right in front of the house.
> Sudden as the crack of dry wood.
> The rugged and restless man.
> Death who fights both with the head and the tail.[5]

Ogun is believed to be a rugged *orisa* who lived partly in the forest and partly in the city. His food was of the most casual kind: roasted yams, fried maize and beans, and, of course, flesh of all animals both wild and domesticated. His favorite meat was the flesh of the dog, which is still used today as an important item of sacrifice for the hunter's divinity.

Although Oduduwa was the creator of Ife, Ogun is closely connected with the settlement of many other towns and villages of the Yoruba. He himself later moved out of Ife and founded the city of Saki. He is also closely connected with the city of Ire which is sometimes regarded as his home. But an *ijala*[6] poem points out that this is untrue:

> Ire is not the true home of Ogun.
> The Ogun cult was taken there by others.
> Saki is the true home of the father.

Apart from Ire and Saki, Ogun is connected with other Yoruba settlements due to the fact that most of these settlements were founded by the hunters. Ogun and his cult of hunters therefore have an interest in the continuity of Yoruba culture, whose cities they helped to found. This is the reason why in every Yoruba community, the hunters, regarded as the protectors of the community against all forces of disintegration, performed the duties of policemen and sometimes even the functions of a standing army.

Ogun stands for the attributes of bravery, physical ability, and truthfulness. In traditional Yoruba society, the hunters were regarded as the most trustworthy and dependable people. By the nature of their profession they also possess physical ability and discipline. So strongly is the trait of honesty associated with Ogun that a Yoruba, whatever his religious faith, will swear on a piece of iron to evidence his truthfulness.

Ifa, otherwise known as Orunmila, is perhaps the most important of the divinities. He was among those who originally descended into Ife, where he lived for many years at oke Igeti. But he soon left Ife for Ado. Hence the saying: Ado is the home of Ifa.

Ifa surpasses the other divinities by his great wisdom. He is known as Akerefinusogbon (the small one with a mind full of wisdom) and Akoniloranbiiyekaneni (he who teaches one wisely like one's own relation). His great wisdom was bequeathed to him by Olodumare, through whom Ifa witnessed the act of creation. Ifa therefore knows all the secrets of the universe.

When the *orisa* were coming to Ife, Orunmila was charged with the function of bringing peace, order, and civilization to the young earth. Ifa built his great wisdom into a system of divination through which human beings can "talk" with their divinities, a system bequeathed to humanity when Orunmila finally left *aye* for *orun*. At first, his departure from the earth caused great confusion, but when his children went to *orun* to plead for their father's return, their

225

father gave them *ikin* (the sacred palm nuts of divination) which then became the symbol of Ifa here on earth.

Through *ikin* and *opele* (the divining chain), human beings have communication with the divinities. Each divinity has a chapter in the 256 *Odu* (categories) of the Ifa literary corpus. The poems in each chapter stipulate the sacrifices to be performed by the supplicant in order to gain the support of the divinities. Thus, Ifa is the storehouse of the tenets and the mythology of all the Yoruba divinities. Through the Ifa divination system, Orunmila acts as the spokesman of the divinities and enables humans to maintain steady contact with their *orisa*. Hence the meaning of the following Ifa poem:

Ifa is the master of today.
Ifa is the master of tomorrow.
Ifa is the master of the day after tomorrow.
To Ifa belong all the four days
Created by the divinities on earth.

Ifa gives the Yoruba religion order, meaning, purpose, and a codified philosophy. Without the communication it provides with the divinities and the ancestors, the whole system probably would have collapsed. Ifa divination has survived despite centuries of Christian and Islamic influence, and the *Odu* system represents the unwritten book of Yoruba religious philosophy. It is a system whereby a people without alphabetic writing before the mid-nineteenth century preserved the ingredients of their own culture, philosophy, mythology, and folk medicine.

The Ifa literary corpus consists of 256 chapters or *Odu*. It is believed that each *Odu* contains 600 poems or *ese*. The Ifa priest,.the *babalawo,* commits to memory as many poems as possible from each *Odu* and recites the appropriate ones to his clients whenever they consult him for divination. He first manipulates either the divining chain or the sacred palm nuts to find the signature of an *Odu*. He then chants as many poems as he knows from that *Odu* while his client watches him and follows the plot of each story attentively, waiting to find one which will be relevant to his own problem. At this stage, the client stops the *babalawo,* who then explains the meaning of the poem to his client and prescribes a sacrifice.

The belief of the Ifa priest and his client is that the divinities and the *ori* (inner head) of the client will speak through the *Odu* system in order to solve the problem of the client. In traditional Yoruba society, people consulted Ifa at every important stage in their lives. Such occasions included naming, marriage, and burial ceremonies. They also consulted Ifa when going on journeys. Kings were made by the kingmakers only after consultation with Ifa. Wars were declared only when Ifa agreed that they should be declared; and even on the battlefield, the generals kept their own retinue of Ifa priests who advised them before they made each movement against the enemy.

The elaborate system of Ifa divination requires maintaining an enlightened and well-disciplined priesthood. Hence, the initiation and training of Ifa priests is very demanding, and the preliminary phase takes about ten years to complete. During this period, the novice is taught how to manipulate the instruments of divination, the identification of each *Odu,* and he learns by heart a good number of *ese* (poems) from each. He also learns the sacrifices pertaining to each *ese* and the method of offering the sacrifice so as to make it acceptable to the divinities. The trainee also learns something about herbal medicine. At the end of the training, the would-be priest "enters the forest of Ifa" where he is initiated as a full-fledged Ifa priest. This initiation is naturally based on possession brought about in chanting and dancing. But initiation marks only the beginning of what is actually a lifelong training. Many Ifa priests undergo another period of training which gives them an opportunity to specialize in a branch of Ifa studies, generally medical practice.

The rigorous training of Ifa priests, which usually takes them to several parts of West Africa, makes them the traditional academic elite of Yoruba society. They are the physicians, psychiatrists, historians, and pharmacists of the communities to which they belong. Ifa can therefore be considered as the Yoruba traditional academic system.[7]

The closest divinity to Ifa is Esu, who is also known as Elegbara:

The war lord who can make himself both short and tall,
Tall and short at the same time.

Esu is the mediator: between humans and the *ajogun* (evil forces), between humans and the divinities, and sometimes between the *ajogun* and the divinities. Esu represents the order, justice, peace, and stability without which these three forces cannot coexist. Without Esu there would be chaos, and so his shrine has a conspicuous place in every Yoruba city or village. One of Esu's praise names, which indicates the importance the Yoruba attach to his presence in the community, is "Laalu," a shortened form of Ola-ilu, which means "the honor and glory of the community."

Obatala, the creation divinity, has sometimes been described as the Yoruba archdivinity.[8] His other name, Orisanla (the great òrìsà), reinforces this belief concerning his supremacy among the Yoruba. But the roles of Esu as the keeper of the *ase,* and of Orunmila as the voice of the divinities, are equally, if not more important than Obatala's role of creation.

Some writers have speculated that Obatala probably represents an earlier Yoruba political regime which was overthrown by the Oduduwa dynasty. The annual ceremony of Obatala and his connection with the Ogboni cult have been interpreted to support this theory.[9] The myth of the creation of the earth by Oduduwa when Obatala failed at it because of drunkenness, may have the same symbolic significance. However, it is clear that the Oduduwa dynasty came to rule among the divinities who landed at Ife and their descendants.

After settling at Ife, there were marriages between the male and female divinities. The female divinities were fewer in number than the male, and the male divinities sometimes snatched away the wives of their neighbors. Thus, Ifa took Ore away from her husband Ogun. The offspring of marriages between the male and female divinities later intermarried with human beings. But their descendants being of divine lineage, they are considered *orisa* as well. To the present day, the rulers of Yorubaland are regarded as such descendants, most directly from Oduduwa.

Oduduwa, also known as Olofin, lived at Ife all of his long life. Although he too was sometimes threatened by death, he lived for several hundred years, becoming so old that he looked petrified.

Oduduwa's most important contribution was in the realm of politics, for he was the ancestor of the Yoruba divine rulers.

Tradition does not preserve much about the life of Okanbi, the only son of Oduduwa. His father outlived him. But Okanbi had seven children. Johnson gives the names of these seven children as Olowu, Onipopo, Alaketu, Onisabee, Orangun, Oba-Ibini, and Oran-anyan![10] The most powerful of them was Oran-anyan.

Oran-anyan is remembered today by the elegant stone carving which lies at the present Ile-Ife. This carving, known as *opa Oran-anyan* (the staff of Oran-anyan), is generally believed to have been originally his walking stick. Evidently carved several centuries ago as a memorial to the great Yoruba warrior, it is now one of the most valuable art works of the holy city of Ife.

The most famous of the children of Oran-anyan was Sango. He became so important in Yoruba traditional religion that his cult is now more popular than the cults of Oran-anyan and Oduduwa. He was the fourth Aláàfin of Oyo, the great metropolis founded by his father. It would appear that he lived for a while at a nearby place known as Oko, for oral tradition associates his name constantly with that town. After reigning many years in Oyo, Sango abdicated the throne under mysterious circumstances.

Sango was always a divinity, both as the king of Oyo and after his death. Like his father, he was believed to be a giant among men. Hence he is known as:

Arira, the very tall one
Who was the son of Oran-anyan in the city of Oko.[11]

Sango was a restless, impatient, pugnacious, and greedy man:

When you were hungry,
You consumed seven pots of fried corn.
When you were suffering from pains in the liver,
You drank six pots of *gbegiri* soup.
When you were not at ease,
And not at rest,
You ate one hundred and twenty bitter kola.[12]

Sango shares with Esu some trickster attributes. He is alternately good and bad, kindhearted and callous, generous and mean. But what his devotees admire most in him is his extraordinary physical and magical powers. His physical ability surpassed the powers of all men. When he spoke, fire came out of his mouth. He fought his enemies with thunderstones which he hauled down from the sky during rainstorms. But despite his extraordinary powers, Sango had many enemies and several plots were hatched against him. The following Ifa poem alludes to one such plot which Sango foiled with the use of two hundred stones:

> The Ifa priest named Patambole Okiribiti
> Performed Ifa divination for Arira,
>> the very tall one,
> Who was the son of Oran-anyan in the city of Oko.
> When Sango was in the midst of a plot,
> When Olubambi was amongst enemies,
> He was told to take care of the divinities.
> He was told that it would be good
> If he offered sacrifice.
> After he had offered the prescribed sacrifice,
> He was victorious.
> He said that was exactly
> How his Ifa priests employed their good voices
>> in praise of Ifa.
> The Ifa priest named Patambole Okiribiti,
> Performed Ifa divination for Arira,
>> the very tall one.
> Who was the son of Oran-anyan in the city of Oko.
> When Sango was in the midst of a plot,
> When Olubambi was amongst enemies,
> What did Arira use to conquer his enemies?
> Two hundred stones.
> Two hundred stones
> Were used by Arira to conquer his enemies.
> Two hundred stones.[13]

In another plot against Sango, he was forced to abdicate the capital and move farther north in the direction of the land of the Nupe. He was followed by his favorite wife, Oya. Sango rode on horseback on this last journey of his life. But when he got to the foot of the àáyán tree, he pondered over the shame involved in his abdication and decided to return to his ancestors. He, therefore, like all his predecessors, entered inside the earth's crust and disappeared.

When Oya and other supporters of Sango got to the place, they found only his horse and a long chain with which he had descended beneath the surface of the earth.

Sango is the enemy of thieves, liars, and traitors. In traditional Yoruba society, it was believed that Sango would punish such dangerous elements by throwing down his thunderstones against them. Whenever there is an incident of lightning striking a person or a house, the priests of Sango are called upon to search for the *edun* (thunderstone) which is believed to have caused the lightning. The Sango priests will also tell the victims the nature of the crime they have committed. The offenders will then be presented with a list of the sacrifices they must offer in order that their offence may be forgiven.

One of the most important functions of Sango among the Yoruba is to cleanse society of criminals and to validate the ethical values of honesty and complete fidelity among friends and kinsmen. Perhaps even more important is the maintenance of the authority of the Aláàfin of Oyo. Sango was the most powerful Aláàfin, and subsequent rulers of Oyo have used the Sango cult to extend the power of the Oyo ruling dynasty. The fact that the Aláàfin of Oyo is crowned by the Sango high priest at Koso (the Sango temple) demonstrates the importance of this divinity to the Oyo throne. Sango, Magba (his high priest), and the Aláàfin of Oyo are all saluted with the same royal greeting: *"Kabiyesi."*

The cult of Sango is important among the Yoruba of Brazil and Cuba. In 1968, the high priest of the Sango cult of Bahia, Dasooredas Maximilianos Dos Santos, came to Oyo where he met his counterpart, Chief Eesuola Odejin, and had his title confirmed by the Magba. His mother, from whom he inherited his title, had likewise come to Oyo in 1956 and had her title of Baale Sango confirmed by the Aláàfin of Oyo. An important link is now being forged between the Yoruba traditionalists of West Africa and their kinsmen across the Atlantic.

We have so far been discussing male divinities. But as already mentioned, there are male as well as female divinities in the Yoruba pantheon. The number of female divinities is less than that of their male counterparts. Furthermore, the sex of some divinities is not quite clear. For example, Obatala is sometimes presented as a female divinity.

The best known among the female divinities are the three wives of Sango: Oya (the Goddess of the River Niger), Osun (the Goddess of the Osun River), and Oba (the Goddess of the Oba River). Other important female divinities are Yemoja, Eléékò, and Oge.

Oya was the favorite wife of Sango. She is believed to have come from Ira, a place said to be in Nupe territory. Oya is reputed to be a powerful and ferocious woman. When Sango was the king of Oyo, she was the most important power behind the throne; indeed she was more powerful than her husband.

After the return of Sango to *orun*, the Yoruba believe his wife found no more purpose in life and chose to become the River Niger, which is known to the Yoruba as Odo Oya (the river of Oya). Old Oyo (deserted in the 1830s) where Oya reigned with her husband is less than fifty miles from the banks of the Niger.

Oya is the Yoruba divinity responsible for strong winds. Whenever there is a tornado or a strong wind, the priestesses of Oya are called upon to offer sacrifices so that there may be peace, calm, and quiet once again. Her favorite food is *egbo* (mashed corn).

Oya is the symbol of the power of women and of dignified motherhood. Her image usually shows her carrying a large calabash bowl on the head. The calabash is one of the most useful implements of the astute Yoruba women traders; in the image of Oya it is a symbol of the physical strength of women, of their enterprise and ability to prosper.

Osun is also believed to have been at one time the wife of Sango; later she became the river which bears her name, a major river of Yorubaland. One of the most important Yoruba towns near the Osun river is Osogbo, where the worship of Osun has been for centuries a yearly national festival observed amidst drumming and poetic chants. Osun is primarily associated with *ide* (brass), a valuable metal to the Yoruba. Many of their important art objects, including the iconography of Osun, are cast in brass, and people who use this metal must offer sacrifice to her.

Osun is believed to greatly love children and is the symbol of motherhood. Most of her devotees are mothers, or barren women who worship her in the hope of a cure. The devotees of Osun fondly call her *iỳaà mi* (my mother). Several *ese Ifa* depict Osun as a mother washing her numerous children. Since the Yoruba attach great importance to *ire omo*, the blessing of children, Osun, as a lover of children, reinforces this aspect of the value system.

Another important female divinity, Oge, believed to have come from the city of Igbonna, is worshipped only by barren or once-barren women whom she aided. Her particular symbol is the horn of the *ira* (a wild animal of the horse family). The horn is washed and rubbed with camwood ointment by the supplicant, who carries it on her back chanting to the rhythm of the poetry associated with this divinity. The cult of Oge further indicates the importance of fertility to Yoruba culture. A Yoruba woman's greatest dread is to be barren and this cult provides such unhappy women with a means for poetic creation, devotion, and hope.

We have so far discussed the major Yoruba divinities, those found in almost every dialect area of the culture. But there are hundreds of minor divinities who are peculiar to certain local areas. Space will not permit us to discuss them. Generally, however, the situation is the same as we found in connection with the major divinities. Each *orisa*, whether major or minor, performs certain functions in Yoruba society and perpetuates or validates certain ethical values or beliefs of the Yoruba people.

## PERSONAL DIVINITIES: *ORI* AND *EGUNGUN*

Apart from the major and minor divinities, there is, however, another dimension to the existence of the *orisa* among the Yoruba. Each individual has a personal divinity known as *ori* (literally "head"), the spiritual counterpart of the physical human head, which governs and directs his life, and acts as a link between him and the divinities. Unlike the other divinities who are chosen by the individual here on earth, every person chooses his own *ori* before he leaves *orun* for *aye* to be born. After an individual has been molded by Obatala, he goes to the home of Ajala where he selects an *ori* for himself before he finally sets out on the journey to the earth. But Ajala, the molder of heads in heaven, is believed to be carefree and irresponsible. Since the clay heads of Ajala are bad as well as good, choosing a good or bad *ori* becomes largely a question of chance, but the choice determines the individual's potential for either success or failure in life. However, the *ori*, whether good or bad, represents only a potential, since there are other matters which bear on the outcome.

Since the *ori* is each individual's personal divinity, it follows that whatever the *ori* has not sanctioned cannot be sympathetically considered by the *orisa*. The *ori* is therefore an intermediary between every individual and the divinity whom he worships. The *ori* takes the requests of each individual to the divinities, who in turn present them to Olodumare, the Almighty God. Here again, as in the Yoruba social order, we see a hierarchy of power and authority.

Whether or not the individual has chosen a good *ori*, he must still labor to realize his potential: hence the concept of *ese*. Just as every individual has chosen an *ori*, he also has his own *ese* (literally "legs") with which he will have to struggle in life to aid his *ori* in the realization of his destiny. *Ese* represents the principle of activity and struggle without which even the best *ori* cannot unfold its good potentialities. As for those who have chosen bad *ori*, they have to work harder and struggle more with their *ese* (and, of course, perform more sacrifices) before they can achieve success in life.

Every individual who reaches maturity before dying, and who lived a normal life,[14] becomes an ancestor. He is buried inside the family home[15] and joins the band of the ancestors of his own lineage in *orun*. The ancestor has greater authority than any living being. Furthermore, he becomes a divinity to his own family. Masks and costumes are made for him and he becomes what the Yoruba call *egungun*.

Once every year, each family propitiates its own *egungun* and parades their colorful costumes and art objects throughout the community. This parade is virtually a national ceremony among Yoruba communities. During the annual *egungun* ceremony, barren women, the infirm, and other people with difficult problems offer sacrifices to the ancestors' divinity who then prays for them and assures them that their problems will be solved.

The annual *egungun* ceremony is a dramatization of the lives of the ancestors here on earth. The ceremonies also provide an opportunity for interaction between the living and the dead. The outcome is a regeneration of society under the influence of the heavenly powers who have come down during the ceremonies to visit their children here on earth. The ceremonies therefore emphasize continuity in the traditions of the society and reinforce the values of kinship.

The *egungun* is a divinity in a different sense from the *orisa*. While the *egungun* is a human being who by death becomes a divinity, the *orisa* are divinities by right of birth.

The *egungun* is essentially a benevolent divinity. He is interested in the perpetuation of the ethical values of the society where he once lived. The *egungun* protects his children from the attack of the *aje* (the witches) and the *ajogun* (the malevolent supernatural powers). He also pleads for his children with the *orisa*. The *egungun* can therefore be regarded as another intermediary between man and the *orisa*. Together with the *orisa*, they watch over human society and prevent the "evil" supernatural powers from destroying its ethical values.

EVIL FORCES: *AJE* AND *AJOGUN*

Against the benevolent forces of the divinities and the ancestors, there is a system in Yoruba belief which caters to an opposing force. This counterforce to the powers of the divinities are the *aje* (the witches) and the *ajogun* (literally "warriors against man").

The *aje* are believed to be women who have certain supernatural powers which enable them to fly about at night in the shape of birds and who congregate to deliberate on the ruination of man and his handiwork. The bird form of the witches, the symbol of their power, is known as *eburu*, and the witches themselves are bynamed *eleye* (the "bird people").

> The one who kills and eats human beings all alone.
> Famous one at night.
> The one who eats raw liver without vomiting.

The very short lady,
Who goes about when the marketplace is deserted.

The *aje* are believed to be the implacable enemies of man and his destruction the sole objective of their existence. They kill and eat the children of their victims, and even their own. In fact, it is believed that before a woman is admitted into the *aje* cult she must offer one of her own children to the cult members.

Since the *aje* received their powers directly from Olodumare, it is impossible for humans to combat their menace. Neither pleading nor sacrifice, it is believed, can have any effect on these pitiless witches; one may only point them out and thereby put them to shame.

The word *ajogun* is a collective term used to refer to all the evil things most dreaded by the Yoruba. These include *Iku* (Death), *Arun* (Disease), *Ofo* (Loss), *Egba* (Paralysis), *Oran* (Trouble), *Epe* (Curse), *Ewon* (Imprisonment), and *Ese* (any other type of evil or affliction). All these things are personified in *ese Ifa* as supernatural powers which, like the *aje*, oppose the powers of the divinities and the ancestors.

Like the *aje*, the *ajogun* have a vested interest in the ruination of mankind. The difference between the two evil powers is that while the *aje* are not always affected by sacrifice, the *ajogun* can almost invariably be propitiated. Once the *ajogun* have accepted sacrifice, they leave a human being untouched. Esu is the divinity who acts as a middleman between humans and the *ajogun* (as he does between humans and the divinities). Indeed, the *ajogun* are sometimes regarded as the "errand boys" of Esu. Since Esu punishes anyone who does not perform sacrifice, and since he acts as the universal policeman of Olodumare, one can easily see why he will use the *ajogun* against human transgressors. Hence, the *ajogun* can be regarded as Esu's police force, punishing offenders against the divine will.

There is a point, however, where the interests of Esu and the *ajogun* begin to diverge. Esu will not molest any human who abides by the accepted values of society and who also performs sacrifice. The *ajogun,* however, will attack anyone (whether or not he has violated the divine rules) whom they have marked out as a prey for their evil ends. This means that the *ajogun* can act independently of Esu, but even in such a case, once the individual involved has performed sacrifice, Esu will quickly come to his aid and ward off the *ajogun*. Esu has complete power to punish the *ajogun* should they disobey his orders.

## THE CONCEPT OF *EBO*

The Yoruba believe that *ebo* (sacrifice) is an important human obligation. In the first place, *ebo* is regarded as food for the divinities, so normally the offering would be of a food that the particular divinity favors.[16] The divinities are propitiated in this way at least once a week. In addition, there is a festival held for each divinity every year, during which a larger offering is made. The ancestors are propitiated every day with the little bits of food which are thrown on the floor for the *ara-ile* (the people of the inside of the earth) during every meal. During the annual *egungun* festival, everyone propitiates his own ancestors with a larger food offering.

Secondly, *ebo* rewards the divinities for their constant watch over the community. Therefore, whenever anyone consults the divinities for help through the Ifa divination system (or any other form of divination),[17] he must offer sacrifice to the divinities. The Ifa literary corpus condemns people who, after enjoying the benefits of the counsel of the divinities offered during divination, refuse to fulfill their own obligation concerning the offering of sacrifice. Such people are open to the attack of the *ajogun* and the punishment of the divinities.

Thirdly, *ebo* is regarded as a means whereby one may repair the inherent defects of one's *ori*. In fact, the only hope for those people who chose bad *ori* from *orun* is to offer much sacrifice in addition to working hard as must everyone.

In the fourth place, *ebo* is a means of making up for one's mistakes as one goes along in life. While the Yoruba do not have the concept of eternal damnation, they regard any violation of the social and divine order as sin *(ese),* which may be expiated by the performance of sacrifice that reconciles the individual once again with the divinities and the ancestors.

Fifthly, *ebo* is food for the *ajogun*, who are the implacable enemies of man. Once sacrifice has been offered, the *ajogun* will leave the individual untouched. Ifa divination poetry therefore states that *ebo* is a form of exchange. When we perform sacrifice, we are using the sacrificial items in exchange for our own lives. When the *ajogun* accept the sacrifice, they will release their human victim.

Finally, *ebo* is also regarded as food for one's own friends, neighbors, and kinsmen. In other words, sacrifice is not meant for the divinities alone. The occasion of the offering of sacrifice provides the community with an opportunity to renew the bonds of kinship among the living and also with the ancestors. One *ese Ifa* makes the astonishing statement that the essence of sacrifice is to feed the mouths of fellow human beings.

> What do we worship at Ife?
> Their mouths.
> Their mouths is what we worship at Ife.
> Their mouths.
> I gave to the calabash,
> I gave to the plate.
> Their mouths.
> Their mouths can no longer fight against me.
> Their mouths.
> I gave to people inside the house.
> I gave to those on the road.
> Their mouths.
> Their mouths can no longer fight against me.
> Their mouths.[18]

## THE CONCEPT OF *IWA*

The Yoruba believe that sacrifice, a good *ori*, and continuous struggle by means of *ese* are not enough to guarantee a good life. *Iwa* (good character) is needed to achieve dignity, purpose, and meaning in life. Any person who lacks *iwa* is regarded as a failure. Furthermore, *iwa* is demanded of everyone by the divinities. Indeed, for the Yoruba, good character is regarded as the essence of religion, since it is the sum total of the ethical values for which the divinities stand.

But what do the Yoruba regard as good or bad character? The

following lists are a partial indication:

### GOOD CHARACTER

*Iteriba* (respect for authority)
*Inurere* (good thoughts toward others)
*Idarijin* (forgiveness)
*Iranlowo* (helping others)
*Ikonimora* (love or toleration of others)

### BAD CHARACTER

*Ole-jija* (stealing)
*Ile-dida* (treachery)
*Okanjua* (covetousness)
*Iro* (lying)
*Ibinu* (anger)

One of the most important aspects of good character is respect for authority, whether it be that of the elders, the ancestors, and the divinities, or that of administrative or political bodies. In a hierarchical social system dominated largely by the elders and the divine rulers, respect for elders is necessary in order to maintain stability. It is the belief of the Yoruba that if one does not respect the elderly or other persons in positions of authority here on earth, one will have neither faith in nor respect for the divinities. Furthermore, any person in authority can make life so difficult for a disobedient person that the wishes of *ori* and the design of the divinities for that individual will fail to materialize. This is the meaning of the following saying which holds that any person who is in a position over another is also in a position of authority over one's own divinity as far as earthly power is concerned:

The person who is greater than one
Is greater than the Ifa worshipped in
      one's household.

The Yoruba also believe that there must be complete trust and faith between people in any relationship of intimacy or kinship. The divinities, and especially the ancestors, are interested in this for the

239

survival of the culture and its lineage system. Thus, the Yoruba frown at *ile-dida* (acts of treachery). In traditional Yoruba society, a traitor is put on the same level as a thief and any other disturber of the social system. Ile (the earth) herself punishes those who betray their friends, while *alajobi* (the ancestors) kill those who betray their kinsmen.

## THE CONCEPT OF *IRE*

A discussion of Yoruba traditional religion would not be complete without going into the Yoruba system of values. What are the elements of this system apart from the moral values partly covered under *iwa*? The things that are most valuable to the Yoruba as elements of the good or successful life are collectively known as *ire*. The most important of them are *owo* (money), *omo* (child or children), *àlàáfià* (good health), and *aiku* (long life).

One may wonder how Yoruba society which was, and still is, predominantly agricultural, gives such importance to money. The answer is that although Yoruba society was agricultural in terms of the occupation of many people, the Yoruba have lived for centuries in large cities, where in particular they have needed a ready means of exchange, in the form of money.

To the Yoruba, money is important because without it one cannot take care of one's children and one's health. Having children is fundamental; it is one of the most important things for which we are created by the Almighty Being, and, of course, the divinities and the ancestors are interested in the continuity and survival of society.

But the most important of the *ire* is *aiku* (good health and long life), because without good health one can neither have money nor be able to take care of one's children. Good health helps one to live a happy life. Longevity gives one the opportunity to become an elder of the community and thereby to enjoy the respect and honor due to the elders. What is more, if one dies very young, one cannot become an ancestor, which means that one cannot by death move into a status of greater authority. Therefore, the benefits of *aiku* even go beyond this life. This is the reason why long life is regarded as the most important of the *ire* and is described as "the blessing of long life, which is the greatest accomplishment of life."

Ifa divination poetry is full of reference to the three *ire*: the Ifa corpus explains to us that anyone who keeps to the divine will and does not disturb the social order will be blessed with the three *ire*, whereas those who disobey the divinities and the ancestors will lack them. The *ire*, therefore, are essentially an individual's reward for his obedience to the divinities. It can therefore be said that one worships the divinities so that one's life may be clothed with the *ire*, which alone can ensure a meaningful and pleasurable life here on earth and continued existence in the other world in the form of a grand and authoritative ancestor.

[1] Incorporating material from the author's oral presentation and the following discussion, and an interview between the author and Francesco Pellizzi.

[2] *Encyclopaedia Britannica*, 1973 ed., s.v. "Yoruba."

[3] Cf. Frank Willet, *Ife in the History of West African Sculpture* (London: Thames & Hudson, 1967).

[4] Wande Abimbola, *Ijinle Ohun Enu Ifa, Apa Keji* (Collins: Glasgow, 1969), p. 76.

[5] Collected from Chief Lamidi Ogundiya Abimbola, the Asipade of Akeètàn (Oyo, August 1972).

[6] *Ijala* is the poetry of hunters chanted in praise of *Ogun* and the brave hunters of today and yesterday.

[7] Cf. Wande Abimbola, "Ifa As A Body of Knowledge and as an Academic Discipline," *Lagos Notes and Records* (2/2, 1968).

[8] See Idowu, *Olodumare, God in Yoruba Belief* (London: Longman, 1963).

[9] Cf. Joel Adedeji, "Folklore and Yoruba Drama: Obatala as a Case Study" in R. M. Dorson, *African Folklore* (Doubleday, 1972) pp. 321-347, wherein the author proposes that the annual ceremony of Obatala is a symbolic dramatization of the overthrow of his dynasty.

[10] S. Johnson, *History of the Yoruba* (London: Routledge, 1921).

[11] Abimbola, *Ijinle Ohun Enu Ifa, Apa Kerin*, pp. 55-6.

[12] Collected from Madam Ogunboade, Ile Onisa Akeetan, Oyo, 1971.

[13] Abimbola, *Ijinle Ohun Enu Ifa, Apa Kiini*, pp. 88-9.

[14] For example, those burnt by fire, the albino, the leper and those who drowned are not buried inside the family house and may not therefore become ancestors.

[15] The Yoruba bury their dead (except for those mentioned above) inside their

own homes. The graves of the dead ancestors therefore become shrines to the whole family.

[16]It is believed that if the offering is of food that the divinity dislikes, he or she becomes enraged and may kill or maim the person responsible for the unfriendly act. Thus, if one wants Esu to harm one's enemy, one may offer, in the latter's name, unfavored food to Esu.

[17]*Ifa* divination is not the only form of divination among the Yoruba but it is by far the most important.

[18]Abimbola, *Ijinle Ohun Enu Ifa, Apa Kiini*, pp. 74-5.

# Contemplation through Actions:
# North American Indians

## Joseph Epes Brown

What we refer to as religion cannot, in the case of the American Indian, be separated from the forms and dynamics of everyday life, or from almost any facet of the total culture; nor as we shall see more clearly, may there be separation from the phenomena of the natural environment. This situation is typical of those religious traditions which still remain close to their primal origins, and which have subsisted at a technological level that does not allow alienation from the environment. One cannot therefore find in these cultures the kinds of systematic theological structures which have become central to most of the historical religions. We could distill out and formulate in our terms such structures, since they are latently there, but the people themselves do not overtly make such abstractions from life and experienced reality. Religious concepts and values, then, are given substance through the direct visual or pictorial image, through the "symbol," which includes the auditory word or "echo," all of which have reference always to the forms and forces, the voices of Nature.

Take the Sun Dance festival on the Crow Indian reservation. This is a ceremonial that lasts three or four days. It is celebrated around a central tree, a special tree, which is considered to be the axis of the universe. It is considered the *very center of the world*. For three or four days, the participants focus, in a ritual manner and through a simple dance form, on this axis, on this center. It is an extraordinarily powerful support for contemplation or for meditation which might lead to contemplation. These still-living rites are intensified by sacrificial acts and by the fact that for the entire period of three or four days the participants go without eating or drinking.

A further barrier to our understanding of primitive traditions may be seen in the fact that within the context of the historical and generally monotheistic religions, only two mutually exclusive theistic possibilities seem to be affirmed. That is, religions are *either* monotheistic or polytheistic, and generally monotheism has been taken as the sign of advancement in civilization. Primitive religions, however, and specifically here the American Indian traditions, do not fit into either one of these categories. Rather, these traditions represent a form of theism wherein concepts of both monotheism and polytheism intermingle and fuse without being confused. Belief in a single unitary God, therefore, does not conflict with, nor exclude, the possibility of belief also in a multiplicity of gods or "spirits." Among the western Lakota and eastern Dakota of the Plains, for example, the term *Wakan-Tanka,* the Great Spirit, or Great Mystery, is an all-inclusive concept which refers both to a Supreme Being and to the totality of all the gods or spirits or powers of creation. Such conceptualizations embracing both unity and diversity are typical of the polysynthetic nature of the languages of these peoples, and thus of their modes of conceptualization and cognitive orientations. A man such as Black Elk, therefore, was able to affirm: "Wakan-Tanka, you are everything, and yet above everything." Abundant recorded materials make it evident beyond any doubt that this type of ultimate affirmation of a Supreme Being was held before the coming of the white man and the Christian missionary, not only among the Lakota, but among most, if not all, American Indian peoples. The contemporary Navajo artist Carl Gorman, speaking from a culture very different from that of the Plains peoples, has recently written:

> It has been said by some researchers into Navajo religion, that we have no Supreme God, because He is not named. This is not so. The Supreme Being is not named because He is unknowable. He is simply the Unknown Power. We worship him through His Creation. We feel too insignificant to approach directly in prayer that Great Power that is incomprehensible to man. Nature feeds our soul's inspiration and so we approach Him through that part of Him which is close to us and within the reach of human understanding. We believe that this great unknown power is everywhere in His creation. The various forms of creation have some of this spirit within them . . . . As every form has some of the intelligent spirit of the Creator, we cannot but reverence all parts of the creation.

244

The implications of this type of primitive religion are far reaching and have relevance to certain theological and existential problems of the historical religions. The one problem which particularly concerns us here is the absence today commonly within the historical religions of an adequate metaphysic of nature. Specifically in the Judeo-Christian tradition, such a metaphysic was certainly present in its origins but is now in oblivion. Such neglect has left the way open, as we currently have seen in an abundance of tragic examples, to abuses of the natural environment.

Unlike the conceptual categories of Western man, American Indian traditions generally do not fragmentize experience into mutually exclusive kinds of dichotomies, but tend rather to stress modes of interrelatedness across categories of meaning, never losing sight of an ultimate wholeness. Our animate-inanimate dichotomy, or our categories of animal, vegetable, and mineral, for example, have no meaning for the Indian who sees that all that exists is animate, each form in its own special way, so that even rocks have a life of their own and are believed to be able to talk under certain conditions. Creatures we relegate to the category "animal" or "bird" and consider inferior to man, the Indian refers to as "peoples" who, in a sense, have a recognized superiority to man. It is generally believed that in the order of creation they were here before man, and in these cultures what is anterior in time has a certain superiority over that which comes later. (It is this belief that accounts for the enormous respect shown to the aged among native American peoples.)

This mode of interrelatedness may be seen in the Lakota's discernment of a certain unity underlying that which we perceive generally as very different kinds of beings or phenomena. For example, spiders, the elk, a bison, birds, flying insects, and even a cottonwood tree have a unifying element, for all these manifest certain relationships to the wind or breath.[2] There is in fact a qualitative and comprehensive science of the winds among these peoples which has as its ultimate unifying principle the understanding that as the wind moves, or exerts power over, the forms of nature, and yet in itself is unseen, so it is with the Great Spirit whose unseen presence gives life and movement to all that is. Such

245

modes of conceptualization are often conveyed through mythical expressions which anthropomorphize the four winds, naming them as brothers identified with the four directions of space, each with his own particular qualities or forces, but ultimately the four brothers are seen to be the sons of a single named father figure. There are, of course, other members of this particular family of unlikely associates unified by the wind or breath as principle. Always, however, such configurations are expressed in terms of directly experienced natural phenomena.

In relation to many of the points expressed above, it is important to note that the generally understood meaning of the symbol, as a form which stands for, or points to, something other than the particular form or expression, is incomprehensible to the Indian. For the Indian's cognitive orientation, meanings generally are intuitively sensed and not secondarily interpreted through analysis; there tends to be a unity between form and idea or content. Here the "symbol" is, in a sense, that to which it refers. The tree at the center of the Sun Dance lodge, then, does not just represent the axis of the world, but *is* that axis and *is* the center of the world. The eagle is not a symbol of the sun, but is the sun in a certain sense; and similarly, the sun is not a symbol of the Creative Principle, but is that Principle as manifested in the sun. When a Navajo singer executes a sand painting of one of the gods, or *Yéi,* the painting does not represent the god, but the god is really present there and irradiates towards all participants at the ceremony his particular grace or power.

It is not that these concepts of the symbol, or of mythic time, are in real contrast to the same concepts of the "historical" religions. The contrast rather is between traditional people generally and modern man who attempts to live in a desacralized world, and who governs his life through the artificial segments of "clock-time," through lineal projections rather than circular. If the American Indian traditions speak to us with special force today, it is partly due to the reactions of many against the fragmented quality of our own society. Indian traditions, and of course other "exotic" outside traditions, appear to be more total and less hypocritical; they seem to represent a gratifyingly integrated and intense participation across a very wide spectrum of experiences. It is noted that aspects of the Indian's world do not become sacralized only within the context of special liturgical occasions, although obviously there are always special occasions where intensity is generated, but rather, and as is generally the case with peoples close to their primal sources, it is the total world of experience that is seen as being infused with the sacred.

Given the above considerations, it should now be clear that if we are to speak with greater precision about modes of contemplation and action for American Indians it will be necessary to examine in detail, and through more specific examples, their modes of understanding their natural environment, and the quality of their structured relationship to specific forms.

It may be said that with the American Indians we are dealing ultimately with a quality of cultures wherein action and contemplation are interrelated and integrated. Or, if we wish to make a sharper distinction between meditation and contemplation, it may be said that special ritual and ceremonial acts, as well as the actions of everyday life, constitute meditative acts which open, to the exceptional person at least, possibilities for pure contemplation. A man who is a hunter, for example, is not just participating in a purely mechanical subsistence activity, but is engaged in a complex of meditative acts, in which all aspects of his activity, whether they be preparatory prayer and purification, pursuit of the quarry, or the sacramental manner by which the animal is slain and subsequently treated, are infused with the sacred. Not all men perhaps, but a person such as a Black Elk was thus able to describe the act of hunting as being—not representing—life's quest for ultimate truth. Hunting is a quest, he insisted, which requires preparatory prayer and sacrificial purification; the diligently followed tracks are signs or intimations of the goal, and final contact or identity with the quarry is the realization of Truth, the ultimate goal of life. Similar examples of hunting as a meditative rite could be presented from the Southwestern peoples, and Frank Speck has found the same attitudes among the Naskapi, hunters of the Labrador peninsula.

Similar kinds of meditative or contemplative attitudes are present over a vast range of other activities. The southwestern Pima or Papago, or any of the basket-making peoples, perceived in their acts of gathering grasses and vegetable dyes, and in the weaving process itself, the ritual recapitulation of the total process of creation. The completed basket is the universe in an image; and in the manufacturing process the woman actually plays the part of the Creator. Similarly, in establishing the dynamic interrelationship between the vertical warp and the horizontal weft, the Navajo blanket weaver participates in acts which are in imitation of the creation of the universe itself. It may be, as indicated above, that the practitioner of such kinds of traditional crafts will not be able to analyze or interpret consciously such "symbolism"; nevertheless, through the force of myth and oral traditions, such values are intuitively sensed and participated in with the total being and not just with the mind.

When a Plains Indian woman decorates a robe with porcupine quills, she is not just involved in making a useful object aesthetically pleasing, but as a member of a women's quillwork "guild" she is obliged to fast and pray before commencing her work, and she must retain a contemplative attitude as she works with the brightly dyed quills. Because of the formal and initiatory nature of the quillworker's guild to which she belongs, the woman will probably be aware of the identity made by the people between the porcupine and the sun, and that the sun is a manifestation of the Creative Principle. The quills, therefore, which she is laying on in geometrical patterns established by tradition, are really rays of the sun and thus eminently sacred. The quillworker has, as it were, trapped the sun, understood as a spiritual principle, upon a garment now of utilitarian, aesthetic, and spiritual value. These are values which are real and operative both to the maker and the wearer of the garment. Neither art nor what we call religion are here divorced from each other or from life.

Similar modes of spiritual conceptualization are involved in the making of dwellings and ceremonial structures, whether it be the teepee, the domed sweat lodge, or the Sun Dance lodge of the Plains; whether it be the round or octagonal hogan of the Navajo, or wickiup of the Apache, or the long houses of woodland peoples such as the Iroquois or Menomomini. All such dwellings are created in imitation of the process of the creation of the world itself, and all such structures are conceived as sacred.

Such dwellings also serve as supports for meditation. The Plains teepee is a house form which is a model of the universe. Its circular ground plan represents the world or, microcosmically, man himself. The fire at the center of this world is the presence of the Great Spirit at the heart of man himself. Living with such a form, I assert, makes it almost impossible to forget this transcendent dimension to life.

Dome-shaped lodges are still used today in which red-hot rocks are placed so that man may purify himself not only physically but also mentally and spiritually. In this rite, the lodge itself is the world, conceived as a world of obscurity from which man should purify himself. It is believed that after the ceremonies of purification, in this dark lodge of the world, man should go forth into the light of day, into the light of wisdom. He should undergo a rebirth, as it were. He is a new person as he goes out of that lodge and plunges into the cold waters of a nearby river. There lies behind these forms a transcendent quality of wisdom, the vertical dimension.

In any one group, all of its ceremonies involved three stages. And these three stages, each of which is dependent upon the preceding one, are: purification (there are forms and ceremonies which then lead the individual to realize an expansion, an identity, as it were, with the universe itself); supporting rites for self-expression; and ritual acts, which lead ultimately to what one might call identity, a state of unity with that Great Mystery underlying all the forms of creation. Purification, expansion, and identity are the three stages, and I would say that where a tradition possesses these qualities it is an authentic tradition. It possesses the means by which man may attain a true spiritual realization.

A multitude of similar types of meditative acts with their supporting forms could be presented across the great diversity of cultures and in relation to a vast range of expressions and activities. A rich array of major rites and ceremonies of special intensity could similarly be presented for these many groups: examples are the synthetic and profound spiritual meanings expressed in the rites of the sacred pipe, or the elaborate four-day communal and sacrificial rites of the Sun Dance in the Plains; another is the seven- or nine-day Navajo ceremonies for reestablishing the health of a person who has become ill through being in a state of disharmony with the universe. One should also describe the core spiritual dimensions to the complex initiatory rites, such as the *midiwiwin,* for many of the Woodland peoples. There is, however, one additional mode of participation in the sacred which should be cited, for it is a foundation to all that has been presented above, and it brings us perhaps closest to the heart of these cultures. I am referring to the retreat or "vision quest" which, in the extent of participation by the people generally, gives to these cultures a spiritual dimension of special intensity.

It is through the vision quest, participated in with physical sacrifice and the utmost humility, that the individual opens himself in the most direct manner to contact with the spiritual essences underlying the forms of the manifested world. It is in the states achieved at this level that meditation may be surpassed by contemplation. Thus Black Elk has said that the greatest power above all in the retreat is contact with silence, ". . . for is not silence the very voice of the Great Spirit?" In certain cultures this retreat is initiatory in character for the young men or occasionally for young girls, who seek spiritual sanction for a new and sacred name which should come to them; in the Arctic, or among some southwestern peoples this retreat is participated in only by those who seek the necessary spiritual power for becoming special religious practition-ers, a shaman, a "medicine man," or a "singer," the term used by the Navajo and the Apache. Among many groups the retreat was specifically associated with the quest for a "guardian spirit," although this is not as general a phenomenon as the vision quest in itself. Among the Plains people the vision quest was most intensely developed; it was an activity that was expected of every young man, and frequently of every young woman, participated in not just once at a certain time in his or her life, but indeed with frequency throughout the life of the individual. No person in these societies, it was believed, could have success in any of the activities of the culture without the special spiritual power received through the quest. It was this special development in the Plains that led Robert Lowie to refer to the trait as "democratized shamanism."

The minimal formal elements of the retreat involved the guidance of a spiritual mentor, preliminary rites of purification, the seeking out of an isolated place, usually on a mountain top, and the observance of a total fast. At the place of the retreat, special patterns for the participant's actions, and often special forms of prayer, were indicated to the supplicant by his mentor. Essentially, the person was to expose himself, normally for four days and nights, to the elements and to the forms and forces of nature; he should be attentive to whatever might appear to him, no matter how insignificant the being or phenomenon might seem to be. If a dream should come to the participant while asleep, this too could be of import. Although the dream was considered to be of lesser power, or as auxiliary to the true vision, nevertheless the person should be attentive to such experiences and should be able to relate them to his guide, who might explain their spiritual implications. Indeed, many of Black Elk's dreams seemed to be very close to the vision experience. I recall one such power dream which he recounted to me: "I was taken away from this world into a vast teepee, which seemed to be as large as the world itself, and painted on the inside were every kind of four-legged being, winged being, and all the crawling peoples. These peoples who were there in that lodge, they talked to me, just as I am talking to you."

Not all who sought, or "lamented" for, a vision received the experience. When the experience did come, however, it was in the form of some being, one of the birds or animals, or of the powers and phenomena of the natural world; usually the being spoke to the supplicant, giving a message revealing some aspect of wisdom which that form manifested or possessed. The supplicant, it was believed, thus established an identity, not just with the form in itself, but with the spiritual essence of the form which conveyed a specific quality of spiritual power. Gradations of such powers were recognized in accord with the nature of the experience and the type of being which appeared. Frequently, the animal or bird might become the individual's "guardian spirit," which would protect him in the events of his life; it might instruct him in specific virtues, or convey skills and qualities of special importance to the activities of the society. Spiritual powers could be accumulated through the frequency of such vision experiences, and thus always the great leaders of the community were pointed to as persons who had received powers through many visions. Without the vision a man was considered to be a nobody and could be successful in nothing. Something of this power received by the individual was communicated to the people generally, not only through the special quality of personality of the individual concerned, but also by his being required to publicly externalize the experience through a special dance, in the sacred songs received, or through the paintings which he made on his shield or garment. Also, to insure the continuing activation of the vision power within the individual, some part of the animal would be taken and worn on his person, or kept carefully wrapped in a special bundle. Occasionally such bundles could be acquired by others to whom a vision had never come, for it was believed that the spiritual power, once manifested to a particular person, was then operative in and by itself, so long as certain prescribed requirements for the keeping of the bundle were met.

In summary, it may be said that within the context of American Indian cultures the vision experience served in an especially forceful manner to render transparent to the individual some facet of the phenomenal world, revealing aspects of a spiritual world of greater reality underlying this world of appearances. It is in and through such qualities of experience that, consciously or not, those barriers are dissolved which have tended to set apart what in experience is seemingly an "outer world"; the vision experience, then, integrates and interrelates these "inner" and "outer" worlds into one experience. The life of Black Elk has revealed this process to us with special clarity. The beings, or whatever might be involved in the vision, serve as intermediaries revealing aspects of reality through which the ultimate reality of the Great Mystery (*Wakan-Tanka*) may be contemplated, if not comprehended. The ray of the sun, in this sense, is none other than the Sun itself.

Understood in its total context, we have here a type of religion, with its specific modes of spiritual realization, in which there is procession in a circular continuum through the domains of action, meditation, and contemplation leading again to action. It is the mysteries of the natural world which provide all of the spiritual means:

> We should understand well that all things are the works of the Great Spirit. We should know that He is within all things: the trees, the grasses, the rivers, the mountains, and the four-legged animals, and the winged peoples; and even more important, we should understand that He is also above all these things and peoples. When we do understand all this deeply in our hearts, then we will fear, and love, and know the Great Spirit, and then we will be and act and live as He intends.[3]

— Black Elk

[1]Carl N. Gorman, "Navajo Vision of Earth and Man", *The Indian Historian* (Winter, 1973).

[2]Spiders, newly hatched, are carried on long filaments by the winds; the mysterious whistling call of the bull elk, through the use of his breath, attracts the cows to him; a bison cow, breathing over her calf in a cold winter, can enclose the young animal in a protective film-like sac; birds and insects with their wings utilize and exercise control over the winds; and through the winds a cottonwood tree in season sends out its seed wrapped in "cotton."

[3]Joseph Epes Brown, *The Sacred Pipe* (Norman, Oklahoma: University of Oklahoma, 1953), p. xx.

# Last-Minute Reflections

Among problems discussed at the Colloquium, the one that arose most often was that of the authenticity of existing spiritual ways and religions. Leo Schaya spoke to the matter: "Please allow me to draw my personal conclusion on the subject of our Colloquium in the light of the Jewish tradition according to which, at the end of time, the Prophet Elias will return to earth. He will raise his voice to announce peace, and he will raise it so loudly that he will be heard from one end of the world to the other. In the Bible God says, through the mouth of the Prophet Malachi, 'Behold, I will send you Elijah [Elias] the prophet before the great and terrible day of the Lord comes. And he will turn the hearts of fathers to their children and the hearts of children to their fathers . . .' (Mal. 4:5-6).

"Now according to this verse from the Scriptures, this descent towards the end of time of the Eliatic teaching and influence will be general; it will take place through all the 'fathers', all the authentic and living traditions. Elias will raise his voice so loudly that he will be heard to the ends of the earth. He will proclaim the peace of all religions, he will proclaim their essential and transcendental unity and truth, which at the final advent of the Messiah will be revealed in an immanent, new, and universal form.

"In fact, Elias, apart from his person, signifies a function which can be incorporated in several persons. This is what is referred to, for instance, in the Gospel where Christ designates John the Baptist as Elias, and where, after the beheading of St. John, he speaks again of Elias who is to come. Thus Christianity shares this tradition with Judaism and at the same time extends the function of the esoteric, invisible master, to include the role of St. John the Apostle who is to live secretly until the end of the world. The Eliatic function appears likewise in Islam in the guise of al-Khidr, secretly and everlastingly living, and of al-Mahdi who is to come in order to make ready the Messianic kingdom. Elsewhere the Qur'an testifies to a certain superiority of al-Khidr over Moses, as does Judaism itself, when affirming that the whole of Moses' Torah will represent but a single line of the sacred book that Elias will bring to the world."

Nevin Danner of Indiana University appealed to the Colloquium to be tolerant of those who are confused in their search for fulfilment: "As a minister at a Midwestern campus, I have a sense of urgency which comes from being very close to persons in all sorts of movements and cultural and religious crosscurrents. Their sense of anxiety and haste has infected me. They are my companions, and I should first like to commend to you the pseudoreligionists, the radicals, and the protesters. These persons are neither your friends nor your enemies, at the moment. In fact, there is a degree of fear and awe among them for your traditions. But they do not know you as persons. As for the God about whom you speak so much, they are not yet ready to trust Him, or the organizations which represent Him, as the true channels for justice, peace, and love which could transform their human longing and potentials into ecstasy.

"They, like you, are aware that they live in a strange era of history that is at the same time post-Freudian, post-Darwinian, post-Marxist and post-technological. They, too, seek some passage to the East for a new existence and a new history. They are suspicious, as you are, of the pseudo-existence and the uncertain direction of the cultural and political leaders of this era. They have experienced, and more intensely perhaps than you, the semi-apocalypse of present existence and they dread, because they are young, the meta-apocalypse immediately ahead.

"Those for whom I speak have some answers, some questions, some experiences, and some demands to share with you. Their quest in many ways is parallel to yours. They have much to give and much to receive.

"These wanderers and seekers now need your encouragement, judgment and, most importantly, your companionship. Do not dismiss them until you know them."

Raimundo Panikkar expressed his apprehensions concerning the establishment of criteria of orthodoxy and heterodoxy, saying: "I think that we have already achieved a certain harmony and depth, so as to be able to formulate positions which need further study. But I would like to say that I have still a certain difficulty in adopting only these criteria. I feel that history is on my side to prove that, even within the particular traditions, reforms and movements which began as a rupture and which are considered heretical and even apostatic, afterwards have been recuperated into those very traditions. This leads me to the unavoidable problem of interpretation, and here is one problem to which the modern world addresses itself with great accuracy. At the same time it has not yet found any real solutions. I would like only to point to the problem of interpretation within one particular tradition.

"Here I should like to introduce another impalatable, intangible element which can only be determined a posteriori and never a priori, the factor of time as an intrinsic and constitutive element in judging the criteria of an orthodoxy within a tradition. This implies that at a certain moment we may have to admit that we do not have the tools to say whether a certain phenomenon is heretical or not, and this is a distressing problem."

A. K. Saran reacted to some varying opinions on the debated issue of the criteria for orthodoxy in tradition by saying: "I think that the criteria for deciding between true and false traditions and between true and false prophets cannot be laid down logically or dialectically because any such set of criteria has to come from within each particular tradition. . . . Therefore I would suggest that this should be regarded as a matter of faith. . . . It is only if men of discernment are there, and there is faith in them, that we can distinguish between the true and the false. Particularly in this context we cannot lay down criteria, and yet we need a criterion to distinguish between truth and error. If we were to say that everything was well, we should be allocating to ourselves a position that could only be taken by the perfectly enlightened ones. Only at that level does the distinction between true and false cease. That is why we cannot wait until history decides which of the current movements, which of the heterodoxies of today will be regarded as orthodoxies tomorrow and be integrated within tradition, and which will be rejected. History does this for us. But my point is, can we wait until history does it? We are confronted with this question *here and now;* we should be able here and now to steer clear of false trails and stick to the correct path.

"My plea is that while we cannot tackle the question of laying down the criteria as a logical or a philosophical matter with a rational solution, this should not lead us into the fallacious belief that there is no need to distinguish the true from the erroneous or the false."

Joseph Epes Brown, afraid that a misunderstanding might arise concerning American Indian and African religious traditions, felt compelled to clarify the situation: "There is one area that I think needs further clarification, for there has arisen what might be an unfortunate kind of dichotomy. It was mentioned that there are the great traditions and the small traditions. As I recall, size here was possibly a question of geography.

"I do not think that this statement was intended to create a dichotomy, but it does raise the question of the standing of those traditions which have commonly been called 'primitive'. I would like to suggest that possibly we could establish the distinction between the historical religions and what we could call the tribal religions without suggesting any kind of value judgment. The traditions of Africa have very often been referred to as primitive or tribal. But there are, in Africa, great traditions that are associated with great civilizations, traditions which are extremely sophisticated and rich. We have not usually spoken of them as historical traditions because their character as such has been obscured through the forces of history, or they have been totally misunderstood or misinterpreted under the spirit of colonialism. So I would like to extend Leo Schaya's excellent statement to the tribal religions, the American Indian religions, for example. In fact, as in Africa, many of these traditions are not exactly in the category of what one would call tribal. There are traditions here that are associated with civilizations occupying vast areas, such as the Inca.

"I would like to emphasize that whether they are tribal or not, represented by small groups or in a limited physical space or not, they should be acknowledged as providing legitimate life ways and attached in every aspect to transcendent principles."

Lobsang Lhalungpa offered this concluding statement: "Our contribution to the promotion of tradition will be truly exemplary and inspiring if we continue to strive unceasingly toward enlarging our knowledge and understanding of other traditions, and also toward responding more positively to the growing thirst among many for real life.

"Finally, I wish to say that each tradition is complete in itself, yet each can discover its own values through understanding of other traditions. I would relate an ancient Buddhist story which illustrates this point and strikes a note of warning to us all.

"Once a follower asked the third Buddha to interpret his dream. He had dreamt that there were elephants trying to push through small holes in a big wall, but, astonishingly, after having done so they found themselves trapped in the holes by their tails, which they could not pull out completely. 'This', said the Buddha, 'is the self-attachment of the religious tradition.'

"The message of this Colloquium that we may carry away with us in our heart should include this vital point. Let us not only discern everything that takes place in the name of tradition anywhere, but also ponder deeply whether we or the traditions have failed, or are beginning to fail, in giving service to humanity."

Finally, the harmony and graciousness which prevailed throughout the week of meetings at the Rothko Chapel were beautifully evoked by André Scrima: "When two people really meet, when the encounter really takes place, an 'angel' (i.e., a more 'divine' face added to human face-to-face) is born in heaven. When afterwards, people fail to generate from this encounter a creative joy, a creative research, and a way for enlightenment and truth, the angel, or the angels, starve and even die. I do not want to count the angels that have been born in heaven during the period of our Colloquium, for statistics have no place in the realm of quality, but let us take care not to slay them."

*Yusuf Ibish*

# Afterword

While each Colloquist's contribution to this book stands by itself, taken in its entirety the volume properly inaugurates a genre which is more than, say, the learned illustration of pragmatic ecumenism: it is the fruit of an exceptional encounter of world religions at the esoteric level. It not only brings into focus a huge amount of first-hand information otherwise scattered throughout scholarly periodicals, but also carries the ecumenical dialogue to a level of depth and essentiality, of sympathetic communication, and of tolerance unprecedented in events and writings of this kind.

Nobody chose to ignore the deep-seated differences between traditions; on the contrary, all the authors seemed acutely aware of the irreducible originality of each tradition. But while the main endeavor of the representatives of various religions was to situate each mystical discipline within its traditional ground, and also to exhibit the "flowers of action" that stem from this rerooting, they all became aware of a sacredness presiding over this enterprise, a result that far transcended what could be expected from the well-worn philosophical principle of "unity in diversity."

Frithjof Schuon's idea of the "transcendent unity of all religions at the esoteric level" functions naturally as Ariadne's thread for many articles included in this volume, but is itself developed and modified in quite unexpected ways. Actually, through the investigation of the active "traces" left by the esoteric trends in the world, one comes to understand that it is not unqualifiedly the hermetic which unifies religions, while the exoteric, the active, would be the mutually estranging factor, the pretext for discord. The acceptability of the

259

exoteric is in fact much more universal than that of the occult or the hermetic. By its very nature the hermetic isolates, segregates; it opposes secret practices to other secret practices — implying, if not an insuperable elitism, at least some form of group or individual exclusivity. Whereas, whatever is or becomes translated from the esoteric level into the actual practice of any segment of mankind, provided it remains inspired by its genuine mystical vision, may appear as infinitely more acceptable to other segments.

What really separates, sharpens, and aggravates the differences between religions are not necessarily the cults, rituals, or practices thereby inspired. What continues to be the cause of innumerable conflicts among nations or groups possessed of religious intransigence is to be found at the level of doctrines, dogmas, ideologies. Whenever a religion becomes ideological it develops in itself principles for rejection which derive from the discriminative nature of ideology itself. The question, then, for any ecumenically-oriented religion is how to prevent the political-ideological model from becoming its dominant form of expression, while maintaining intact its historic originality. In its relevance for this problem lies the whole meaning and fruitfulness of the concept of "tradition."

In a paper presented at the Colloquium which could not be included in this book,[1] Huston Smith argued against both the theological and the phenomenological views on world religions. One could not agree more with the pyramidal scheme he proposed to represent graphically the fascicle of convergences-divergences between religions, which, according to Schuon, become evident as we travel back and forth between their esoteric and exoteric levels. No doubt, there is a point of convergence in the Absolute, which neither the theological nor the phenomenological viewpoints are able to reach or to comprehend totally. "The Absolute Unity that God is defies visualization or even consistent description," Smith writes; and he is, for a certain level, undoubtedly right about this impossibility. However, there is a variety of religious phenomenology, derived from Husserl, which provides a method for transcending the level of mere description and even that of the famous "vision of essences." After performing the necessary reduction of time and space — as well as those of the psycho-sociological determinants and of the empirical self — in passing over to the intersubjective sphere, we absolutely touch upon the level of transcendentality to which Schuon alludes. Whatever this level may be called, it is certain that precisely here occurs the constitution of the absolute as absolute, i.e., transcending all the limitations, whether historical or doctrinal. The mystical encounter of religions and the essential attributes (or nonattributes) of Godhead can be attained only by means of this transcendental reduction. Phenomenology, thus, is not mere description; it implies among other things a kind of reduction — as radical, it seems to us, as mystical purification itself, and as far-reaching.

A particular circumstance of this meeting was very significant and, hopefully, has been adequately reflected in the book: the fact that the contributors, as well as being eminent scholars in the field of the history of religions, are most all contemplatives, each immersed in one particular tradition. They spoke, then, with a double authority: that conferred by an in-depth study of several mystical traditions, and that coming from the charismatic power which emanates from the practicing mystic's way of life. On the latter it would be useless to comment: it speaks of itself.

As Raimundo Panikkar remarked at one point in the discussion, what emerged was a *sui generis* understanding of what comparative religion has come to mean: not merely the business of comparing religions, but the study of ultimate problems (man, peace, freedom, salvation, joy, life, and death) under the guidance of *more than one* religious tradition. "It is," he went on to say, "this kind of an attitude that makes interreligious dialogue and the common search for truth one of the purest religious experiences." In other words, the time is past when we could simply juxtapose bodies of religious doctrine and compare their anatomical features. A personal "reactivation" of one or more religious experiences different from one's own has come to be recognized as a prerequisite for what could be termed a "physiological" description and comparison of religion, one certainly much more meaningful for the contemporary quest than the dusty facts of classical comparative studies.

The prevailing intention in the elaboration of this volume was to show how mystics of the most varied traditions conceive —

theoretically and practically — the *ascent* from everyday life to the summits of contemplation, and how they visualize and effect the *descent* from the height of ecstatic states-of-awareness to the everyday aesthetic, moral, and even political activities in the world of the common. This ascending-descending motion, this to-and-fro movement of contemplation and action, far from being an opportunistic theme in a world of increasing desacralization which idolizes action for utilitarian purposes alone, is inherently a movement of life. If anything has been conveyed with particular suggestive force in the papers by Scrima, Nasr, Bando, Izutsu, and others, it is this central theme. By directly addressing it, the Colloquium responded directly to the heaviest objection leveled against spirituality in today's world: that of being out of touch with the concerns of every man and woman, with the practical world, and with the struggle for social justice and a better lot for the dispossessed. If only on this point, the volume brings an informed answer, not on the specific ways of dealing with social injustice (this remains the task of organized groups in concrete circumstances), but on the inner attitudes which make this kind of action possible and necessary at the same time.

One of the future perspectives opened up by the Colloquium is a comprehensive discussion of the nature and problems of evil in changing contemporary societies in the light of the mystical trend in various religions. The claim of the mystic likely to make the most sense to contemporary man is perhaps not the supreme and noetic one, the achievement of the contemplation of universal truth in a glimpse of superessential intuition, but rather that of being able to *dispel evil* whenever and wherever mystical awareness is at work. This is a theme seldom dealt with directly (except in Buddhist circles, where it functions as a traditional concern), but it may well constitute the essential question of comparative mysticism and metaphysics for some time to come.

A connected topic is that of appraising the authenticity of any religious tradition. Obviously, the Colloquium, by its chosen theme, was oriented to an intense focus on the past. This was not an arbitrary preference of a group of esoteric scholars assembled for the purpose of scorning modernity; rather it was an intrinsic demand —

perhaps itself the very proof of modernity — of the theme proposed. The precise requirement was a firm, but not unyielding, distinction between what Lhermitte calls "vrais et faux mystiques" and "vrais et faux possédés." The purpose was not to single out authentic representatives of traditions and to excommunicate others. But the criteria have to be laid down — at least in principle — for what one dreams from the standpoint of one's own internalized heritage to be the true path of mysticism as opposed to imposture.

The problem is eternal; it only becomes more or less acute at different moments in history, and it is vastly greater than what its mere psychological connotations would seem to imply. At this point in history, it involves the whole set of objective criteria for the appraisal of a tradition, as well as for its uses in a context that is severed both historically and geographically from that of its origins. How much continuity, both devotional and cultural, is required for a tradition to survive and to be aptly proclaimed alive? What went wrong with the Western tradition on this continent, and at what point, that it has departed in seemingly irretrievable ways from the sacredness of its roots? Where did it go astray? Did it eventually reach a point of no return? These questions were asked meaningfully by Jacob Needleman in the discussions of the Colloquium. Leo Schaya proposed positively that we are not only entitled but obliged to reestablish a set of criteria that would distinguish an orthodoxy from an apostasy. Schaya identified the revelatory, the scriptural, the exegetic, the soteriological, the hierarchical, and the communal as the component elements of every genuine tradition, excluding those religions that are not based on Revelation and those traditions that are exclusively oral. The problem is far too complex and delicate to be solved at one shot. The merit of the Colloquium lies, however, in having raised it at various levels in the discussions. There were, of course, reactions against the setting up of rigid criteria for orthodoxy: we are naturally loath to start off on a redefinition of heresy nowadays. And yet we all resent the phoniness of commercialized imports, the kind of undigested Eastern merchandise that has flooded the American and European markets with subproducts of "instant bliss," "instant salvation," and ways and techniques to improve efficiency in business and other profane endeavors to which pompous names, borrowed from mystical traditions, are applied.

This being the case, criteria for discrimination between true and false mysticism and traditions may be more than needed. Certainly, one must be critically aware of the danger of throwing out new religious forms developed as a consequence of the reception of old traditions in a traditionless environment, and of the cross-cultural fertilization among traditions of different weight and importance. The best one can do in this respect is to *manifest* a model, not to impose it or to draw restricting, dogmatic lines derived from the definition of a sole path. The clearest lesson of the Colloquium, which belongs to the essence of mystical religion, seems to have been an appeal for the widest tolerance: and, as Abimbola remarked, in discussion, a whole gamut of meaning was unfolded concerning tradition itself as a category. Nasr, for instance, described tradition not in the Latin sense as something that has to be accumulated over the years but as "something of divine origin, which is rooted in Heaven and grows and therefore becomes a living presence." Tradition was dealt with essentially as a science of the real (both visible and invisible, let us add). Maybe, as Zolla suggested, "tradition is the final cause of our lives through the ecstasy of their epiphany." Further , it is the innate authority, singularly lacking in today's "advanced" civilization. Tradition implies the capacity to follow the diagnosis and the spiritual prescription integrally, through one's innermost capabilities — faith and grace.

One should not forget for a single moment the limitations of any single culture's viewpoint. The essay by A. K. Saran (not included in this volume) emphasized this point; it warned against taking for granted the Western concepts of freedom and creation (doing and making) and brought out the vacuousness of the concept of freedom when understood as "freedom of choice." Both the *Bhagavadgîtâ* and the *Tao te ching* agree in considering that action and inaction imply each other in harmonious and inextricable ways, and that a doctrine of mystic detachment entails the nullity of individual choice as well as the irrelevance of any evolutionary theory of human progress.

In an essay of classical simplicity, Mahadevan argues, following

Sankara, that the realization of the nondual Self is not a matter of the will: knowledge depends on the object, while action that does not bind is independent from the fruits of action. This teaching of and striving for the absolute independence of action from its consequences may be the highest point of Eastern wisdom.

Shojun Bando's treatment of the duality of faith responds to the same question of ultimacy in religion: it is beyond man's will to experience the simultaneity of death and rebirth. But in order for it to occur, the necessary condition is a complete severance from the attachments of life. This teaching is in agreement with both Taoism and the Christian tradition according to the Johannine Gospel, Augustine, and Meister Eckhart. A closely similar pattern is found in the rapid and the gradual paths of Tantric Buddhism as they are outlined by Lobsang Lhalungpa. These are in some way consonant with that of Freudian analysis, in so far as the highest state of mystical awareness is "awareness of unawareness." The esoteric path brings forth, without unnecessary asceticism, the silent realization of one's deepest potential — the Buddha-nature in ourselves. It goes without saying that whatever parallels one may draw with modern existentialism, a tremendous difference subsists: this path has to be fulfilled, at variance with the "human potential" ideal in Western philosophies, in a totally *selfless* way.

Toshihiko Izutsu introduces us to a very clear typology of Zen schools: the real novelty of his paper consists in the way in which the intellectual and nonintellectual approaches to the koan method are intertwined. Zen is presented by Izutsu as the most vivid refutation of the myths of passivity in mysticism: the emptying of the mind through the "absurdist" practices of the different Zen schools all amount to an "awakening of mindfulness"; and this heightened activity of the mind translates magnificently into the Zen arts — painting, calligraphy, gardening, archery, swordsmanship, etc. — a powerful source of aesthetic inspiration for all times and places.

An attempt to bring together under the same empathetic movement the concept of karma and the person of Jesus, as fundamental tenets of two world religions between which seems to loom an unsurmountable gap, is presented by Raimundo Panikkar. He asserts, firstly, the absolute primacy of contemplation over action as the only way in which one may at least begin to understand the other not as "other" but as a "self"; secondly, he proceeds to disentangle the idea of karma from that of reincarnation, and thus to reinterpret it in terms of the continuity and mystery of individual life itself; thirdly, on the basis of this hermeneutic approach, he is able to link it with the *identity of Jesus*, whose resurrection comes to mean at the same time the mystery of his presence and his absence, and the continuity of being and nonbeing as the essence of life. No *word* is ever to be taken literally, he says. In this respect, the contemplative's power and superiority is that "he knows without knowing." The understanding of two (or more) traditions means precisely the discarding of discriminatory knowledge, the recognition of the supreme powerlessness of the intellect confronted with the mystery of another view, another refraction of the *event*, in a total refusal of idolatry.

In a complex and multifaceted argument, Elémire Zolla describes the *met-hodos* (primary path) of contemplation as the feminine element within the Western tradition. It would be preposterous to try and summarize an intricate string of cogently argumentative descriptions. Let us simply say that a whole dimension of the Western tradition is unfolded before our eyes, ranging from the aesthetics of contemplation to the pertinent understanding of *labor as sacrifice*, and ending up with a description of the ecstasy of contemplation in a Neoplatonic vein.

In a personal essay, not included in this volume, Jacob Needleman gave a description of the ineffable and unforgettable effect on a Californian of a pilgrimage to Mount Athos.

> I felt warmed by the tremendous effort this Athonite monk was obviously making to communicate to me. I began to grasp the teachings of orthodox Christianity in a way that had never before been possible to me. In the long silences I watched the darkness settling in the room and enjoyed the balmy night wind that began to blow off the sea. But during these silences there were several moments when I glancingly observed something important take place in myself: I saw the believer begin to arise and step forward.

The mystery conveyed, the deep lesson in humility, the passion and patience in awaiting conversion among the menial things of life, leave one with an impression of a total otherness embedded in the

Greek Orthodox way, an otherness perhaps inaccessible to the West in its total atemporality.

In an admirably concise essay, André Scrima retraces the history of the Hesychastic anthropology of the Eastern Orthodox tradition, insisting on the significant history of the Philokalia with abundant allusions to the techniques of prayer in Eastern Christian mysticism. The study is a jewel of inspiration both in the philosophy of mysticism and the philosophy of the encounter of Eastern and Western culture.

The passage to Islam is effected by a highly specialized comparative treatment of the Kabbalah and the Sufi doctrine, focused on the theory of the divine names and the exegesis of Talmudic and Qur'anic writings, by Leo Schaya. The convergence unveiled between the spiritual world of the Jew and that of the Muslim into one object of contemplation, through the intermediary of their theories of Holy names, brilliantly demonstrates the fruitful synthesis of two apparently divergent approaches to religion, the contemplative and the active, as well as the true transcendental unity of two great world creeds.

Seyyed Hossein Nasr underscores in his study the unitary perspective of Islamic religion, particularly in its esoteric aspect. The essentially gnostic character of Islamic spirituality endows all possible actions stemming from it with a definite flavor of contemplation. The complementariness of the two aspects, however, while never leading to a separation in the ways of life, manifests itself on the contrary in the sacredness of all aspects of life as inspired by contemplation, the supreme model of which is the life of the Prophet.

Yusuf Ibish performs the tour de force of showing how the whole gamut of higher religious essences, as well as of natural phenomena, is encompassed in Ibn al-ᶜArabî's theory of journeying, a theosophical teaching which conveys the message of unity through the metaphor of a journey whose stations are each a stage in the religious consciousness of mankind. Al-Sayyedah Fatimah Al-Yashrutiyyah wrote a beautiful invocation to Sufi prayer in which the human intellect is supposed to travel "inside itself" towards the Infinite. She shows Islamic esotericism to be a total fusion of the contemplative and the active-practical, this latter embracing forms as different as jurisprudence, psychology, morals, the history of knowledge, meditation, and love.

In an effort geared at reconstructing the impressive architecture of an African theology, Wande Abimbola presents the history and function of various gods and goddesses in the Yoruba cult, shunning the separation of action and contemplation in time or space. He also shows how the high Yoruba priests are initiated into the complex meanings of the sacred Ifa poems in ceremonies that, through the use of certain forms of intoxication, are intended to lead to divine possession and to the awakening of mystical ecstasy.

Finally, in a piece of eulogy directed at the American Indian metaphysical conception of nature, Joseph Epes Brown gives instances of intimate fusion between the active and the contemplative in the attitudes of several North American Indian tribes, the religions of which are described as involving a circular continuum between meditational practices, action, and contemplation, all focused on the Great Mystery as Ultimate Reality.

In general, the authors took a view of contemplation which was more cultural than technical, more metaphysical than theological. In spite of the unmistakable emphasis on the past, hardly any major contemporary problem has been left entirely out. Even so, the inevitable lacunae appear as a result of time and space limitations, not as sins of intention. The missing themes suggest themselves for future encounters, such as, for example, the relationship between spirituality and culture. From the climate opened up recently by discussions around the sacred, it is possible to show that an expansion of the *cross-cultural* dialogue between religions is already taking place.

By rerooting the many varieties of mystical experience in the ground of their respective traditions, this volume will have shown above all that mysticism is not a matter of arbitrary individual preference in the world today, nothing like an aesthetic gratuitous act. This collection of essays in comparative metaphysics makes an exemplary case for an involved sacred science.

*Ileana Marculescu*

[1]For omitted papers see complete edition: *Traditional Modes of Contemplation and Action*, eds. Y. Ibish and P.L. Wilson, distributed by Thames and Hudson Ltd., London.

# Authors

WANDE ABIMBOLA is a Nigerian and an authority on Yoruba tradition. He studied in England, the United States, and in Lagos, where he received his Ph.D. in 1970. He has contributed to several anthologies on Yoruban literature and folklore. Among his books are: *Ijinle Ohun Enu Ifa,* Apa Kiini (Glasgow: Collins, 1968); *Ijinle Ohun Enu Ifa,* Apa Keji (Glasgow: Collins, 1969); *Sixteen Poems of Ifa* (Paris: UNESCO, 1973).

SHOJUN BANDO studied in Tokyo and in England. He has taught in Japan and in the United States. He is the Associate Editor of the Eastern Buddhist Society as well as the Vice-Head-Priest of Bando Hoorji (Shin Buddhism). His works include: *Indo Busseki Jumpai Kiki* (Travels among Buddhist Sacred Places in India), 1955; *Bibliography in Japanese Buddhism* (co-author), 1958; *Chi to Ai no Katachi* (Forms of Wisdom and Compassion), 1966; *Zettai Kiye no Hyogen — Kyogyoshinsho* (Kyogyoshinsho, an expression of Absolute Devotion), 1969.

JOSEPH EPES BROWN is a well-known scholar in the fields of anthropology and history of religions; the main focus of his work is the spiritual legacy of the American Indians. He met Black Elk and recorded his account of the seven rites of the Oglala Sioux. At present, Dr. Brown is a professor of religious studies at the University of Montana. His books include: *The Sacred Pipe* (Norman: University of Oklahoma, 1953); *The Spiritual Legacy of the American Indian* (Wallingford, Pa.: Pendle Hill, 1964); *The North American Indians: The Photographs of Edward S. Curtis (Aperture,* Vol. XVI, no. 4, and Philadelphia Museum of Art, 1972).

YUSUF IBISH teaches at the American University of Beirut and is a student of Islamic Culture. Born in Damascus, Syria, he studied at the American University of Beirut where he received his B.A. and M.A. in political science. He received his Ph.D. from Harvard University in Middle Eastern studies, concentrating on Islamic political theory and institutions, and wrote his thesis on al-Baqillani's doctrine of the Imamate (Harvard, 1961). His books include: *Al-Baqillani's Doctrine of the Imamate* (Beirut: 1964); *Islamic*

*Political Theory* (Beirut: 1955); *The Political Doctrine of Baqillani* (Beirut: American University of Beirut, 1966); *The Life and Travels of Sheikh Rashid* (Beirut: 1970).

TOSHIHIKO IZUTSU, a leading scholar in the field of comparative philosophy and a famous Islamicist, was born and raised in Tokyo and attended Keio University where he received his M.A. and his Ph.D. He has taught at the Institute of Islamic Studies, McGill University, Montreal, and is currently with the Imperial Iranian Academy of Philosophy in Tehran. He is a member of the Institut International de Philosophie in Paris, of the Société International pour l'Etude de la Philosophie Médiévale in Louvain, Belgium, and an Eranos Lecturer. Of his books the following have appeared in English: *Language and Magic* (Tokyo: Keio Institute of Cultural and Linguistic Studies, 1956); *God and Man in the Koran* (Tokyo: Keio, 1964); *The Concept of Belief in Islamic Theology* (Tokyo: Keio, 1965); *Ethico-Religious Concepts in the Qur'an* (Montreal: McGill University Press, 1966); *The Key Philosophical Concepts of Sufism and Taoism* (two volumes) (Tokyo: Keio, 1966-67).

LOBSANG P. LHALUNGPA was born in Lhasa, Tibet. He was educated in Tibet, and he joined the ecclesiastical service of the Dalai Lama's government. After the flight of the Dalai Lama to India he devoted himself primarily to the preservation of Tibetan culture in India and Nepal. He taught at the University of British Columbia, Vancouver, and then moved to New York, where he is working on a series of translations of the Tibetan classics into English. He is the author of *Life and Teachings of Mahatma Ghandi* (New Delhi: 1970) and *Life of Milarepa* (New York: Dutton, 1977).

T.M.P. MAHADEVAN is a leading Indian educator and philosopher. He was born and educated in Madras. He received his Ph.D. from the University of Madras in 1937, and at present he is director there of the Center of Advanced Study in Philosophy. Professor Mahadevan has taught and guided several generations of students, not only in India, but also in the United States and Mexico. In 1967 he was awarded Padma Bhusan by the Government of India in recognition of his valuable contribution to Indian Philosophy and Religion. Among his publications are the following: *The Philosophy of Advaita with special reference to Bharatitirtha-Vidyaranya* (Madras: Ganesh, 1957); *The Philosophy of Beauty* (Bombay: Bharatiya Vidya Bhavan, 1969); *The Insights of Advaita* (Mysore Prasaranga: University of Mysore, 1970); *Ten Saints of India* (Bombay: Bharatiya Vidya Bhavan, 1971).

ILEANA MARCULESCU, born in Romania, received the Ph.D. degree at the University of Bucharest, her thesis on teleological principles in biology. She also taught there in both the biology and philosophy departments. Subsequently she has been a visiting fellow at the Center for Democratic Institutions, Santa Barbara, California; a lecturer in philosophy at the University of California; and a Harry Emerson Fosdick Visiting Professor of Philosophy and Religion at the Union Theological Seminary, New York City. Currently she lectures in philosophy and religion at Sweet Briar College. Her recent work includes *The Book of Sweet Repose,* a book on Eastern Orthodox Hesychasm (Paulist-Newman Press, forthcoming).

SEYYED HOSSEIN NASR, born in Tehran, is one of the leading Muslim scholars in the field of Islamic science, philosophy, and Sufism. He studied in the United States, graduating with honors in physics from M.I.T. and receiving his M.A. and Ph.D. from Harvard University in the history of science and philosophy. Formerly Chancellor of Aryamehr University, he is now Director of the Imperial Iranian Academy of Philosophy, Tehran. His books include: *Three Muslim Sages* (Cambridge: Harvard University Press, 1964); *An Introduction to Islamic Cosmological Doctrines* (Cambridge: Belknap Press of Harvard University Press, 1964); *Islamic studies; essays on law and society, the sciences, and philosophy and Sufism* (Beirut: Libraire du Liban, 1967); *The Encounter of Man and Nature, the Spiritual Crisis of Modern Man* (London: Allen and Unwin, 1968); *Science and Civilization in Islam* (Cambridge: Harvard University, 1968).

RAIMUNDO PANIKKAR was born in Barcelona of an Indian father

and a Spanish mother, and studied in Spain, Germany, India, and Italy. He has a Ph.D. in chemical science as well as in philosophy, and completed his Ph.D. in theology at the Lateran University in Rome. Ordained as a priest in 1954, he left Europe for India. Between 1964 and 1971 he commuted between Benares, India, Rome, and Harvard University. He is presently Professor of Religious Studies at the University of California at Santa Barbara. He is the author of some twenty books, including: *The Unknown Christ of Hinduism* (London: Darton, Longman, and Todd, 1964); *The Trinity and World Religions; Icon-Person-Mystery* (Madras: The Christian Literature Society, 1970); *The Trinity and the Religious Experience of Man* (Maryknoll, N.Y.: Orbis Books; London: Darton, Longman, and Todd, 1973).

LEO SCHAYA, born in Switzerland and a resident of Nancy, France, is a renowned scholar in the field of comparative religion. He is one of the world's leading authorities on Kabbalism and Sufism. His field of interest also includes Christian, Taoist, Hindu, and Buddhist spirituality. Among his books are the following: *L'homme et L'Absolu selon la Kabbale* (Paris: Editions Buchet/Chastel, Correa, 1958) translation into English, 1961; *The Universal Meaning of the Kabbalah* (London: Allen and Unwin Ltd., 1971; New York: Penguin Books, 1971); *La Doctrine Soufique de l'Unité* (Paris: Maisonneuve, 1962) translation into English to appear.

ANDRÉ SCRIMA, Archimandrite of the Orthodox Church and former personal representative of the Patriarch Athenagoras at Vatican Council II, is currently Professor of Philosophy and Religious Sciences at the University of St. Joseph in Beirut, Lebanon. He was born in Romania and studied at the Universities of Bucharest, Paris, and Benares. He is a member of the International Academy of Religious Sciences in Brussels. His works include: *Essai sur l'anthropologie apophatique* (Bucharest: 1956); *L'avènement philocalique* (Paris: 1959); *Le mythe et l'épiphanie de l'indicible* (Paris: 1965); *Le Nom-Lieu de Dieu* (Paris: 1969); *L'apophase et ses connotations selon la tradition Spirituelle de l'Orient chrétien* (Paris: 1970); *L'infaillibilité: inscription conceptuelle et destination eschatologique* (Paris: 1971).

AL-SAYYEDAH FATIMAH YASHRUTIYYAH received no formal education, yet she must be one of the most cultivated and spiritually educated Muslim women. Absorbed in devotion and Sufism, she has been an instrument of spiritual guidance for several generations of Muslims and is one of the pillars of the Yashrutiyyah order. Born in Acre, Palestine, she is the daughter of the famous Tunisian Shadhili Sheikh ᶜAli Nur Al-Din al-Yashruti, who was born in 1779 and who settled in Acre to start the Yashrutiyyah Zawiya. She is the author of three books in Arabic, none translated.

ELÉMIRE ZOLLA is a well-known Italian scholar and linguist in the field of comparative literature. At present he is Director of the Institute of Foreign Languages and Literature at the University of Genoa, and he holds the Chair of American Literature and Germanic Philology. Since 1969 Professor Zolla has been the Director and Editor of *Conoscenza Religiosa,* a leading Italian journal in religious studies which is published in Florence. He has published the following works: *I Mistici* (Milano: Garzanti, 1964); *La Storia del Fantasticare* (Milano: Bompiani, 1964); *Volgarità e dolore* (Milano: Bompiani, 1966); *Le Potenze dell'Anima* (Milano: Bompiani, 1968); *The Writer and the Shaman, A Morphology of the American Indian* (New York: Harcourt Brace Jovanovich, Inc., 1969); *The Eclipse of the Intellectual* (New York: Funk and Wagnalls, 1969); *Che Cose'è la Tradizione* (Milano: Bompiani, 1971).